W9-DEO-259

broken bodies
broken dreams

violence against women exposed

Office for the Coordination of Humanitarian Affairs
Integrated Regional Information Networks

A United Nations OCHA/IRIN publication

Lead writer:	Jeanne Ward (all chapters)
Associate writers:	Jackie Kirk (chapter 6) Leah Weinzimer (chapter 12) Christopher Horwood (chapter 14 / 15) Zoe Flood (chapter 15)
Lead researcher:	Leah Weinzimer
Contributing photographers:	Zana Briski, Georgina Cranston, Jan Dago, Donna Ferrato, Mariella Furrer, Evelyn Hockstein, Annie Liebowitz, Mirjan Letsch, Anthony Lloyd, Julie Podlowski, Brent Stirton, Jennifer Szymaszek, Sven Torfinn, Leah Weinzimer, Magnum (various photographers), Panos (various photographers), Agence France Presse (various photographers), Network Photographers (various photographers)
Editor:	Lisa Ernst
Project manager and book design:	Christopher Horwood (IRIN)
Printing:	Progress Press Co. Ltd. Malta. May 2007
Layout:	Eugene Papa (UNON Nairobi)

Available in English and French
Cover image: Sex worker in Bangladesh
Cover photographer: Martin Adler / Panos

ISBN 9966-7108-0-9

© OCHA/IRIN. 2005

IRIN is a humanitarian information and advocacy support service providing news and analysis, through on-line articles, special reports, printed publications, film documentaries and radio. IRIN is part of the United Nations Office for the Coordination of Humanitarian Affairs (OCHA). For more information visit: www.irinnews.org

For specific information concerning this publication contact: brokenbodies@irinnews.org

Ah love, let us be true to one another!
For the world which seems to lie before us like a land of dreams
So various, so beautiful, so new,
Hath really neither joy, nor love, nor light nor certitude,
Nor peace, nor help from pain,
And we are here as on a darkling plain
Swept with confused alarms of struggle and flight
Where ignorant armies clash by night.

Dover Beach, Matthew Arnold (1822-1888)

Acknowledgements

This publication is part of OCHA/IRIN's longer term commitment to the fight against gender-based violence, offering products that are aimed to increase awareness and information of different forms of violence against women and girls. Acknowledgements and thanks are due to Jeanne Ward for her intense commitment to the research and writing of the majority of this book and to the dedication of a team of researchers working with IRIN's Analytical Unit in Nairobi, Kenya. These include Leah Weinzimer, James Neuhaus and Zoe Flood. Special thanks go to those photographers who contributed images to the book free of charge, including Annie Liebowitz, Jennifer Szymaszek, Brent Stirton, Julie Podlowski, Jan Dago and all photos from AFP. Thanks also to Sarah Muscroft for helping us locate photographs from OCHA archives and particularly to Lisa Ernst for tireless editing. Our appreciation also goes to the staff at the United Nations Nairobi Printshop for their assistance with the layout and printing of this book.

For the many testimonies and images that were collected in different countries while compiling this book, our thanks go to those photographers who reported stories while on assignment. Our greatest thanks goes to the women and girls themselves, who consented to share their personal stories with us. These women have suffered, and will continue to suffer, different forms of violence and are unlikely to directly benefit in their lives, from any contribution this project makes to global advocacy. In preparing this book the authors have made every effort to adhere to the spirit of ethical presentation of images of victims, while at the same time recognising the importance of exposing the realities of violence against women.

We thank the specialist reviewers of each chapter of this book, who freely offered their time and expertise to ensure the writing is both accurate and balanced. Any errors in this publication are the responsibility of the authors. The reviewers were Sunita Kishor (son preference), Jane Warburton and Amanda Bissex (child prostitution and pornography), Kate Burns (female genital mutilation and violence against women in times of war), Vijayendra Rao, Mirjam Letsch and Madhu Kishwar (dowry crimes and bride-price abuse), Sandra Bunch and Naana Otoo-Oyortey (child marriage), Fatma Khafagy and Angel Foster (crimes of "honour"), Irene Weiser, Lori Michau and Claudia Garcia Moreno (intimate-partner violence), Rachel Jewkes (sexual assault and harassment), Cathy Zimmerman (trafficking of women and girls), Charlotte Feldman-Jacobs and Susan Igras (female genital mutilation), Michael Flood (perpetrators), Bonnie Fisher (abuse of older women), Sonia Navani and Heidi Lehmann (violence against women in times of war).

This project was generously supported by various donors, of which the Swiss Agency for Development and Cooperation was the first to capture the vision of what this book could become. Important financial support was also given by the Italian government, the European Community Humanitarian Office (ECHO), the United Nations Women's Fund (UNIFEM), the United Nations High Commissioner for Refugees (UNHCR), the United Nations Fund for Population Activities (UNFPA) and the Inter-Agency Internal Displacement Division (IDD). Without such support this book would not have been possible.

contents

Introduction   1

Chapter 1   Son preference   11

Chapter 2   Sexual abuse of children   19

Chapter 3   Child prostitution and   35
             pornography

Chapter 4   Female genital mutilation   51

Chapter 5   Child marriage   61

Chapter 6   Violence against girls in   73
             schools

Chapter 7   Sex trafficking of women   85
             and girls

Chapter 8   Dowry crimes and   101
             bride-price abuse

Chapter 9   Intimate-partner violence   115

Chapter 10   Crimes of "honour"   135

Chapter 11   Sexual assault and   147
             harassment

Chapter 12   Abuse of older women   165

Chapter 13   Sexual violence in times   177
             of war

Chapter 14   Perpetrators   205

Chapter 15   Turning the tide   225

Endnotes   237

broken bodies
broken dreams

violence against women exposed

Foreword

When images of the world's disasters flash across our television screens, more often than not, we are presented with a rough sketch of the humanitarian crisis. Rarely do the cameras venture beneath the surface to look at the hidden impact of a humanitarian crisis on affected communities. If they did they would find that virtually without exception, it is women and girls who are the most vulnerable.

In many countries today, the breakdown of law and order exposes women to untold discrimination, exploitation and violence which is often committed with impunity. In Darfur and the Democratic Republic of the Congo, for example, sexual violence and rape have been deliberately used as weapons of war and as a means of destroying the very fabric of communities. In Nepal, a decade of civil unrest has disrupted schooling and forced girls into domestic servitude, while declining law and order has led to a sharp rise in sexual violence. Poverty and hardship in Central Asia, Eastern Europe and in parts of South Asia have fueled a global trafficking industry that is defined by high levels of exploitation and abuse.

This is merely the tip of the iceberg. Violence against women is so widespread in different societies — in all our societies — that one is sometimes left with a sense of helplessness as to where to begin to act. But we must act and we must act with a sense of urgency in both the private and public spheres.

Broken bodies, broken dreams offers a powerful testimony, through photographs and text, of the different types of violence that define the everyday existence of countless women and girls. It examines the nature of this violence through the cycle of women's lives, including discrimination at birth and at school, domestic violence, sexual assault, trafficking, servitude and abusive cultural practices.

We are now in an era like no other in human history, where governments and civil society are starting to act together to uphold and fight for human rights. We are also in an era of unprecedented communication and access to information, which allows us to document the full extent of how gender-based violence affects women's lives.

This book serves to raise awareness and provoke action in addressing the causes of gender-based violence. as well as assisting and defending the millions of women targeted by violence. These are our sisters, our mothers, our daughters. History will judge us harshly if once aware of the nature and scope of this violence, once outraged by its injustice, we do not choose to act against it.

Jan Egeland

Jan Egeland
United Nations Under-Secretary-General for Humanitarian Affairs and Emergency Relief Coordinator

"States should condemn violence against women and should not invoke any custom, tradition or religious consideration to avoid their obligations with respect to its elimination. States should pursue by all appropriate means and without delay a policy of eliminating violence against women … " Declaration on the Elimination of Violence Against Women, proclaimed by General Assembly resolution 48/104 of 20 December 1993, Paragraph 4

"While I was still standing up he was taking off my skirt. When I refused, he pushed me to the ground amd then removed it. He took me by force. I felt so much pain when he raped me. He just left me there." Eleven-year-old survivor of rape, Democratic Republic of Congo

"Rape, then, is the logical consequence of a system of definitions of what is normative. Rape is no excess, no aberration, no accident, no mistake — it embodies sexuality as the culture defines it." Andrea Dworkin

"He beat me so hard that I lost my teeth. … He beat me most severely when I was pregnant … The first time he beat me, and I lost the baby." Survivor of intimate-partner violence, Uzbekistan

"Violence against women is global in reach, and takes place in all societies and cultures … It affects women no matter what their race, ethnicity, social origin, birth or other status may be … Much more remains to be done to create and sustain an environment where women can go about their lives free from this scourge." Kofi Annan

"He hit me, he kicked me, he would leave me half-dead. I almost lost our first baby two times … He only hit me when I wasn't pregnant … He would throw me against the wall, pull my hair, kick me." Survivor of intimate-partner violence, Nicaragua

"The prevalence of rape and sexual violence during armed conflict is not a new problem, but it is as serious as it has even been...Perpetrators of sexual violence during armed conflict are violating international law. States must hold them accountable, and there must be resources for victims to seek justice." Carol Bellamy

"It was then that they took off my skirt and began raping me, with my baby on my back throughout. … I was raped by three men and my [four-year-old] daughter was raped by the other three at the same time, lying next to me on the ground. While one raped each of us, the other two would point their guns and hold us down with their feet." Survivor of rape by militiamen in the Democratic Republic of Congo

"Where after all do universal human rights begin? In small places, close to home … such are the places where every man, woman and child seeks equal justice, equal opportunity, equal dignity without discrimination." Eleanor Roosevelt

"Safety and security don't just happen: they are the result of collective consensus and public investment. We owe our children — the most vulnerable citizens in any society — a life free from violence and fear. In order to ensure this, we must become tireless in our efforts not only to attain peace, justice and prosperity for countries but also for communities and members of the same family. We must address the roots of violence. Only then will we transform the past century's legacy from a crushing burden into a cautionary lesson." Nelson Mandela

"Forced sex is the norm. It is the way people interact sexually." Teenage girl, South Africa

"We need to voice the violence, to hear the stories of all those affected by violence … Spreading the word, breaking down the taboos and exposing the violence that takes place among us is the first step towards effective action to reduce violence in our own societies."
Gro Harlem Brundtland

"My husband would beat me to the point that he was too ashamed to take me to the doctor. He forced me to have sex with him and beat me if I refused … Even when he was HIV-positive he still wanted sex." Survivor of intimate-partner violence, Uganda

"Because women's liberation is a movement of the powerless for the powerless, its attraction is not immediately clear to the powerless, who feel they need alliance with the powerful to survive." Rosemary O'Grady

"Once I became so desperate, I did not want to continue living. I went down to the bridge to commit suicide." A woman from Bangladesh who was forced into prostitution at the age of 12

"The significant problems we face cannot be solved at the same level of thinking we were at when we created them." Albert Einstein

"If we kill female babies immediately after their birth, the chance of having a male son is very high." A father, India

"[Rape] is nothing more or less than a conscious process of intimidation by which all men keep all women in a state of fear" Susan Brownmiller

"I feel threatened because if he did not kill me this time he will kill me the next time … We women are alone. There is no one to protect us." Seventeen-year-old survivor of intimate-partner violence who was stabbed by her husband, Nicaragua

"We must be the change we wish to see." M. K. Gandhi

A man holding prayer beads walks past a beggar woman in Afghanistan. Often associated with the now-ousted Taliban regime, the strict separation of men and women and the widespread enforcement of the burkha predates the Taliban and continues to be enforced in one of the world's most traditional Islamic countries. In Afghanistan the predicament of widows and female-headed households is precarious as women struggle to survive in a context where their opportunities and freedoms are severely limited and controlled by men.

Image: Iva Zimova/Panos

introduction

This book is a ripple. Its portraits and testimonies join the global groundswell that has formed in response to the injustice of violence against women. This violence is a worldwide pandemic, one that transcends the bounds of geography, race, culture, class and religion to touch virtually every community, in virtually every corner of the globe. Too often sanctified by custom and reinforced by institutions, it thrives on impunity. Today, as in history, violence against women may constitute one the "most universal and unpunished crimes of all."[1]

It has been estimated that at least one in every three women around the globe "has been beaten, coerced into sex, or otherwise abused in her lifetime."[2] In many settings, the percentage is even higher. From birth to death, millions of women are directly exposed to violence, and an even greater number are forced to live with the fear its pervasiveness instils. As numerous investigators and activists have highlighted and as this book graphically reiterates, violence against women may begin even before birth: In certain parts of the world, sex-selective abortions of female foetuses, female infanticide, and fatal neglect of girl children have caused dramatic imbalances in sex ratios between males and females. Some researchers place the global number of "missing" females — those who should currently be living but are not because of discriminatory practices — at between 50 million and 100 million.[3]

During childhood, girls may be up to three times more likely to experience sexual abuse than boys, and some data indicate that they are the majority of all incest victims.[4] Of the almost two million children being exploited in prostitution and pornography worldwide, 80 percent to 90 percent are girls in most countries.[5] In the rapidly increasing global trafficking market, well over a half-million human beings are forcibly or coercively transported across international borders each year — an estimated 80 percent of these victims are women and girls, and most of them are believed to be trafficked into the commercial sex industry.[6]

In adulthood and even into old age, women continue to be at risk of specific forms of violence simply by virtue of being female. Most of their abusers are known to them — they are boyfriends, husbands and other family members, people from their community and, in the case of older adults, those specifically designated as caregivers.

The inconceivable repercussions

The human injustice of such violence is almost inconceivable in its scale. An estimated 100 million to 140 million girls alive today have undergone some form of medically unwarranted genital cutting.[7] In 2000, a United Nations report estimated that on average five Indian women a day were killed in "accidental" kitchen fires by husbands or in-laws whose demands for dowry had not been met.[8] In other parts of the world, thousands of women are murdered each year in the name of family "honour", and in most instances, their murderers receive little to no punishment. In times of war, women are increasingly targeted for rape and other assaults so extreme in their brutality that in the Democratic Republic of Congo violence against women has been coined "murderous madness".[9] Only a negligible fraction of these perpetrators will ever be prosecuted for their heinous crimes.

Just as difficult to conceive are the public-health implications of violence against women. Complications from pregnancy and child-bearing are the leading cause of death for 15- to 19-year-old girls worldwide, a fact made all the more alarming by widespread child marriages.[10] A projected 82 million girls around the world who are now between the ages of 10 and 17 will be married before their 18th birthdays.[11] The health risks of marriage are not limited to pregnancy. In 1997, the United States Surgeon General concluded that violence committed against women by their intimate partners poses the single largest threat to all American women, and similar conclusions have been drawn from studies in Europe and Australia.[12] According to a 1993 World

The development implications are no better. In the words of the United Nations Secretary-General, any society which fails to take measures to protect the safety and wellbeing of half of its members "cannot claim to be making real progress."[14] Violence against women drains a country's existing resources and handicaps women's ability to contribute to social and economic progress. According to the United Nations Special Rapporteur on Violence Against Women, women are nine times more likely than men to leave their jobs as a result of sexual harassment.[15] In some industrialised settings, the annual costs of intimate-partner violence alone have been estimated in the billions of dollars. State expenses for one act of rape in the United States, when accounting for both tangible and intangible costs, may amount to US $100,000.[16]

However immense in scope and impact, violence against women is not inevitable. At the same time that activists have been struggling to expose its magnitude, they have been working towards its elimination. An important part of these efforts has been defining exactly what violence against women entails and, in the process, identifying its root causes.

Defining violence against women

One of the great victories of women's rights activists over the last 10 years is that "the political climate surrounding the rights of women has shifted from refusing to admit that violence against women is a problem, to an almost universal understanding that it is the ultimate expression of the subordinate status of women globally."[17]

In 1993, the United Nations General Assembly adopted the watershed Declaration on the Elimination of Violence Against Women, in which violence against women was defined as "any act of gender-based violence that results in, or is likely to result in, physical, sexual, or psychological harm or suffering to women, including threats of such acts, coercion, or arbitrary deprivation of liberty, whether occurring in public or private life."[18] In emphasising the centrality of gender, the definition speaks to the necessity of examining the societal and relational contexts in which violence against women and girls occurs.

In adulthood and even into old age, women continue to be at risk of specific forms of violence simply by virtue of being female.

One conundrum of the United Nations definition — especially when taken out of the context of the entire Declaration — is its circularity: Neither gender-based violence nor

Development Report, violence "is as serious a cause of death and incapacity among women of reproductive age as cancer, and a greater cause of ill-health than traffic accidents and malaria combined."[13]

violence against women is actually defined. Despite, or perhaps because of this, the term gender-based violence has come to be used synonymously with violence against women. When removed from the

Young girl with baby, Democratic Republic of Congo. In most developing countries, girls take on household and caregiving tasks in addition to or instead of going to school. As the divisions of labour become more apparent, so do the differences between the opportunities and aspirations of boys and girls

Image: Georgina Cranston/IRIN

Women at work in Goma, Democratic Republic of Congo. Many women in conflict situations are highly vulnerable when they venture in search of firewood, water and other necessities.

Images: Georgina Cranston/IRIN

Declaration's tautology, however, gender-based violence stands alone to describe harm perpetrated against any person — male or female — that is instigated or exacerbated by exploiting social roles ascribed to men and to women. As such, the term may not only refer to violence against women, but also to certain manifestations of violence against men.

To the extent that this book focuses on violence against women, the term gender-based violence, when it is applied herein, refers to women. While recognising that boys and men in some instances may be exposed to gendered violence, women's inferior status virtually everywhere in the world means that they are its primary targets. The term is therefore used

Throughout history, acts of gender-based violence have been explicitly endorsed or implicitly condoned by the male-dominated societies in which they are committed.

in this book to emphasise the fact that violence against women is fundamentally related to discrimination, the foundations of which are deeply rooted in nearly universal attitudes and behaviours that reinforce women's subordination. The preamble to the Declaration makes this clear: "Violence against women is a manifestation of historically unequal power relations between men and women, which have led to domination over and discrimination against women by men and to the prevention of the full advancement of women."[19] The Declaration goes on to say that "violence against women is one of the crucial social mechanisms by which women are forced into a subordinate position compared with men."[20]

Thus, gender is one of the most significant factors around the world in the perpetuation of violence against women and girls. It is not the only criterion for evaluating and addressing the nature and prevalence of violence against women, however. Additional measures include class, race, poverty, ethnicity and age. In fact, where gender bias intersects with these "other sites of oppression", levels of discrimination are likely to be compounded, "forcing the majority of the world's women into situations of double or triple marginalization."[21]

Grasping the context of gender-based violence

Any effort to understand violence against women must be located within the larger framework of gender inequality. Women are the majority of the world's poor. Seventy percent of people living in poverty — those surviving on less that $1 per day — are women.[22] In many countries,

women are less likely than men to hold paid and regular jobs within the formal employment sector — where the benefits and security of employment are most reliable — and therefore more likely to suffer the financial instabilities inherent in the informal economy.[23]

In addition, women represent more than two-thirds of the world's illiterate.[24] While gender disparities in education are shrinking globally, in many parts of the world they still "yawn wide".[25] The predictable outcome of women's lack of education, especially when combined with other forms of discrimination, means that they are almost entirely excluded from the corridors of power: Women hold only 15.6 percent of elected parliamentary seats globally.[26] Without admission to decision-making structures, they are less able to determine and enforce the laws and policies that are meant to protect them.

As a result, in many countries women are not accorded the same basic legal rights and social privileges as men. In some settings, women have no right to own or inherit housing, land or property. In fact, they own only 1 percent of the world's land.[27] Not surprisingly, the majority of the one billion inadequately housed persons in the world are women.[28] In a number of countries, marriage laws discriminate against them, in terms of the legal age of marriage, for example, as well as the right to divorce.

Against a backdrop defined by widespread inequities, women's ability to assert their rights is crippled. The conclusion of the World Economic Forum's 2005 study on the global gender gap elucidates the problem: "The reality is that no country in the world, no matter how advanced, has achieved true gender equality, as measured by comparable decision making power, equal opportunity for education and advancement, and equal participation and status in all walks of human endeavour."[29] Such is the context in which gender-based violence breeds with impunity.

Women's rights: from invisible to indivisible

Throughout history, acts of gender-based violence have been explicitly endorsed or implicitly condoned by the male-dominated societies in which they are committed. This is in part because these violations most often occur in private spheres — traditionally considered beyond the purview of international and national law. It is also due to the self-interest and self-preservation of patriarchy. According to the World Health Organization, "Something that greatly encourages violence — and is a formidable obstacle in responding to it — is complacency.

Often, this complacency is strongly reinforced by self-interest."[30] Violence against women is a method by which men assert their social control; when it goes unchecked it is a method of propagating that control. In the absence of justice and in the presence of fear, women may not challenge the presumption of male dominion because to do so would put them at further risk. And so, the vicious circle of gender-based violence continues.

Women's rights activists are working to break this cycle. By insisting that violence against women constitutes a fundamental violation of basic human rights — human rights codified by men in international law — they have succeeded in making the invisible both visible and indivisible. They have brought violence against women "outside its protective shell of culture and tradition and focused attention on state responsibility to work to eliminate it."[31] Article 4 of the Declaration on the Elimination of Violence Against Women unequivocally asserts, "States should condemn violence against women and should not invoke any custom, tradition, or religious consideration to avoid their obligations with respect to its elimination."[32]

The Declaration goes further in making explicit what gender-based violence entails. It includes, but is not limited to "physical, sexual and psychological violence occurring in the family, including battering, sexual abuse of female children in the household, dowry related violence, marital rape, female genital mutilation and other traditional practices harmful to women, non-spousal violence and violence related to exploitation; physical, sexual and psychological violence occurring within the general community, including rape, sexual abuse, sexual harassment and intimidation at work, in educational institutions and elsewhere; trafficking in women and forced prostitution, and physical, sexual and psychological violence perpetrated or condoned by the state, wherever it occurs."[33]

Breaking the silence: promoting empowerment

In the words of one female victim of violence, "The less we speak about it, the more it hurts." This is as true at the societal level as it is for the individual. Even so, calling attention to violence against women presents risks, especially when individuals — and the cultures they represent — aggressively insist that their attitudes and actions related to the subordination of women are integral to their customs and traditions and that challenges to those traditions are an intrusion of foreign values.

The concept of human rights is not foreign to any culture, however, and not all traditional practices are harmful to women. The line cannot be strictly drawn between foreign and traditional ideals. The essential ideological divide is instead one that is internal to every culture around the world — where one set of beliefs seeks to justify discrimination

"States should condemn violence against women and should not invoke any custom, tradition, or religious consideration to avoid their obligations with respect to its elimination."

against women and an opposing set of beliefs seeks to uphold the fundamental equality and human rights of all people, both women and men.[34]

This book is based on the premise that human rights are both universal and indivisible. It draws on the decades of work by researchers and activists committed to exposing and eradicating violence against women. It insists — once again — that the issue of violence against women be acknowledged and confronted. The results of such confrontation have never been, and never will be, a "zero-sum game" for men, or for societies.[35] Putting an end to gender-based violence will bring us that much closer to a stage of human social development in which "the rights, responsibilities, and opportunities of individuals will not be determined by the fact of being born male or female."[36] The goal is to create a world where all people, regardless of their gender, are free to achieve their full potential. n

Children sorting rubbish in Pakistan. Girls are more likely than boys to be found, outside school, starting work from a young age.

Images: Evelyn Hockstein/IRIN

Women make up two-thirds of those who are illiterate in the world. Gender disparities in education are reducing globally, but in certain countries the differences remain high. The absence of educational opportunities is one of many inequalities that define childhood for millions of girls — and is symptomatic of cultures that are patriarchal in both ideology and structure.

Power by the gun leads to abuses in communities without recourse to civil authority.

Image: Brent Stirton

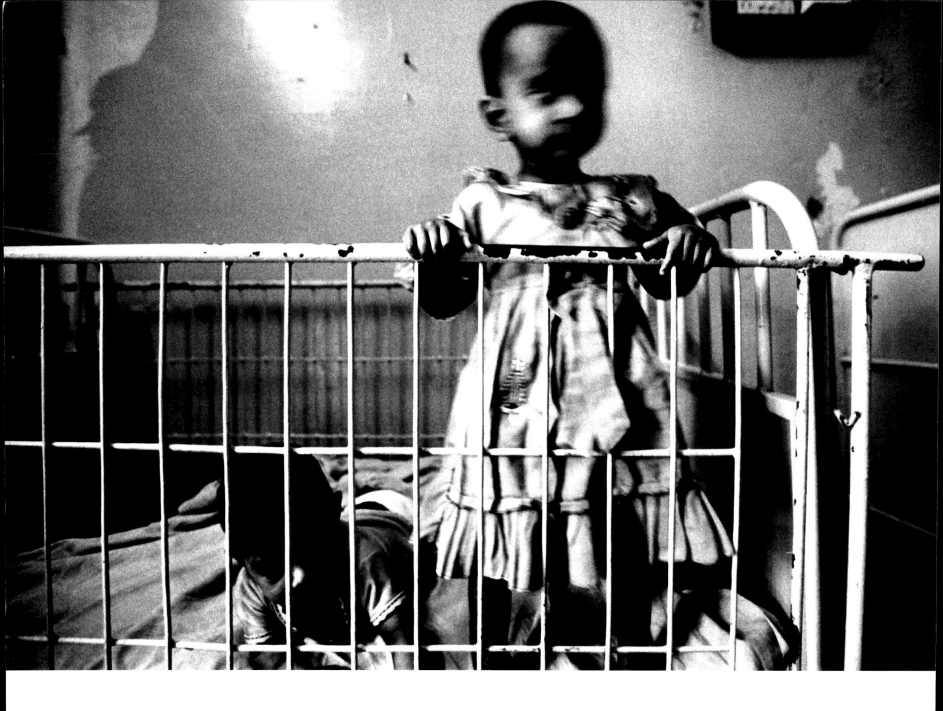

A small girl who was found on a roadside shares a cot at an orphanage in India. Every year, thousands of girls are abandoned, killed or aborted as parents make harsh choices reflecting son preference.

Image: Zana Briski

son preference

According to the wisdom of various Asian proverbs, to have a son is "good economics and good politics" and "as essential as taking food at least once a day." A boy's birth is attended by a variety of celebrations and likened to "a sunrise in the abode of gods." For girls, however, the axioms are very different. Being labelled an *abu-banat* in Arabic is to be insulted as the "father of daughters", and one adage in India likens raising a daughter to "watering the neighbour's garden."[1] In certain parts of Pakistan, an "endearment" for daughters roughly translates as "May you die."[2]

The expendable girl child

Around the world, many girls die because of the lesser value accorded to them. The United Nations Children's Fund (UNICEF) estimates that more than one million female babies succumb each year as a result of inequitable access to healthcare, differential feeding and other forms of neglect.[3] Some researchers put the global number of "missing" females — those who should currently be living but are not because of discriminatory practices — to between 50 million and 100 million, telling "a terrible story of inequality and neglect."[4]

Existing in various forms and across many cultures, son preference includes a broad spectrum of customs and rituals, the foundations of which are favouritism towards male children with concomitant disregard for daughters. In almost all cultures, it is the sons who carry the family name, making male progeny essential to the propagation of the family lineage. In many societies, a daughter is destined in marriage to live with her husband's family. The responsibility for the care of aging parents often falls to sons, who not only support their parents in their dotage, but also perform their parents' burial rights, especially in communities throughout Asia and Africa. At the very least, not having a son is a source of vulnerability for parents in this life; at its worst, it may prevent mothers and fathers from "securing peace in the next world."[5]

While scientific data on the prevalence and effects of discriminatory practices against females is very difficult to obtain, population sex ratios, birth sex ratios and infant- and child-mortality rates often are used as indicators to assess son preference. According to the World Health Organization (WHO), regions where son preference is most apparent include Asia (China, Bangladesh, India, Korea, Nepal, Pakistan, Taiwan), the Middle East (Iran, Jordan, Syria, Saudi Arabia, Turkey) and parts of

Africa (Algeria, Egypt, Libya, Morocco, Tunisia, Cameroon, Liberia, Madagascar, Senegal), as well as Latin America (Bolivia, Colombia, Ecuador, Mexico, Peru, Uruguay).

Although the most typical demonstration of son preference is the neglect of daughters, its most extreme form is female infanticide, or the intentional killing of baby girls.[6] Infanticide of either sex, whether for

> "We no longer kill the girl baby with the poisonous sap of the oleander plant, as traces of the poison can be detected. We make the death appear natural. For instance, we starve the baby to death or asphyxiate it."

economic, social or other reasons, has been prevalent across cultures throughout history. Even today, infants under one year of age in the United Kingdom are "four times as likely to be victims of homicide as any other age group — almost all killed by their parents."[7]

Infanticide specifically targeting females, however, has largely been supplanted — at least for those who have access to modern technology — by preventing the birth of girls through sex-identification testing and sex-selective abortion, representing "a substitution of prenatal discrimination for postnatal discrimination."[8] Most pronounced in India, China, Korea and Taiwan, much of the contemporary research on prebirth sex selection, as well as its historical cousin, female infanticide, focuses on the world's two most populous countries: India and China.

Prebirth sex selection and female infanticide in India

Based on extrapolations from the 1991 census, approximately 35 million to 45 million females were concluded "missing" in India, a finding which repeated itself in the 2001 tally. In that year, 933 women were enumerated for every 1,000 men. Ratios in specific states in the north of India were even more dramatic and as low as 861 women per 1,000 men.[9] Some of those among the missing are never even born: An estimated 106,000 female foetuses are aborted in India every year following sex-identification testing.[10] A significantly lower number may be killed as newborns — poisoned, suffocated, burned or buried alive. According to one father, "If we kill female babies immediately after their birth, the chance of having a male son is very high."[11]

Outlawed by the British in 1870, female infanticide still retains a foothold in some areas of northwest India, where the practice has a long history. In a human rights survey in 2000, the State Department of the United States estimated that there are 10,000 cases of female infanticide annually in India.[12] One traditional practice was to feed unwanted girls milk laced with poison or shredded paddy husk, the latter slitting a baby's tender throat as it was swallowed.[13] In the face of modern post-mortem examination technology, however, today's methods have become more strategic. A woman from Tamil Nadu dispassionately explained how things have changed: "We no longer kill the girl baby with the poisonous sap of the oleander plant, as traces of the poison can be detected. We make the death appear natural. For instance, we starve the baby to death or asphyxiate it."[14]

Female infanticide, however, has not been perpetrated with complete indifference. Elaborate traditional ceremonies were designed to absolve parents of wrongdoing. According to one Indian custom, after an infant girl is killed, the parents bury her in the room in which she was born and replaster the floor with cow dung to purify the site. Thirteen days after the death, a village priest — a Brahman — must cook a meal using *ghee* (clarified butter) and eat it in the room. By doing so, he "takes the sin of killing the baby upon himself."[15]

Given this moral ambivalence towards killing girl infants, it is not surprising that modern methods of foetal sex identification and pregnancy termination have replaced infanticide as the preferred way for some families in India to control the number of daughters they have. Abortion under certain circumstances was legalised in India in 1971.[16] Since then, it has become a burgeoning business, especially for the purposes of sex selection. From 1982 to 1987, the number of sex-determination clinics in Bombay grew from fewer than 10 to 248.[17] One study from that period revealed that of 8,000 abortions performed in Bombay in a single year, 7,999 were female foetuses.[18] In a study of one Bombay hospital, 430 out of 450 female foetuses were aborted, while none of 250 male foetuses were — even when there was evidence of a genetic problem.[19]

Birth order also plays its part in sex-selective abortions. The higher the birth order, the greater likelihood a female foetus will be aborted.[20] While it is generally accepted that one girl is needed "to light the lamp" in each home, a second or third daughter might be viewed as a liability.[21]

Although national legislation criminalising sex-determination testing was introduced in the mid-1990s, recent research suggests that sex-

Social workers in India counsel a pregnant woman who they believe is at high risk
of commiting female infanticide. Her seven-year-old daughter waits by her side.

Image: Zana Briski

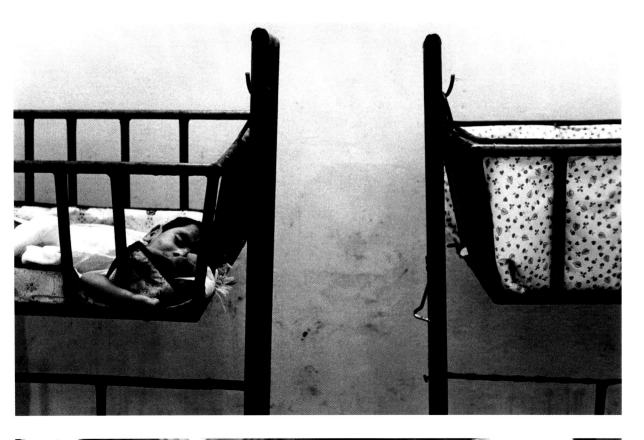

Another abandoned girl sleeps in rudimentary conditions at an orphanage in India. She faces an uncertain future in a culture where many baby girls start life with comparatively fewer opportunities than baby boys.

Image: Zana Briski

Plastic baby-boy dolls for sale to pilgrims praying for fertility at the tomb of Fuxi, who according to Chinese legend is the creator of the human race. In a 1997 report, more than 50 million females were concluded "missing" from China's current population.

Image: Mark Henley/Panos

selective abortion continues to flourish in India as a method for controlling family composition.[22] Some experts argue that disproportionate sex ratios where men increasingly outnumber women will eventually elevate the status of women by creating a greater demand for wives, leading to positive reforms in the dowry system in India.[23] Others contend, however, that sustained sex-ratio imbalances do "not improve the status of women, [but rather] … reflect it."[24] In the last century, such imbalances increased steadily from 972 women per 1,000 men in 1901 to 930 women per 1,000 men in 1971. For the following 30 years, they remained virtually unchanged, fluctuating between 927 and 933.[25] In the meantime, dowry payments have increased significantly, and dowry crimes and many other forms of violence against women do not appear to be abating.

Beyond perpetuating gender-based discrimination, sex-selective abortion triggers a host of other negative repercussions for women and girls. Because the primary modes of sex determination among the lower classes are amniocentesis and ultrasound — the first unavailable and the second unreliable until the second trimester — sex selection often leads to late-term abortions, which in turn can cause an array of reproductive-health problems for pregnant women. In addition, more girls may be wed at a younger age due to a scarcity of marriageable women, further contributing to the poor status of women as these young brides are less likely to complete their education and are likely to suffer increased morbidity and mortality associated with early child-bearing.[26]

The declining sex ratio could also stimulate an increase in prostitution, as well as other forms of exploitation and violence against women.[27] In India, women reportedly have been "imported", internally and from Bangladesh, to areas where sex ratios are dramatically low. According to one account, these women are "treated as slaves, and subjected to physical and sexual abuse."[28] Whether or not trafficking and other forms of violence against women can be attributed directly to sex-ratio imbalances remains an area for further investigation.

Prebirth sex selection and female infanticide in China

While female infanticide existed in China before 1949, the installation of the People's Republic of China heralded a significant decline in excessive female mortality — at least until the 1980s. At the end of 1979, the government implemented its "one-child policy", penalising couples for bearing children "outside the plan". Pressured to limit their number of children, many couples took whatever measures were necessary to ensure that they had a son. By the mid-1980s, the use of sex-selective technology was widespread, and from 1985 onwards, China's sex-ratio imbalance conspicuously reasserted itself. The ratio of boys relative to girls increased from 111.3 boys per 100 girls in 1990 to 116.9 boys per 100 girls in 2000.[29]

In a 1997 report, the WHO estimated that more than 50 million Chinese women were "missing" from the current female population. An analysis from 1999 noted, "The imbalance between the sexes is so distorted that there are 111 million men in China — more than three

"The imbalance between the sexes is so distorted that there are 111 million men in China — more than three times the population of Canada — who will not be able to find a wife."

times the population of Canada — who will not be able to find a wife."[30] According to the 2000 census, as many as seven provinces had sex ratios at birth exceeding 120 boys for every 100 girls, and these imbalances rose proportionately for higher-birth-order children.[31]

International adoption of girl babies may account for some of the sex-ratio disparities in China. So, too, might the estimated million or so "orphaned" girls who are consigned to state institutions so abysmal that one documentary film referred to them as "dying rooms".[32] Another explanation for sex-ratio imbalances in China has been the underreporting of female births, where girls might not be counted because they were never officially registered by their parents. However, recent data from China's Family Planning Commission revealed, surprisingly, that in almost all of China's provinces, more male than female births were underreported from 1990 to 1999.[33] This evidence suggests that the high numbers of "missing" females in many provinces can be attributed primarily to sex-selective abortions.[34] In certain parts of China, according to one reporter, "Gynaecology clinics offering ultrasound tests do a flourishing business, and are more common in many neighbourhoods than convenience stores."[35]

China has instituted a number of policies to prevent sex-selective abortions, most recently in January 2005, when it banned abortions beyond the 14th week of gestation. As a result, there has been an apparent increase in the number of underground abortion services in "back-alley" settings where, according to one Chinese doctor, "safety is very poor, because the ability of these little clinics to respond to emergencies is very poor."[36] The health hazards associated with late-term abortions are among the many risks to which women and girls are exposed. As in India, sex imbalances in China may be exacerbating the trade of women, both internally and across borders.[37] According to official Chinese statistics from 1990 to 1999, on average 8,000 women per year were rescued from forced marriages by authorities. It is impossible to know what proportion has yet to be rescued.[38]

Root causes: the lesser value of women and girls

An undeniable psychological effect of son preference on women and girls is the internalisation of the meagre value accorded them by society. It could be argued that women carry out sex-selective abortion or female infanticide because of low self-esteem. It is probably more accurate, however, to say that these practices are for many women a sober acknowledgement of the miseries they suffer in oppressive patriarchal societies. Acting on the belief that, in the words of one woman, "It is better they die than live like me," mothers who abort female foetuses or kill their girl babies may think they are actually doing them a favour.[39] One Bombay gynaecologist echoed such wrenching pragmatism: "You can't wish away centuries of thinking by saying boys and girls are equals. ... It is better to get rid of an unwanted child than to make it suffer all its life."[40]

"You can't wish away centuries of thinking by saying boys and girls are equals. ... It is better to get rid of an unwanted child than to make it suffer all its life."

Beyond female psychology, various other theories have been proffered to explain the popularity of sex-selective abortion. First among them is the availability of the sex-identification technology itself. This explanation, however, does not clarify why these practices are not prevalent in more developed areas in China, such as Shanghai and Beijing, as well as in many developed countries where sex-detection technology is widely available.[41] Moreover, legislation already exists to control the use of the technology. In the late 1980s China outlawed sex-determination tests, followed by India in 1994. These measures have not had a significant impact on sex ratios and, as is illustrated in China's "back-alley" clinics, they may make sex-selective abortion more clandestine and expensive, thereby increasing its danger to women. Sex-detection technology does not cause son preference — instead it intensifies "the manifestation of gender bias where this bias is already strong."[42]

Rapid fertility decline is also cited as an explanation for sex-ratio imbalances, particularly in Asian countries. But in Indonesia, Sri Lanka and Thailand, where son preference appears to be nearly nonexistent, a rapid decline in fertility has not led to abnormal sex ratios at birth.[43] Nor can sex selection be solely or even primarily attributed to poverty. Taiwan and Korea are "some of the most developed places in Asia, yet sex-selective abortion is very widespread ... greater economic development, affluence, education, and knowledge do not necessarily ameliorate son preference or reduce the use of sex-selective abortion."[44]

The burden of dowry also has been used as justification for sex-selective abortions. In India, sex-determination clinics solicit clients with slogans like "Better 500 now than 5,000 later", where the number 500 indicates the price of a sex-determination test and the number 5,000 indicates the cost of a bride's dowry payment.[45] This does not explain, however, why sex-ratio imbalances are high in China and South Korea, where bride price, rather than dowry, is the norm, and where the expenses of a son's wedding may exceed that of a daughter's several times over.[46]

Research suggests that poverty actually may protect some Indian girls, especially in settings where they participate in subsistence agriculture and therefore are valued as producers.[47] Wealth, on the other hand, poses a significant risk, and imbalances in sex ratios are most acute among the higher classes in India.[48] In the Punjab region, one of India's more economically advanced states, approximately one in five female foetuses is thought to be aborted following sex-identification testing.[49]

In a study of the middle class in Punjab, the top two reasons cited for aborting a female foetus were "male-dominated society" and "social stigma attached to having a daughter."[50] In China, research indicates that the most seriously perceived gender inequality for many women is that they anticipate they will be deeply discriminated against if they fail to have a son.[51] Regardless of levels of development, patriarchal systems sustain these attitudes. Clearly, any lasting efforts to address sex-selective abortion and female infanticide will require fundamental changes in cultural norms that promote son preference. ◼

An abandoned newborn baby girl lies alone at a hospital in India.

Image: Zana Briski

"Cindy" reaches for the door in a futile attempt to leave her room at the Teddy Bear Clinic for Abused Children in Johannesburg, South Africa, where she will undergo a genital exam to assess the physical effects of the sexual abuse she has suffered. Cindy was brought to the clinic after a nine-year-old boy admitted to playing sexual "games" with her. The boy said he learned the games from his sexually abusive stepfather.

When Cindy does exit the clinic, she will be walking into a future that may prove all the more challenging for having been sexually abused. Like millions of other little girls around the world who have been victimised, Cindy will grapple with the psychological trauma of abuse long after her physical wounds have healed. Compared to girls who have not been violated, Cindy is much more likely to experience a range of short- and long-term behavioural and emotional problems like low self-esteem, depression, suicidal impulses, alcohol abuse, substance abuse and sexual risk-taking later in adolescence and adulthood. She is also more likely to be physically or sexually abused as an adult. Unlike the vast majority of children who have endured such abuse, however, Cindy is lucky. Her trauma has been recognised and is being addressed. With early response, sensitive caregivers and supportive treatment, she has a good chance of not becoming another casualty in the global epidemic of child sexual abuse.

Image: Mariella Furrer

sexual abuse of children

"It was a terrifying experience. When I tried to resist, he pinned my arms above my head. It was so painful and suffocating that I fainted, for I only remember getting up in the morning and finding stains of blood on the bed sheet." Thirty-two-year-old "Laxmi" is remembering the sexual abuse she experienced at age 13. While her description captures the fear and violation associated with rape, what she is describing is her wedding night: The attacker was her adult husband.[1]

While it is widely accepted that child sexual abuse exists in virtually all societies around the world, varied cultural practices lend different interpretations to its meaning. These ethnic disparities make understanding and addressing the global problem of sexual abuse against children a daunting task.

The silent scourge

The term "child sexual abuse"* generally is used to refer to any sexual activity between a child and a closely related family member (incest) or between a child and an adult or older child from outside the family. It involves either explicit force or coercion or, in cases where consent cannot be given by the victim because of his or her young age, implied force.[2]

What constitutes sexual abuse varies across cultures, and legal interpretations of the age of consent also differ. Where laws stipulate an age, the range is from age 12 to age 16 and, in a few countries, up to age

18.[3] While some experts consider peer assault among minors to be within the realm of child sexual abuse, many laws do not recognise this type of violence as such unless there is a significant age difference — usually three or more years — between those involved.[4]

Determining the scale of child sexual abuse worldwide is complicated, not only because it is difficult to define the abuse cross-culturally, but also because of its hidden nature. Children typically do not have the wherewithal to defend themselves against abuse, and they often lack the resources to report or even acknowledge their victimisation. In many instances, a victim's dependent relationship to the perpetrator makes it that much more unlikely that the abuse will be reported. Protective surveillance — either by parents, caregivers or health, social and child welfare systems — is also challenging because many sexually abused children do not have visible injuries. Detecting such mistreatment

*The forms of child sexual abuse presented here are of a noncommercial nature. Child prostitution and pornography are discussed in Chapter 3. The trafficking of girls and women is discussed in Chapter 7.

"requires a high index of suspicion and familiarity with the verbal, behavioural, and physical indicators of abuse."[5] As such, most victims of child sexual abuse suffer in silence.

Nature and scope

Methodological and ethical challenges associated with interviewing young children make research into child sexual abuse difficult. As a result, most population-based analyses are retrospective: Adults (age 18 and older) and, in an increasing number of surveys, adolescents (usually age 15 and over), are asked whether they had ever been exposed to "unwanted" sexual activity during childhood. "Childhood" in these studies varies from under 18 years of age to under 12 years of age.[6] Unwanted sexual activity is often broken out by researchers into two main categories: "contact" abuse, including vaginal or anal penetration with a penis, finger or an object, or giving or receiving oral sex; and "noncontact" abuse, such as being forced to watch pornography, to disrobe or to view each others' genitalia.

Outcomes of these studies vary widely. According to data collated from 25 countries worldwide, estimates of exposure for girls range from as low as 2 percent in Samoa and Serbia and Montenegro to 30 percent or higher in Barbados, Costa Rica and Switzerland. For boys, estimates range from 1 percent in Norway to 20 percent in Nicaragua.[7] It is generally impossible to compare these statistics because none of the research is standardised. Exactly what constitutes child sexual abuse and which types of abuse are included differs from study to study.[8] Based on available data, the World Health Organization estimates that approximately 25 percent of girls and 8 percent of boys around the globe have been subjected to some form of child sexual abuse.[9] Given its hidden nature, these numbers most likely underrepresent the true scope of the problem.

Regardless of its limitations, the growing body of research on child sexual abuse has shed light on some common characteristics of this type

While women do commit sexual violence against children, the vast majority of abusers are men, regardless of the sex of the victim.

of violence. Girls, for example, are significantly more likely to be abused than boys. In many parts of the world, however, boys may be even less likely to report violence than girls, making the true extent of child sexual abuse against boys a critical area for further study. In one notable survey of secondary school and university students in Sri Lanka, 12 percent of girls reported sexual abuse as children, compared to 20 percent of boys.[10] But these findings are exceptional. A review of international studies found that girls are one-and-a-half to three times more likely to report child sexual abuse than boys.[11] Research from the United States indicates that compared with boys, girls are at twice the risk of sexual victimisation throughout childhood and at eight times the risk during adolescence.[12] Police statistics from countries as culturally dissimilar as Lithuania, South Africa and the United States show that the majority of all reported rapes are committed against girls, a sizeable proportion of which are under age 12.[13] In addition, research indicates that girls are at much greater risk of incest than boys. Cross-culturally, from 40 percent to 60 percent of sexual abuse in families involves girls under age 15.[14] Perpetrators who abuse boys are more often from outside the family, although in the Sri Lanka research cited earlier, boys identified family members as the primary perpetrators.[15] Both boys and girls with physical and/or learning disabilities are especially vulnerable.[16]

While women do commit sexual violence against children, the vast majority of abusers are men, regardless of the sex of the victim.[17] Contrary to popular perception, few perpetrators are strangers. Most are fathers, stepfathers, grandfathers, uncles, brothers, cousins, neighbours or family friends. They may be men who exploit their positions of power in the community, such as teachers, religious leaders or doctors. They also can be older children and young men — boyfriends, schoolmates or other acquaintances.

The peak age of vulnerability to child sexual abuse has been estimated at between age seven and age 13, but abuse at younger ages may be significantly underreported because of issues of detection, disclosure and, in the case of retrospective studies, recall.[18] Media coverage of "virgin cure" infant rape in sub-Saharan Africa has drawn special attention to the problem of sexual abuse of very young children in that part of the world. The "virgin cure" is certainly not limited to Africa. Evidence suggests that it is currently practised in Asia as well as the Caribbean and apparently was not uncommon in Renaissance Europe.[19] Allegedly related to a myth that intercourse with a virgin girl is a cure for HIV/AIDS and other sexually transmitted diseases, the extent of virgin-cure infant rape has been contested by researchers in South Africa.[20] Its prevalence remains unknown there as well as in other in parts of the world, but the effects are unarguably devastating for a baby:

Dr Lorna Jacklin, paediatrician and founder of the Teddy Bear Clinic for Abused Children in Johannesburg, South Africa, examines a two-and-a-half-year-old girl who was sexually abused by a man living in the same house as her family. The girl's mother realised something was wrong when her daughter began to simulate sexual movements and became hyperactive. Dr Jacklin believes that the child had been penetrated digitally or that the tip of a penis had been forced into her. During the checkup, the little girl spread her legs without hesitation — as she had been trained to do by her abuser.

Images: Mariella Furrer

"To penetrate the vagina of a small infant, the perpetrators first need to create a common channel between the vagina and the anal canal by forced insertion of an implement. Rape in this manner can be immediately life threatening. The tearing of the perineal body, rectovaginal septum, and anterior anal sphincter can cause infants to die from haemorrhage or abdominal sepsis despite medical care."
The Lancet, 2002

Image: Mariella Furrer

"To penetrate the vagina of a small infant, the perpetrators first need to create a common channel between the vagina and the anal canal by forced insertion of an implement. ... Rape in this manner can be immediately life threatening. The tearing of the perineal body, rectovaginal septum, and anterior anal sphincter can cause infants to die from haemorrhage or abdominal sepsis despite medical care."[21]

The problem of underreporting

Even if children are able to articulate their experiences and to recognise that they have been violated, they may correctly realise that reporting the abuse could result in rejection by caregivers who are more intent on protecting the family's reputation than preserving the rights and welfare of the victim. For example, when "Joan" from Zambia finally managed at age 16 to tell her mother that she had been abused by her stepfather since she was nine years old, her mother threw her out of the house. Joan never reported her case to the police.[22]

While parental denial is a cross-cultural phenomenon, the issue of family rejection is all the more distressing for many child sexual abuse victims in sub-Saharan Africa, where a disproportionate number of these children have been orphaned by the HIV/AIDS pandemic. Another 16-year-old from Zambia described the dilemma of young girls who have lost their caregivers and are left with very few choices:

"After my mother died, I went to my mother's mother. In 2001, she died, so I stopped school. ... Then we went to my auntie, my mom's younger sister. ... Most girls find that they start keeping up [having sex] with stepfathers or uncles. Most are raped — they have no say. They think if you [go] to the police, there will be no one to [take care of them]. So they keep quiet."[23]

Sometimes reluctance to come forward also can be related to overwhelming fears of punishment by the perpetrator, who may threaten to hurt or kill a child for speaking out. In places where the honour of a family or community resides in the sexual purity of its female members, revelations of child sexual abuse can result in extreme forms of retaliation against a victim, no matter how obvious her innocence. In one case from Pakistan in 1999, a 16-year-old girl with severe learning disabilities who was raped in the Northwest Frontier Province was brought to her community's judicial council. Even though

the crime was reported to the police and the perpetrator was arrested, the council decided that she had brought shame to her tribe, and she was killed in front of a tribal gathering.[24]

In a 1998 study conducted in the United States among children age 10 to age 18, 48 percent of boys and 29 percent of girls who had been sexually abused said they had never told anyone — not even a friend.[25] Those who acknowledge abuse often do so years after it has occurred, by which time the constellation of personal and social problems typically associated with child sexual abuse already may have begun.

Short- and long-term impact

Child sexual abuse has a host of negative physical and psychological repercussions, including reproductive-health problems, depression, suicidal tendencies, anxiety, posttraumatic stress disorder, sexual dysfunction and substance abuse. Girls who are sexually abused in childhood may be more likely to engage in sexual risk-taking later in

> When "Joan" from Zambia finally managed at age 16 to tell her mother that she had been abused by her stepfather since she was nine years old, her mother threw her out of the house.

life, compounding their long-term risk of sexually transmitted diseases and early pregnancy. One study from the United States found that girls who experience childhood sexual abuse are nearly three times more likely than nonvictimised girls to become pregnant before age 18.[26]

Of the various forms of child sexual abuse, studies show that forced abuse and penetration, repeated incidences of abuse and parental incest have the most severe impact on victims. Another factor that worsens severity is a marked age difference between the victim and perpetrator. Lack of support from family members or caregivers also increases the potential for distress among child abuse victims.[27] On the other hand, a positive response can bolster a child's natural resiliency and coping skills. Unfortunately, in too many instances, children do not receive the support they need.

Protection and prevention

The Convention on the Rights of the Child, adopted by the United Nations in 1989 and ratified by every member state except the United States and Somalia, requires countries to "undertake to protect the child from all forms of sexual exploitation and sexual abuse" and further obliges them to "take all effective and appropriate measures with a view to abolishing traditional practices prejudicial to the health of children."[28] In acknowledging and respecting cultural differences, however, the Convention does not specify a universal age for sexual consent, nor does it delineate harmful traditional practices. A "child" or "minor" is defined as "every human being below the age of 18 years unless, under the law applicable to the child, majority is attained earlier." As a result, while the Convention is one of the most accepted and effective of all international agreements, its directives regarding child sexual abuse may be open to cultural interpretation, allowing some of the practices that promote child sexual abuse to continue.

In the words of one expert, "There is a sense in which abusers often extend, rather than reject, socially tolerated attitudes towards adult-child relations."[29] Given that girls are at a significantly greater risk than boys of child sexual abuse, it is probably also true that male abusers of girls are reinforcing, rather than rejecting, socially accepted gender

In Kenya in 1991, 19 schoolgirls were killed and 71 others were raped by a gang of male students. In her comments about the incident, the deputy principal stated, "The boys never meant any harm against the girls. They just wanted to rape."

norms related to male dominance and violence. One glaring example of this was a widely publicised case at a secondary school in Kenya in 1991, where 19 schoolgirls were killed and 71 others were raped by a gang of male students. In her comments about the incident, the deputy principal stated, "The boys never meant any harm against the girls. They just wanted to rape."[30]

Perceptions that condone and reinforce gender-based violence exist even among those working in the systems whose stated purpose is to protect and assist victims. Within health and social-services sectors, the judiciary and law enforcement, discriminatory attitudes may limit, or even preclude, appropriate response. In South Africa, for example, where a notoriously small proportion of sexual-assault incidents are reported to police, a 2002 study found that cases involving girls aged 11 to 17 are often "treated as suspect" because of the belief that these older girls are sexually active and, therefore, potentially complicit.[31]

The conviction rate for all rapes reported to the police, whether of a child or an adult, is around 7 percent in South Africa.[32] In the United States, it is approximately 16 percent for reported cases — but when estimates of unreported rapes are factored in, only 6 percent of all rapists are likely to go to jail.[33] Convictions for child rape are especially challenging because of issues of evidentiary substantiation. Even so, the burden of proof may sometimes be so extreme as to beg the question of whether social customs that condone violence at least partly contribute to the failures in child protection, as in this case from Nigeria:

"Sometime in 1999, an uncle sexually assaulted [his niece] of six years. The matter was taken to court and prosecuted. In giving judgement, however, the magistrate set the accused person free for lack of corroboration. This was in spite of the bloodied panties, the testimony of the mother who noticed the pains while bathing her, and the medical evidence from a government hospital. The magistrate said [corroboration] meant testimony from another person who witnessed the alleged act …"[34]

Thus, any efforts to address child sexual abuse must include building the capacity of law enforcement and the judiciary, as well as social services, to promptly and effectively deal with suspected or confirmed cases. Just as importantly in relation to long-term prevention, states must make a serious effort to understand the motivation behind the behaviour of abusers and put in place appropriate prevention programmes.

In many countries, prevention and response initiatives are already well underway. Nevertheless, many children's advocates are concerned about how long it may take before these initiatives will yield tangible results. As such, they have turned considerable attention to raising awareness among children, their families and communities. Grassroots activities include public education about the underlying causes of child sexual abuse, parental-monitoring programmes, life-skills workshops for adolescents and support groups for high-risk children. Another widely applied preventive strategy involves school-based education for children on concepts and skills that promote protection from sexual abuse.

As an institutional entry point for victims and their families, healthcare systems are critically important.[35] An agency's ability to provide immediate medical support — such as treatment for sexually transmitted diseases, including post-exposure prophylaxis for HIV/AIDS and, with older girl victims, emergency contraception — can do much to limit the potential negative health impacts of the abuse. By treating a victim with

Burial of three-year-old Sbongile, who was raped and murdered in November 2003
in Soweto, Johannesburg. Her funeral had been delayed, as the family was too poor
to pay for it. In the end, a local funeral company offered their services free of
charge. Sexual abuse and murder of extremely young children has been increasing
in South Africa in recent years.

Image: Mariella Furrer

compassion and sensitivity, a healthcare provider can also reduce the victim's immediate distress and act as a role model to family members, whose support is so critical to a child's recovery.

Sexual abuse of children is a global problem that cuts across class, religious, ethnic and national boundaries. Even in the most remote places, child sexual abuse may be widespread. In the British colony of Pitcairn in the South Pacific, for example, six men — almost half the adult male population of the tiny island — were found guilty in 2004 for sex offences against the island's girls. The eldest of the convicted men was 78 years old, and the victims were allegedly as young as five years of age. It was the revelations of one victim to a visiting British policewoman that initiated an investigation, which led to other disclosures. According to one woman who used to live on the island, "The girls are treated as though they are a sex thing ... men could do what they want with them."[36] Whereas some islanders defended the practice as a longstanding tradition, conversations with the victims revealed that many of them suffered from depression, insomnia and suicide attempts.[37]

Addressing the epidemic of child sexual abuse requires societies to recognise, rather than minimise or disavow, its impact on victims. Most importantly, states must acknowledge the rights and vulnerability of their children and take measures to protect them. Otherwise, child sexual abuse will remain a silent scourge.   n

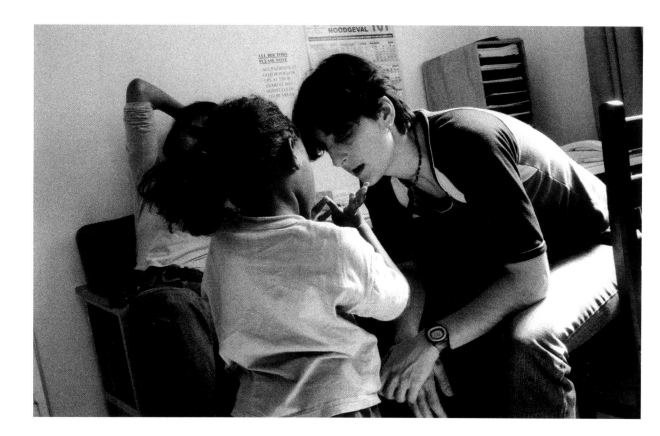

Dr Elli Georgiou at the Karl Bremer Hospital in Cape Town, South Africa, talks to a four-year-old girl who was sexually abused by a six-year-old relative. The girl said she and the boy went behind a fence, where he lifted her skirt, pulled her panties down and "slept with her" (she used a Xhosa expression for this). The boy was too young to be prosecuted or receive treatment at a programme for sex offenders, so his case was referred to the social welfare department, which intended to do one-on-one counselling with the boy. Experts agree that children who exhibit sexual interest long before puberty are likely to have been exposed to prior sexual abuse.

Lisa's fourth birthday party is not taking place at home with family and friends. Instead, she is celebrating at the Teddy Bear Clinic for Abused Children in Johannesburg, South Africa. Her father could not attend the festivities — he is in police custody for repeated sexual abuse of Lisa and her older brother.

Images: Mariella Furrer

A three-year-old girl six days after she was abducted from a friend's first birthday party, raped and badly beaten. Police arrested the perpetrator shortly afterwards. The incident caused a public outcry in South Africa, as the man — who had been in prison for raping a boy — had been released less than a month earlier, after the government granted him amnesty. He was freed on the grounds that the South African legal system considered his attack on the boy to be indecent assault, as the crime of rape only involves female victims. Apparently his release was an error, as amnesty cannot be granted to sex offenders or murderers.

"One evening, at around 7 p.m. in July 2004, I was on the way to collect water. It was about a five-minute walk from my house. I was alone and I had two Jerricans. I filled them with water and took the first home.

"On the way back to collect the second, a young man who was our next-door neighbour came up from behind and grabbed me. I had been walking along a small track, and he took me into the bush. He asked me to sleep with him and I refused. I started screaming. While I was still standing up he was taking off my skirt. When I refused, he pushed me to the ground and then removed it. He took me by force. He was 20 years old. I felt so much pain when he raped me. He just left me there. I left the other Jerrican, ran home and told my mother what had happened.

"That night, I couldn't sleep. My mother went to tell his family, and the boy denied it. The next day I wanted to go to the general hospital, but on the way we met my aunt, who told us to go to DOCS [Doctors on Call Services]. I went there accompanied by my mother, uncle and two aunts. My family did not reject me — they helped me look for medical care. I carry on going to collect water, but not when it is dark."

At DOCS in the Democratic Republic of Congo, "Furaha" received free medical services and was given post-exposure prophylaxis, as well as antibiotics. When she returned to DOCS three months later for an HIV test, her result was negative.

In addition to providing medical support, the staff at DOCS asked a lawyer to help prosecute the case. The police arrested the neighbour the day after the rape and put him in jail. Unfortunately, his parents were able to secure his release, most likely through the payment of a bribe. He is now studying in Bukavu.

Following a school campaign to sensitise school children about sexual violence and teach them what to do if they are abused, more girls have come to DOCS for treatment and advice. A worker there explained that many girls in Goma in the DRC are raped by civilians: "It is a culture where men think they can do anything to a woman and not be accused. The culture has been damaged by war and impunity."

"While I was still standing up he was taking off my skirt. When I refused he pushed me to the ground and then removed it. He took me by force."

A man waits behind bars at the Bellville Police Station in Cape Town, South Africa, after being arrested for the indecent assault of a friend's 10-year-old son. The man had frequently offered to help out his friend by looking after the boy. On at least one occasion, he made the child masturbate him in the shower. Because the boy was too shy to give a verbal statement to investigators, he wrote the details of the assault in a letter.

Image: Mariella Furrer

A young sex worker leans against the bars of a brothel where she lives and works in the red-light area of Dacca, Bangladesh. A significant number of girls in Bangladesh and around the world become sex workers as the result of abduction or coercion. Many exploited girls are held in virtual captivity by their pimps and "mamas", who force as many clients on them as they can find.

child prostitution and pornography

Chapter 3

In 1986, approximately 20,000 children in the Philippines were involved in the sex trade. In 2000, the estimate rose fivefold to 100,000.[1] Between 20 percent and 50 percent of prostitutes in Lithuania are believed to be minors. Children as young as age 11 are known to work as brothel prostitutes, and children from children's homes — some as young as 10 or 12 years of age — have been used in pornographic movies.[2] In Cambodia, the average age at which children enter the sex trade dropped from age 18 in 1992 to age 13 or 14 in 1994, while in Taiwan, the average age is between 11 and 15.[3] In Asia, an estimated one million children in the sex industry are held in conditions that are indistinguishable from slavery.[4] When 100,000 Indian commercial sex workers were asked the age at which they entered the industry, 40 percent said they had started before age 18.[5]

The global child-sex trade

The United Nations Children's Fund (UNICEF) estimates that one million children around the world enter the sex trade every year, the majority of them girls.[6] The International Labour Organization's figures from 2000 indicated that as many as 1.8 million children were being exploited in prostitution and pornography worldwide, with girls representing 80 percent to 90 percent of the victims in most countries.[7] Other estimates have put the number of children engaged in sex work significantly higher, closer to 10 million.[8]

Global approximations such as these are really nothing more than educated guesses. The clandestine nature of commercial sexual exploitation, coupled with the fact that many of the world's sexually exploited children exist in society's blind spot, means that untold numbers of these children — the majority of whom are poor, uneducated, homeless and rejected by society — will never be captured in any statistic. These are just three of their stories:

"Rachel", a 12-year-old Albanian who worked in a local cigarette factory, was taken to Italy and forced to work as a prostitute by her 29-year-old husband three months after they married. If she refused to sell herself on the streets, he beat her. "I worked morning to night every day," said Rachel, who serviced as many as 10 clients daily to earn the US $250 that her pimping husband demanded of her.[9]

"Sarah", from the United States, was 10 years old when she was sexually molested live on camera by her friend's father. The camera was connected to his computer, which allowed him to take simultaneous instructions from members of an Internet-based paedophile club about how to molest her. He later traded the images on the Internet.[10]

child prostitution and pornography   35

"Saida", a Kenyan, dropped out of school when she was 15 to take care of her sick mother. After her mother died, Saida began cooking and selling beans to help support her siblings. Once, when the family had no food, Saida agreed to have sex with a young man in her neighbourhood, with the understanding that he would give her money in return. According to Saida, "He gave me 300 to 500 shillings [approximately $4 to $7] when I slept with him, and this helped. But I worried about diseases since I knew he was sleeping with other women."[11]

Rachel, Sarah and Saida are among the lucky few who managed to extricate themselves from a cycle of abuse. Rachel was rescued by an antitrafficking organization and returned to her family in Albania. She later received financial aid to enrol in a vocational-training programme. Sarah, after initially denying that she had been molested by her friend's father, disclosed the abuse with the support of her mother. Her testimony in turn assisted the police in sending the perpetrator to jail and led to the first major international police effort to apprehend Internet paedophiles. Women in her community told Saida about a local programme to help girls who are either at risk of entering or already are engaged in commercial sex work. Through that project, she plans to take a hairdressing course and to get her three younger sisters back into school.

Most sexually exploited children are not as fortunate. Thea Pumbroek was six years old when she died of a cocaine overdose while being filmed for one of the many pornographic videos in which she was forced to feature. Few people know of her tragic life and death: "She seems to have been treated in death as little more than the object she had been in life."[12]

Defining commercial sexual exploitation of children

Experts agree that sexual exploitation of children is hardly a new phenomenon. It has existed in various forms in every culture around the world as far back as "the most remote stages of the history of mankind."[13] However, the more recent forces of globalisation, internationalisation and free trade have conspired to produce "what appears to be a dramatic increase worldwide" in the buying and selling of children for sexual purposes.[14]

In the modern world, young girls and boys are forced or coerced into prostitution, trafficked for sex within and across borders, sold into sexual slavery or exploited for the purposes of pornography and sex tourism. All of these activities constitute commercial sexual exploitation of children (CSEC).* Although there is no universal definition for the term, CSEC generally describes sexual abuse of children that is primarily economically driven.[15]

Any child who is seduced, coerced or forced to engage in sex for material gain is being commercially exploited. While money is very often the mode of exchange, CSEC also can involve the trade of food,

The more recent forces of globalisation, internationalisation and free trade have conspired to produce "what appears to be a dramatic increase worldwide" in the buying and selling of children for sexual purposes.

shelter, protection, drugs or other goods and services. In some cases, such as the production and sale of pornography, a child may be exploited for commercial purposes without any exchange of money or goods between the child and his/her exploiter.

The person who engages in sexual activity with the child is the direct exploiter. Universally, the majority of direct exploiters are men. Some are paedophiles — adults who are sexually aroused by prepubescent and pubescent boys or girls. Others do not necessarily conform to the conventional definition of a paedophile but nevertheless target children because they believe they are less likely to contract sexually transmitted diseases. Still others may use children simply out of convenience or curiosity and are indifferent to their young age.[16]

There are also networks of other exploiters, such as pimps, traffickers, family members and members of organized crime, who may not necessarily engage in direct sexual activity with a child, but who facilitate child sexual exploitation for financial or material gain. Men are well-represented in the ranks of these "third-party" exploiters, but women also figure prominently as organizers and beneficiaries. In some settings, women are the essential and even primary promoters of the child-sex trade. Too often these women, and to a lesser degree their

_____

*As trafficking of girls and women is discussed in detail in Chapter 7, the focus of this chapter will be primarily on child prostitution and pornography. It is important, however, to note that all forms of commercial sexual exploitation of children are strongly interrelated and that one type often contributes to another. Children may be trafficked for prostitution, for example, and then exploited by sex tourists and made to participate in the production of pornography.

"Angelica", who is 14 years old and works as a prostitute in Rita, Latvia. During the day she meets with friends and plays in the amusement arcades. By night, she works in the red-light district before returning to the flat where she lives, and where one tap of running water serves many families.

Image: Jorgen Hildebrandt/Panos

Pornographic DVDs exchange hands in Kabul, Afghanistan. Some Afghan cities have seen a significant rise in the availability of pornography since the fall of the Taliban regime in 2001. Internet availability and DVD technology have brought about a huge global increase in access to pornography, with sex-related sites consistently being the most visited sites on the World Wide Web.

Image: Fredrik Neumann/Panos

The pimp of a Thai sex worker in Johannesburg, South Africa, is arrested after a police raid. He is being charged with possession of a large number of Asian-made child pornography DVDs.

Image: Mariella Furrer

male counterparts, are "yesterday's exploited children, who are today exploiting the children who will become tomorrow's exploiters."[17]

For many third-party exploiters, greed is a major incentive, reinforced by traditions or beliefs that deny children their basic rights. In some instances, the same circumstances that propel children into the sex trade also drive third-party exploiters: poverty, lack of economic alternatives, little or no education, domestic violence, drug addiction, gender inequities and other forms of social discrimination or exclusion.[18] Despite any shared circumstances, exploiters always have the advantage

Many countries "have come to depend on the sale of women's and children's services almost like a cash crop."

over the children they abuse. By definition, in every case of commercial sexual exploitation of a child, maximum benefits accrue to the exploiter, and the child's rights and wellbeing are abrogated, regardless of whether the child engages willingly in the sexual activity.[19]

As with noncommercial child sexual abuse, issues of consent are considered by law to be irrelevant if the child is under a certain age. In some countries, all pornography and/or prostitution is illegal, regardless of the age of the person involved. In a growing number of countries, trafficking is a crime. Even so, the United Nations Special Rapporteur on the Sale of Children, Child Prostitution and Child Pornography has expressed concern that in many parts of the world child-sexual-exploitation offences are not considered crimes.[20]

Where pornography and/or prostitution are legal, and where there is also a relatively low age of consent, children may be at greater risk of specific forms of commercial sexual exploitation, such as sex tourism. But even in countries where prostitution and/or pornography are banned, the tendency of criminal justice systems to punish sex workers more aggressively than sex exploitersm combined with the "underground" nature of the sex industry, means that children caught in the sex trade in these settings may be among the most difficult of all sexually exploited children to reach and assist.[21]

Child prostitution in the contemporary world

In 1998, the *Economist* estimated that the global sex industry generates $20 billion each year, one-quarter of which is the result of child prostitution.[24] Many countries "have come to depend on the sale of

women's and children's services almost like a cash crop."[25] The highest numbers of prostituted children — some as young as 10 years of age — are thought to be in Brazil, India, China, Thailand and the United States, but the child sex trade is an international problem.[26]

Most child prostitutes are integrated into mainstream prostitution markets. They generally are not targeted by abusers because of their young age. There are exceptions, however. Paedophilia is one. Another is the increasing demand in prostitution markets for "virgins". Young girls are sold over and over again — by pimps, brothel owners, within strip clubs, etc. — under the false pretence of being free from sexually transmitted diseases by virtue of their "virgin" status.[26] Yet another exception is child-sex tourism — where people travel, often with the assistance of Internet-based tour operators, to other countries to engage in commercial sex acts with children. The destinations typically have a lower legal age of sexual consent than the sex tourist's home country or comparatively lax law enforcement. According to the International Tribunal for Children's Rights, "Sex tours enable men and women who would not identify with the label paedophile to travel to exotic places where they feel able to step outside whatever sexual mores may constrain them at home, because they believe these rules do not exist in foreign cultures. Powerful forces of racism, misogyny, neo-colonialism and economic exploitation combine to sell 'exotic' and 'erotic' sex vacations."[26]

In some settings, there are longstanding traditions which dictate that women and girls automatically enter the sex industry — and that men work as pimps for their sisters, wives and daughters. The Rajnat men in Rajasthan, India, for example, have lived off the earnings of the females in their families for centuries. While Rajnat girls historically serviced the princely families in the Raj system, they now service local farmers and merchants. Such is the extent of their involvement in the commercial sex industry that wives are in short supply in certain communities. Even those men who manage to find spouses may be left to care for their children while their wives work within the sex industry. These families raise their daughters to do the same.[27]

Noncommercial markets

Child prostitution also takes place outside commercial markets. In parts of Africa and Asia, some girls are offered or sold into sexual slavery by their families — who are seeking political assistance, economic benefit, spiritual appeasement or all of the above. These children then serve priests, wealthy men or even — in the form of "temple prostitutes" — a deity.[28]

Street children of any culture might engage in "survival sex" for subsistence. So might other poor or socially marginalised children who lack any other resources or support. A study of adolescents in Zambia found that many girls have sex with their male peers in exchange for money or goods. While the girls acknowledged that poverty is their prime motivator, the boys explained that "having sex with girls is a way of proving that one is a man and it is a means of gaining popularity."[29]

"Sugar daddy" relationships further extend this unequal power dynamic. The global phenomenon of the sugar daddy appears to be gaining popularity in sub-Saharan Africa, where older men — hoping to avoid exposure to HIV/AIDS and other sexually transmitted diseases — coerce adolescents into sexual relationships by offering money, cell phones or other gifts. While the risk of exposure to disease may be reduced for the older man, it is more likely to be increased for the girl. Research suggests that girls in relationships with marked age asymmetries have less success negotiating condom use.[30] This, in fact, is true for all sexually exploited girls, regardless of whether their victimisation occurs in commercial or noncommercial settings.

Girls are not the only victims of the sex trade. Although data are still lacking, it is likely that in every country a considerable number of young boys also are sexually exploited. In Sri Lanka, significantly more boys than girls work as child prostitutes.[31] The Dominican Republic, Haiti,

In the United States alone, the estimated revenues of the child pornography market are approximately $2 billion to $3 billion per year, making it one of the country's most lucrative cottage industries.

the Czech Republic, Egypt and Morocco are a sampling of destinations offering sex tourism involving young boys.[32] In Iraq, where the number of commercial sex workers has increased in the midst of political turmoil, hundreds of young boys are believed to be sexually exploited. Many of them work under the menacing control of street gangs. Sixteen-year-old Hassan, whose homosexuality is grounds for death under Iraq's Islamic law, was forced into the commercial sex industry by a man who took pictures of Hassan while they were having sex. The man threatened to send the pictures to Hassan's family if the child refused to be pimped out to other men.[33]

Despite the clear vulnerability of boys — especially those who are impoverished, gay or, for other reasons, cast out of society — the majority of child prostitutes in the world are girls. Their exploitation is in many ways an extension of gender norms and behaviours prevalent in the societies in which they are bought and sold. In Tokyo, for example, where a 2001 survey "found that 72 percent of teenage girls had been groped on their way to school," a sex club offers clients a service called "ripping pants off a school girl". Another option is to molest girls who are holding onto ceiling straps in a simulation of a subway train.[34]

Child pornography in the contemporary world

Not surprisingly, Japan is a major Asian producer of child pornography.[35] Around the world, there are strong links between child prostitution, child-sex tourism and the production of child pornography.[36]

Girls and boys of all ages, including infants, are sexually exploited in pornographic imagery.[37] Both "a crime in and of itself, and … a picture of a crime scene," child pornography stretches back centuries.[38] In the last 30 years, however, it has become a thriving enterprise, with images that are more hardcore than before and increased access to those images via the Internet.[39]

Most paedophiles do not use child pornography to turn a profit. They are more likely to stockpile pictures and films that they can copy and trade, thereby adding to their private collection. Nevertheless, the advent of modern home video and personal computer technology has made child pornography progressively easier to produce and trade without detection. As a result, underground distribution has become more organized and commercialised. In the United States alone, the estimated revenues of the child pornography market are approximately $2 billion to $3 billion per year, making it one of the country's most lucrative cottage industries. Russia is notable as an emerging market, second only to the United States as a source for child pornography.

In modern times, no region in the world is exempt from the production of child pornography. During the industry's early days, most images were of Western children, many from the United States, whose pictures were commercially reproduced in Europe.[40] A minority of other images were from India, Mexico and Africa. With the growth in sex tourism, images of

Fifteen-year-old prostitutes in Birmingham, England.

A slave girl draws water for her master's household in Niger, where many slave children are born of rape. Regardless of their age, female slaves in Niger are exploited tirelessly by their masters for free labour, as sexual servants and as "slave breeders" of the next generation.

Image: Georgina Cranston/IRIN

Asian and Eastern European children were added to the global stock and trade in child pornography, as sex tourists filmed and then distributed their encounters with children.[41] Latin American children also have been exploited on film by both international and local paedophiles and child abusers. In Brazil, street children in particular have been targeted for pornography that is exported to North America.[42]

Many victims of child pornography are boys. In the United States, over 50 percent of child pornography seized in raids depicts boys, and in Canada that figure is 75 percent. In Japan, however, girls are captured in the majority of images.[43] For both boys and girls, their exploitation on film can have a lasting psychological impact. Because of an almost inexhaustible shelf-life, pornographic images can continue to be reproduced and shared, such that "long after the child has grown up, he or she knows that someone, somewhere, may be looking at their picture, witnessing their degradation and distress."[44] This has perhaps never been more true than in the age of the Internet.

Evidence suggests that a significant number of consumers of child pornography are likely to be active child abusers.[45] The Internet facilitates this link, because it "not only acts as a mechanism for making, displaying, trading, and distributing child porn, it also acts as a vehicle for child pornographers to make contact with and ensnare new victims."[46] Child sex abusers can enter Internet chat rooms where children congregate, gain their trust and either solicit pictures of them online or arrange to meet them — sometimes travelling across continents — for the purposes of sexually abusing them.[47] One study from the United States found that one in five children who go online regularly is approached by Internet strangers for sex.[48]

Moreover, the Internet allows paedophiles and child abusers to receive positive reinforcement in a way that can legitimise and normalise their criminal impulses and behaviours. According to one convicted paedophile, "The Internet is great. It's a whole world that sucks you in. Within 24 hours of first going on I'd found child porn. … I found people I could talk to. People who felt like me … I never had so many friends."[49]

Global recognition of the problem

During the last decade of the 20th century, the international community gathered forces to stem the rising tide of commercial sexual exploitation of children. In 1989 the United Nations General Assembly passed the Convention on the Rights of the Child (CRC), which requires its signatories to protect children against all kinds of sexual exploitation and abuse. In 1991, the United Nations appointed its first Special Rapporteur to address the issue. And in 1996, 1,300 people from around the world gathered in Stockholm, Sweden, to participate in the First World Congress Against Commercial Sexual Exploitation of Children.

A ground-breaking outcome of the week-long Stockholm meeting was the unanimous adoption by 122 participating governments of a Declaration and Agenda for Action. The Agenda requires countries to

> The Internet "not only acts as a mechanism for making, displaying, trading, and distributing child porn, it also acts as a vehicle for child pornographers to make contact with and ensnare new victims."

"develop or strengthen and implement national laws to establish the criminal responsibility of service providers, customers, and intermediaries in child prostitution, child trafficking, child pornography, including possession of child pornography, and other unlawful sexual activity."[50] It also calls on governments to "adopt a non-punitive approach to child victims of commercial sexual exploitation in keeping with the rights of the child."[51] This Agenda was reiterated and reinforced five years later by participants of the Second World Congress, held in Yokohama, Japan.

In May 2000, the United Nations adopted a protocol specifically prohibiting the sale of children, child prostitution and child pornography. In November of the same year, it passed the "Palermo Protocol", which focuses on the prevention of and punishment for human trafficking, especially that of women and children. While these international instruments are important steps forward in terms of holding governments accountable to protect children, their ratification is only a small part of a much larger process of addressing the global escalation of the commercial sexual exploitation of children.

In the past five years, considerable progress has been made in implementing protective regulations related to several aspects of commercial sexual exploitation of children. At least 32 countries, for example, have introduced extraterritorial laws that support prosecution of their citizens who commit child sex crimes abroad. The World Tourism Organization has created a global Code of Conduct for the Protection of Children from Sexual Exploitation in Travel and Tourism.

Some countries have increased the legal age to participate in pornography to coincide with the age of majority rather than the (often lower) age of consent. And in some settings hotlines have been established to report Internet websites promoting child pornography.[52]

Despite these gains, the United Nations Special Rapporteur on the Sale of Children, Child Prostitution and Child Pornography observed in his 2003 report that many national laws do not adequately criminalise

In many instances, sexually exploited children are either ignored or treated as criminal delinquents.

offences against children.[53] Even in the growing number of countries that have legislated against child sexual exploitation, challenges remain in its implementation. There is "an alarming lack" of training for law-enforcement officers and members of the judiciary, and child victims may not have access to legal support.[54] Where legal processes are initiated, there may be extended delays and unreliable outcomes, further victimising the children involved. This "process of revictimization of children and adolescents who seek remedial action," according to the Special Rapporteur, "nourishes the vicious cycle of impunity."[55]

One case involving an Australian diplomat who allegedly sexually exploited two Cambodian street children, for example, took two years to bring to court in Australia. In accordance with Australian extraterritorial law, the children were brought to Australia to give evidence. During their aggressive cross-examination, they were unclear as to how the process worked and gave confusing answers. As a result, the judge dismissed the case, acquitting the defendant. The children were sent back to Cambodia, where their futures remain uncertain. One of the children currently travels to and from the border with Thailand, presumably to work as a prostitute.[56]

In many other instances, sexually exploited children are either ignored or treated as criminal delinquents. They bear the myriad physical and psychological wounds associated with their exploitation — rape, physical assault, HIV/AIDS and other sexually transmitted diseases, unwanted pregnancy and multiple additional reproductive-health problems, social stigmatisation, antisocial behaviour, substance abuse, depression and suicidality, to name only a few.[57] Their recovery depends not only on the implementation of effective and protective laws, but also on the ability of organizations to find and support them.

In an effort to document best practices, the organization End Child Prostitution, Child Pornography, and the Trafficking of Children for Sexual Exploitation International (ECPAT) committed itself at the Stockholm Congress to develop a database of country-specific information on national plans to combat the sexual exploitation of children. Its summaries of regional, national and community-based prevention and response programming include, among others, descriptions of advocacy initiatives in Honduras, law-enforcement strategies in Cambodia and peer-education programmes in China. These case studies are an inspiration for future initiatives — so that current generations will receive help rather than recrimination, and fewer children will suffer the experiences of Rachel, Sarah, Saida, Thea, Mary and millions like them. ◾

Young girls and boys in a police cage in Manila's red-light district after being picked up off the streets in the early hours of the morning. Some of them were selling chewing gum or cigarettes; others were likely working as underage prostitutes. The children can be released after posting bail or paying a small fine. Observers in the Philippines report that for $10, the police on duty will "bail out" individual children for paedophiles, who take them to hotels and sexually abuse them.

Image: Peter Marlow/Magnum

When "Mary", a 14-year-old Kenyan girl was very young — she cannot remember her age at the time — her father claimed that she was not his biological daughter and tried to kill her. Running away from her house with no clothes on, she was taken in by "Jane", an adolescent, who bathed, clothed and fed her. Jane worked nights as a child prostitute, and Mary soon joined her. One night, Jane brought Mary to a man's house. Mary, who was high on alcohol and marijuana, doesn't remember much of what happened, only that she was raped repeatedly and then locked in a room. For three days, her hands and legs were tied together and she was raped into submission. Mary's rapist then became her pimp: He sent her out onto the streets at night and forced her to hand over her earnings each morning.

"I was so unhappy, but I had no choice. I wanted to escape. One day when I tried to escape, he caught me and put a knife to my throat. I screamed so loud. A neighbour heard me and came to the house. She took the knife away but didn't help me any further."

A group of child prostitutes who had heard about Mary's troubles informed the police, who arrested her pimp and required him to undergo a medical examination, which confirmed gonorrhoea. Mary, who stayed at the police station for two days and also had a check-up, had contracted gonorrhoea as well. Police contacted the local nongovernmental organization End Child Prostitution in Kenya to help Mary. The agency, which had no funds for a shelter, referred Mary to a rescue centre in Nairobi, several hours away from where she was living. The facility, run by the Irish humanitarian agency GOAL, provides children with basic literacy training and medical support.

"I was so unhappy with my life, but had no possible escape. On the streets I had to keep all of my feelings inside — there was no one to talk to. At last I am okay. I feel so lucky to have been brought here. I still have terrible nightmares about that man when I sleep. If someone talks to me about that time in my life, I go blank and feel dizzy. I cannot think straight. I have never had an education, but I am being given a chance here to learn to read and write. I can't think so far into the future at the moment. I am just so grateful for the help I have been given since my rescue.

"There are so many girls where I come from who have been raped and are living a life like I did. If anyone wants to help, we desperately need a shelter for those children to escape to — a shelter that can offer vocational training, and give them a chance for a better life."

Image: Georgina Cranston/IRIN

"Roxanna" takes a rest while waiting for clients alongside a main road in Managua, Nicaragua. She is 15 years old and walks the streets at night with other teenagers who also work as prostitutes to help their families. Roxanna, like many of them, had been sexually abused when she was younger: "I was raped when I was 13 by two guys. It was seven in the evening, and I was on my way home from the market. I had to stay at home for a month after the rape. We needed money — we were so in debt that I decided to go to the streets." Roxanna's father left the family when she was nine, and her mother is 60 years old and diabetic. "She has ulcers on her legs and can't walk," Roxanna said. "Two months after I started working she asked me how I earned the money. I told her — she agreed there was no alternative. Now I go out every night."

A young woman of the Samburu tribe in northern Kenya undergoes circumcision as an essential cultural rite before marriage. Women hold her mouth closed to mute her cries of pain. The following photos in this chapter were taken of another Samburu girl, "Juliana", during different stages of the same ceremony.

All images in this chapter by Mariella Furrer

female genital mutilation

Dating back centuries among cultures predominantly clustered in West, Central and the Horn of Africa, as well as Egypt, female genital mutilation (FGM) is a traditional rite to which an estimated two million girls are subjected each year. Performed as early as infancy and as late as age 30, most girls undergo the procedure between the ages of four and 12. Roughly 100 million to 140 million women and girls alive today have undergone some form of medically unwarranted genital cutting.[1] The prevalence of FGM varies widely in the 28 African countries where it is practised, from approximately 5 percent in Uganda and the Democratic Republic of Congo to over 90 percent in Djibouti, Egypt, Eritrea, Ethiopia, Guinea, Mali, Sierra Leone, Somalia and northern Sudan.[2] Cases also have been reported in some communities in the Arabian peninsula and South and Southeast Asia, and among African immigrants living in Australia, Europe and the Americas.[3]

Defining FGM

Synonymously identified as female genital cutting or female genital circumcision, "female genital mutilation" broadly encompasses "all procedures involving partial or total removal of the external female genitalia or other injury to the female genital organs whether for cultural or other non-therapeutic reasons."[4] Although many variations in procedures as well as terminology exist within and across the cultures where FGM is practised, a standardised international classification for FGM was collaboratively developed in 1995 by the World Health Organization (WHO), the United Nations Children's Fund (UNICEF) and the United Nations Fund for Population Assistance (UNFPA).

The first method within the classification, commonly referred to as "clitoridectomy", involves holding the clitoris of a girl child between thumb and index finger, pulling it out and then partially or fully amputating it with a swift stroke of a razor, knife or other sharp instrument. The second method, "excision", similarly involves cutting away the clitoris, but further entails slicing off a portion or all of the inner vaginal lips (labia minora).

With "infibulation", the third classification, the inner surface of the outer lips of the vagina (labia majora) is also cut. The wound is then fused together with thorns, dung or other poultices, or stitches — a process that may be reinforced by tying together the girl's legs for a period of up to six weeks. The resulting scar tissue typically covers the urethra and part or most of the vagina. A small hole is retained for the discharge of urine and menstrual blood.[5] A fourth, "unclassified" type of FGM includes a wide range of harmful practices, from piercing or incising the clitoris to burning, scraping or introducing corrosive substances into the vagina.[6]

While it is estimated that 85 percent of all FGM practices worldwide fall within the first two types, approximately 80 percent to 90 percent of girls in Djibouti, Somalia and Sudan, as well as small percentages of girls in Chad, Egypt, Eritrea, Ethiopia, Gambia, Guinea, Kenya, Mali, Nigeria and Tanzania undergo infibulation.[7]

International debate regarding the appropriate terminology to describe FGM is almost as controversial as the practice itself. All official United Nations documents currently use the term "mutilation" to emphasise its medically gratuitous and severe nature. Many working on the ground, however, maintain that the term "cutting" is a more value-neutral and therefore respectful articulation of a practice to which many cultures and individuals remain committed. Others working both internationally and locally have used the term "circumcision". While still popular idiomatically, the use of this term is diminishing in international discourse because its association to male circumcision (removing the foreskin of the penis) minimises the nature and effects of most types of genital cutting performed on women. Comparable genital "circumcision" for men would involve the partial or complete removal of the penis, in addition to the foreskin.[8]

Although male circumcision is considered by some advocates to be a fundamental violation of a boy's right to bodily integrity, its health impacts are currently the subject of heated discussion. Those opposed to male circumcision argue that it has negative impact on men's health and sexuality. Evidence also suggests that when performed in unhygienic settings male circumcision can lead to infections, injuries and even death.[9] A recent study conducted in South Africa, however, concluded that circumcision may have positive effects for males in terms of reducing their risk of contracting HIV.[10]

For females, the evidence is not similarly equivocal. Even the most minimal form of FGM can affect a girl's normal sexual function and put her at risk of a wide spectrum of negative health consequences.[11]

The health effects of FGM

The immediate physical effects of FGM may include severe pain, shock and haemorrhaging. There is also high risk of local and systemic infections, including abscesses, ulcers, delayed healing, septicaemia, tetanus and gangrene. Long-term physical complications may include urine retention and associated urinary-tract infections, obstruction of menses and related reproductive-tract infections, infertility, painful intercourse and prolonged and obstructed labour.[12] FGM also can facilitate the transmission of HIV, especially if infected infants and girls are cut in group ceremonies where circumcisors use the same instrument on all the initiates. Even after it has healed, the scarred or dry vulva of an excised or infibulated woman can be torn easily during sexual intercourse, increasing the likelihood of HIV transmission by an infected partner.

In addition to a host of physical effects, the psychological terror of FGM may also have a lasting impact, including a sense for some girls of no longer having control over their own bodies — especially if they are

> "When you cut a girl, you know she will remain pure until she gets married, and that after marriage, she will be faithful. … But when you leave a girl uncut, she sleeps with any man in the community."

ambushed and forced to submit to the procedure. One young girl from Burkina Faso recalled what she initially thought was a casual visit to a relative's house:

"They asked us to go around for sweets and eggs. When we arrived, three women caught me, bundled me in to the toilet, pinned me down and undressed me. … I saw the knife and knew what was going to happen. I cried out, but I couldn't find the words to speak."[13]

"Medicalisation" of FGM

In some settings, the heightened awareness of the negative health consequences of FGM has led to increased demand for and supply of genital cutting by official health personnel. A 1995 Egyptian demographic and health survey found that young Egyptian girls were three times as likely as their mothers to be cut by a healthcare professional.[14] Data from 2000 suggests that more than half of all cutting in Egypt is done by doctors and nurses. Although cutting by medical professionals does undoubtedly reduce some of the immediate risks of FGM, the WHO and other international entities have advocated strongly against this "medicalisation" of FGM, citing the performance of needless procedures on children as a violation of medical ethics. Medicalisation is also occurring outside of health facilities. In Kenya, for example, circumcisors sometimes purchase antiseptics and tetanus toxoid to prevent infection. This type of activity is much more difficult to address than that of trained professionals.[15]

The wedding ceremony of "Juliana", a Samburu girl in northern Kenya, is drawn out over three days and will include ritual circumcision. She will become the second wife of an older man who lives 130 kilometres from her village. Juliana's responsibility will be to herd his cattle. Members of the community told the photographer of this series that Juliana was 16 or 17 years old.

On the first day, Juliana's head is shaved in preparation for her excision. The skins she will sit on during the cutting are blessed, and her beaded necklaces are arranged.

Despite some trends towards medicalisation, FGM most often is performed by traditional practitioners in poor sanitary conditions and without anaesthesia. As initiates, many girls are forbidden to discuss the process or impact of the procedure, especially with unexcised women.[16] The secrecy of the ritual, the absence of adequate health facilities in many of the countries where FGM is practised and the acceptance of its associated risks and complications may conspire to prevent women from receiving appropriate care for FGM-related complications. Nearly 84 percent of infibulated women in Eritrea, for example, reported receiving no medical assistance for problems related to cutting.[17]

Attitudes sustaining the practice

Custom, religious belief and, at the heart of these, the desire to maintain a woman's purity by restraining her sexuality have prevailed over the negative health effects of FGM to perpetuate the practice. A female circumcisor from Kenya explained that the ritual is a way to ensure purity and fidelity:

"When you cut a girl, you know she will remain pure until she gets married, and that after marriage, she will be faithful. ... But when you leave a girl uncut, she sleeps with any man in the community."[18]

While there is no definitive evidence documenting why or when FGM began, many theorise that it provided families a means to ensure virginity before marriage. Infibulation scars in particular form a "seal" that both guarantees and confirms a bride's chastity, and even the less severe forms of FGM may diminish girls' and women's sexual desire, thus decreasing the likelihood of premarital relations.[19]

Social control of women and girls remains a primary argument for FGM even today. According to a demographic and health researcher in Eritrea, the most common defence for FGM among survey respondents was that "Chastity is a woman's only virtue and all measures have to be taken to maintain it. ... Women have to be protected, and infibulation is the defense mechanism."[20] Chastity is not a universal goal, however. In some communities in Kenya, Uganda and select West African countries, a girl may be expected to produce a child before marriage to prove her fertility. If she successfully delivers a baby, she will then undergo FGM and be married.[21] In these atypical examples, FGM is practised on older girls and women.

Both men and women who embrace the practice say that FGM promotes cleanliness, attractiveness and good health. Implicit in their view is the perception that female genitalia are dirty, unsightly and, if left in their natural state, may breed disease or be susceptible to other maladies. The tradition also increases marriageability. FGM is believed to confer a sense of general calm on its initiates and, insofar as it decreases sexual desire, to limit the risk of extramarital affairs. In the words of one tribal elder in Kenya, "A circumcised woman will choose a partner for love, not for sex."[22]

In some communities, in fact, FGM is a prerequisite to marriage. Failing to comply with the tradition may constitute grounds for divorce and/or forced excision.[23] In others, bride price may be significantly lower for an uncircumcised woman. A smaller vaginal opening is thought to increase a husband's sexual pleasure. Despite this, FGM cannot be assumed to be solely or even primarily "male-driven". Some men currently are acknowledging the negative impact of FGM and speaking out against it, even as societies of women continue to insist that FGM is a critical rite of passage for girls.

Practised by followers of Christianity, Islam and traditional or animist faiths, as well as some Ethiopian Jews, FGM transcends religious belief. Nevertheless, and notwithstanding the fact that FGM predates Islam, research suggests that Muslims in particular associate FGM with *sunnah*, or "required practice". In fact, clitoridectomy is referred to as "*sunnah* circumcision" in Arabic.[24] Although most Islamic clerics actively discourage infibulation and an increasing number of *imams* are speaking out against any form of FGM, some maintain that lesser forms are acceptable. For example, one cleric from Ethiopia, speaking at a regional conference on female genital mutilation concluded, "This conference,

> **"I was circumcised at 13 and have myself circumcised 23 girls since then. This is the only way I earn a living and feed my children. I was at school when my parents were killed – I had nobody to take care of me and entered the secret society."**

and the medical research associated with it, does not show that the *sunnah* circumcision — cutting only the outer part of the clitoris — has caused any medical complications. ... I believe that Islam condones the *sunnah* circumcision; it is acceptable."[25]

Across cultures, religions and continents, one common feature of the practice of FGM is the social conditioning of women and girls to accept and defend it.[26] Longstanding traditions and social norms have ordained

On the second day, Juliana is taken to the door of the hut where she will be excised. She removes her clothing, and cow's milk is poured over her head as a blessing. As she sits down, she is held firmly in place by other women as the circumcisor, another Samburu woman, prepares for the ritual.

Only women are allowed to attend the cutting, where Juliana's *labia minora* and clitoris are removed. In Juliana's case, the process took between five and 10 minutes. The other women cover her mouth to stifle her screams.

FGM as a social imperative that promotes the future wellbeing of girls. In most communities, songs and poems are used to deride and taunt unexcised girls. Myths similarly help to ensure FGM's perpetuation. In Nigeria, for example, some communities believe that if a baby's head touches the clitoris during delivery, the infant will die.[27] Community and family pressure to conform to traditional practices is great for both mothers and girls, and mothers are often the primary actors responsible for their daughters' mutilation. In the words of one mother who was interviewed at a refugee camp in Kenya, "The practice adds to a family's prestige in the community. Who would not want to bring honour to her family?"[28]

There are economic aspects to FGM as well. The practice is an important source of income for circumcisors, who most often are female. In impoverished settings, the financial impetus can be very strong. The social support of the secret societies also can be very compelling, as one 26-year-old female circumcisor explained: "I was circumcised at 13 and have myself circumcised 23 girls since then. This is the only way I earn a living and feed my children. I was at school when my parents were killed — I had nobody to take care of me and entered the secret society. It was from there I got married."[29]

Response: from legislation to prevention

In the 1970s and 1980s, FGM gained international attention as a critical health issue for women and girls. As a result, women's advocates have broadened the discourse surrounding FGM to include gendered considerations of women's subordination and oppression, acknowledging FGM as a violation of internationally recognised human rights, including rights to life, liberty and freedom from torture. Largely in response to the worldwide action of numerous local and international organizations, the WHO launched a 20-year plan in 1997 to accelerate the elimination of FGM. Since its inception, the WHO initiative has informed individual country plans to eradicate the practice.

Implicitly denounced in several international treaties and conventions that condemn harmful traditional practices, including the Convention on the Elimination of All Forms of Discrimination Against Women (1979), the Convention on the Rights of the Child (1989) and the African Charter on the Rights and Welfare of the Child (1990), FGM is explicitly condemned in the United Nations Declaration on the Elimination Against Violence Against Women (1993), the Declaration and Platform for Action of the Fourth World Conference on Women (1995) and the African Charter on Human and People's Rights and its Protocol on Women's Rights (2003).

Many Western countries receiving immigrants from settings where FGM is customary have passed laws forbidding the practice, including Australia, Belgium, Canada, Denmark, New Zealand, Norway, Spain, Sweden, the United Kingdom and the United States. France has used existing legislation to prosecute FGM cases.[30]

At the national level, 14 of the 28 African countries with cultures that perform FGM have instituted legislation prohibiting the practice, most in the last decade, including Benin (enacted in 2003), Burkina Faso (1996), Central African Republic (1966), Chad (2003), Cote d'Ivoire (1998), Djibouti (1994), Ethiopia (2004), Ghana (1994), Guinea (1965), Kenya (2001), Niger (2003), Senegal (1999), Tanzania (1998) and Togo (1998). Nigeria has state laws outlawing FGM (1999-2002), and Egypt's health ministry declared FGM unlawful and punishable under the penal code (1996).

Infibulation was outlawed in Sudan in 1946 and again following Sudan's independence in 1956, but the 1993 penal code does not explicitly prohibit FGM. Nor do several other countries with a high prevalence of FGM have laws proscribing the practice, including Eritrea (95 percent prevalence), the Gambia (60 percent to 90 percent), Guinea Bissau (50 percent), Liberia (50 percent to 60 percent), Sierra Leone (90 percent) and Mali (90 percent). Although no laws in Mali prohibit FGM, the Ministry of Women, Children and Family has developed a national plan for eliminating the practice by the year 2007.[31]

Despite progress in legislation, enforcement of anti-FGM laws in countries where they exist is often poor.[32] Even more importantly, according to the president of the Research, Action and Information Network for the Bodily Integrity of Women (RAINBO), "Social change will not be attained through legal or punitive action alone."[33] Many

History already has proven that outlawing FGM without corresponding community sensitisation may increase the practice.

experts argue that laws preventing FGM are valuable for underpinning education efforts and giving credibility to those working to eradicate harmful practices, but criminalising FGM practitioners can inhibit critical discussion and encourage those involved to "go underground" in

For the rest of the second day, the celebrations continue, with dancing and singing in anticipation of the actual wedding on the following day. Juliana was brought to her hut to rest after the excision.

On her wedding day, Juliana was too weak to stand without support. She had bled all night and was in terrible pain. Women gave her a traditional Samburu drink of cow's blood and milk, which is believed to replenish blood loss. Despite Juliana's condition, the wedding proceeded, and she was carried to the ceremony.

order to continue the practice, making an already dangerous procedure even more perilous.[34]

Confronting cultural traditions

Experts consider the real challenge in eliminating FGM to be confronting deep-rooted cultural traditions. History already has proven that outlawing FGM without corresponding community sensitisation may increase the practice. When FGM was outlawed in Sudan in the late 1940s, thousands of people rushed to circumcise their daughters before the law went into effect.[35] Much more recently, Somali Bantu refugees seeking resettlement to the United States hastened to circumcise their daughters — some as young as one year old — when they were told that FGM was a criminal offence in the United States.[36]

Findings from national demographic and health surveys indicate that women living in settings where FGM is practised most often endorse educational campaigns as the best way to abolish the procedure.[37] However, the education strategies must be tailored to each cultural context. Evidence from multicountry projects supported by the nongovernmental organization CARE, as well as those supported by the Promoting Women in Development (PROWID) project, indicate that education focusing only on negative health outcomes of FGM results in communities adopting forms of cutting with less severe health consequences. CARE and PROWID concluded that it was more useful to frame education within a larger context of the social wellbeing of girls and women, facilitating rather than mandating community members' decisions to abandon the practice.[38]

Almost universally, the most effective community-level anti-FGM sensitisation initiatives, like those of the nongovernmental organization TOSTAN in Senegal, are the outcome of indigenous movements aimed at stopping the practice.[39]

Many activists also agree that the key to ending FGM is increasing women's empowerment. As such, a number of projects include initiatives to help circumcisors find other means to support themselves; education programmes for girls and women' and "alternative rites" that forego FGM in favour of positive initiation rituals.[40] One project supported by the United Nations High Commissioner for Refugees (UNHCR) in Northern Kenya promotes female literacy, a component of which educates refugee women and girls about the integrity and value

of their bodies.[41] Other projects have developed critical strategies for engaging men — especially community and religious leaders — in discussions of the cultural values and traditions that perpetuate FGM. Most activists concur that programmes addressing only one aspect of FGM, such as the legal framework, or one group of stakeholders, such as women, cannot effectively put an end to the practice.[42]

Some activities, such as the alternative rites of passage programme operating in seven districts in Kenya under the auspices of Maendeleo Ya Wanawake Organization (MYWO) and the Program for Appropriate Technology in Health (PATH), appear to have been successful. From 1998 to 2003, Kenya witnessed a 6 percent decline in the number of females who reported undergoing FGM, particularly among women under age 25. Although these declines must be carefully monitored to ensure they reflect an actual waning of the practice, UNICEF optimistically contends that FGM in Kenya (where the practice is outlawed), has decreased by almost half over the past two decades.[43]

Evidence of decline is not universal, however, or even common. This is partly because groups working on the ground reach only a small proportion of the population.[44] These agencies generally are underresourced and struggle with information gaps, most glaringly in

> It was more useful to frame education within a larger context of the social wellbeing of girls and women, facilitating rather than mandating community members' decisions to abandon the practice.

the area of best approaches for ending FGM, as well as in ways to measure the success of programming.[45] Many organizations perceive that existing resources do not provide sufficient information or guidance for combating FGM.

The continued high prevalence of FGM in many countries confirms that any efforts to eradicate the practice must be sustained and strongly supported. The first anniversary of the International Zero Tolerance to FGM Day was celebrated only last year, on 6 February 2004. While such an event is a useful advocacy tool, it remains to be seen whether international "zero tolerance" will translate into support to the individuals and organizations that have dedicated themselves to working on the frontline of the fight to eliminate FGM. ◻

Unable to walk, Juliana was dressed in her wedding skins and carried to the arch of sticks which she and her husband must pass through as part of the marriage ceremony. After the wedding, Juliana was supposed to walk with her new husband and his best man to her new village, some 130 kilometres away.

Considering the condition Juliana was in, the photographer convinced the family that she needed medical care. Juliana was taken by vehicle to hospital, where she underwent an operation to repair a deep cut in her vaginal muscle. The doctor who performed the surgery said it was unlikely Juliana was older than age 12. The following day, she was driven to her husband's village to begin married life.

A frightened-looking girl is prepared for her marriage in India. Many young brides
live in South Asia and sub-Saharan Africa, where on average one in three girls
between the ages of 15 and 19 is already married.

Image: Zana Briski

child marriage

40%: The percentage of girls in Nepal who marry before age 15.

50%: The percentage of girls in the Amhara Region in Ethiopia who marry before age 15.

1 in 3: The proportion of married adolescents in Egypt who are beaten by their spouses.

41%: The percentage of these Egyptian adolescents who were pregnant when beaten.

2,000,000: The number of women suffering from obstetric fistula worldwide.

12: The age of one wife in Nigeria whose husband cut off her legs after she repeatedly tried to escape from him.[1]

What is child marriage?

The Inter-African Committee on Traditional Practices Affecting the Health of Women and Children (IAC) defines child marriage as "any marriage carried out below the age of 18 years, before the girl is physically, physiologically, and psychologically ready to shoulder the responsibilities of marriage and childbearing."[2] An array of international instruments — including the 1948 Universal Declaration of Human Rights, the 1979 United Nations' Convention on the Elimination of All Forms of Discrimination Against Women (CEDAW) and the 1990 African Charter on the Rights and Welfare of the Child — echoes the perspective of the IAC: that marriage decisions should be the preserve of consenting adults.[3] Children have the right to be protected from prematurely assuming the responsibilities of adulthood, especially marriage and child-bearing.

Even though some countries permit marriage before age 18, international human rights standards classify these as child marriages, reasoning that those under age 18 are unable to give informed consent. Child marriages involving parental, partner and/or social influence, collusion or pressure are, de facto, forced — regardless of the extent of enthusiasm or acquiescence of the child designated in marriage. In many settings, however, these basic standards are considered irrelevant rather than universal and — even more pointedly and dismissively — "Western". In Ethiopia, where more than half of all girls are married before age 18 and medical problems associated with early child-bearing are rife, one Orthodox priest insisted, "These days, with Western ideas spreading everywhere, girls stay unmarried as late as 30. It's all very scientific and modern, but in our church it is prohibited. Such girls are neither clean nor blessed."[4]

"Fatima" carries her three-month-old infant on her back. Still a child herself, Fatima was forced to marry when she was nine years old. After becoming pregnant, she ran away from her husband's house to stay with her mother. Fatima remains there while recuperating from the surgery that was required to address complications she suffered during obstructed labour — her immature pelvis was too small to deliver a baby. Both Fatima and her mother are slaves in Niger, where an estimated 82 percent of girls marry before age 18. As is custom, Fatima's master forced her into child marriage to exploit the number of years Fatima can produce slave progeny.

Image: Georgina Cranston/IRIN

The unsurprising upshot of such perceptions resounds in the chatter of 12-year-old Deepali from Bangladesh, who has embraced her society's perception that a girl's worth is measured by her ability to be wed at a young age:

"People say I'm very fortunate to have been born so fair, so beautiful. My parents had no problems finding an eligible husband for me. Unlike my dark cousin Maya, who is 13 and still unmarried! I also don't have to go to school anymore. But Maya — she has to go to school until she gets married."[5]

Others do not embrace their fate as easily as Deepali. Girls in focus group discussions in Afghanistan, for example, repeatedly identified child marriage as a major concern in their young lives. Even those as young as 10 and 11 years of age understood that marriage and schooling for Afghan girls are almost always mutually exclusive.[6] In Afghanistan, as in many other parts of the world, losing out on an education is just one of a broad spectrum of negative consequences of child marriage for a young girl.

The extent of the problem

The implications of child marriage are all the more alarming given its scope: Around the world, a projected 82 million girls who are now between the ages of 10 and 17 will be married before their 18th birthdays. Of the 331 million girls aged 10 to19 in developing countries (excluding China), nearly half will be married before turning 20.[7] Although many marriages coincide with a girl's first menstrual period, girls in some communities may be betrothed in infancy and married as early as age eight or nine.

Many of these young wives live in South Asia and sub-Saharan Africa, where on average one in every three girls between the ages of 15 and 19 is already married. In Central America and the Caribbean, the numbers are only slightly better at an estimated 20 percent.[8] And these averages do not capture the remarkable extremes: Two out of every three girls in Yemen, Mali, Nepal and Mozambique will be married before age 18. In Niger, Bangladesh and Chad, the prevalence of underage marriages is as high as 70 percent to 80 percent.[9]

Child marriage is both a cause and a consequence of poverty. While the marriage of young girls and boys is common in the history of most societies around the globe, the average age of wedlock in the world's industrialised regions has risen along with social and economic development. Only 2 percent to 4 percent of girls in North America, East Asia and Western Europe marry before age 19.[10] By not marrying at a young age, girls in these areas have greater opportunity to complete their education, increase their life skills and develop a sense of personal autonomy. As such, they are better equipped to contribute to society, whether in the public or private spheres. Even among the small

"These days, with Western ideas spreading everywhere, girls stay unmarried as late as 30. It's all very scientific and modern, but in our church it is prohibited. Such girls are neither clean nor blessed."

percentage of girls who do wed at an early age in these regions, entering the marriage is much more likely to be the result of personal choice rather than pressure from parents or community.

Child marriage and its negative consequences are also decidedly gender-biased. The number of boys in child marriages around the world is significantly lower than that of girls. In sub-Saharan Africa and South Asia, for example, only 5 percent of boys marry before age19.[11] For most boys who do become young husbands, child marriage is not the harbinger of misfortune that it is for many girl wives. Boys from traditional societies who marry at a young age are less likely than girls to be strictly bound by their family responsibilities. Whereas girls who marry early automatically attain the status of adults and loose any special protections that come with being a child, boys have more freedom to continue their education and acquire skills that will further their personal and social development.

The legal context

Despite national and international laws pertaining to minimum age and consent in marriage, many young girls around the world are still at risk. In 15 countries, the legal age of marriage is 16.[12] Even when legal protections against child marriage do exist, they may be ambiguous, allow for dual existence of customary and civil law and have limited enforcement mechanisms. Some legal provisions, for example, may allow traditional law to override statutory law, and therefore restrictions against early marriage in state law may not apply to customary marriages.[13]

Moreover, in countries "where there is a discrepancy between the minimum age of marriage for boys and girls, it is consistently lower for girls."[14] According to CEDAW, these discrepancies "assume incorrectly that women have a different rate of intellectual development from men, or that their stage of physical and intellectual development at marriage

"People say I'm very fortunate to have been born so fair, so beautiful. My parents had no problems finding an eligible husband for me. Unlike my dark cousin Maya, who is 13 and still unmarried! I also don't have to go to school anymore, but Maya — she has to go to school until she gets married."

is immaterial."[15] The national laws of Cameroon, Jordan, Morocco, Uganda and Yemen do not specifically accord women the right to consent before marriage.[16] Among the "vast majority" of countries around the world that have codified a woman's equal right to choose a marriage partner, legal provisions are often "merely symbolic" — and as a result unenforced or subject to wide exceptions.[17]

Legislative provisions in many countries allow for child marriage with parental consent, which in the context of traditional societies does little to preserve the rights of girl children. In Algeria, Chad, Costa Rica, Lebanon, Libya, Romania and Uruguay, the law allows a perpetrator of rape — including rape of a minor — to be pardoned of his crime if he marries his victim.[18] In the case of a young victim, stigma, shame, coercion and ignorance of the law, along with a multitude of other factors, may prevent her from exercising her legal right to refuse such a marriage. In Ethiopia, illegal "abduction marriages", where men kidnap young girls and consummate the marriage with rape, remain prevalent in some rural settings. In a study conducted among 227 Ethiopian wives, 60 percent said they had been abducted before age 15, and 93 percent before age 20.[19]

The failure to prioritise women's and girl's rights

Child marriage predominates in traditional societies around the world, where the desires and needs of parents and community may override considerations for the individual development and wellbeing of a girl child. The patriarchal values buttressing these cultures further erode any rights that might otherwise be afforded a young girl. The fact that marrying young maximises a female's reproductive lifespan and thus ensures large families justifies the custom of child marriage and ignores the health impact of such a tradition on young wives.

The prevalence of child marriage also may be linked to the economics of poverty. Young girls in certain communities in Africa will generate more bride price because as virgins they are less likely to have HIV and other sexually transmitted infections. Conversely, African parents in resource-poor settings who are worried about not being able to find men who can afford a high bride price may prevent a daughter from completing schooling for fear that an education will increase her cost.[20] Once a girl has left school, she is much more likely to get married. In the Asian societies where dowry customs dominate, girls may be married off early because dowry increases as a girl matures. In Bangladesh, for example, dowry doubles once a girl reaches the age of 15, because she is considered less "marriageable".[21]

Other motives for child marriage include controlling a young girl's sexuality and curbing any manifestations of independence. Committing a pubescent or even prepubescent girl to marriage reduces the likelihood of premarital liaisons, which is important when the sexual purity of girls and women is seen as a community prerogative and the basis of family and tribal honour. In societies where subservience to husbands is requisite in marriage, young brides offer the additional benefit of being easier to mould into deferential wives.[22]

Child marriage and gender-based violence

Child marriage is a form of gender-based violence that leads to a range of other forms of violence. Research suggests, for example, that sexual assault in marriage may be more common among wives who marry young, due at least in part to the power inequities between older husbands and younger wives. Indian girls from Calcutta who married early reported that their husbands had forced them to have intercourse before they had started menstruating. Despite protestations of pain and lack of desire, 80 percent of these girls said their husbands continued to force them to have sexual relations.[23]

Girls who marry early also may be at greater risk of physical violence at the hands of their husbands and in-laws. In Jordan, 26 percent of domestic violence incidents reported in 2000 were committed against wives who were under age 18.[24] As with sexual violence, this increased risk may be associated with age and power differentials. Lack of social networks and economic assets, as well as low self-esteem, make child brides less likely to leave abusive husbands and more likely to tolerate the abuse. In studies in Benin, India and Turkey, for example, 62 percent to 67 percent of young wives — as opposed to 36 percent to 42 percent

Twenty-year-old "Salamat" lives in Niger as the second wife to a man 28 years her senior. She had no choice in the marriage. Salamat gave birth to her first baby when she was 13 years old. Her husband's first wife, who is 35 and lives in a hut nearby, has had six children.

Footprints of urine made by a girl at the Fistula Hospital in Ethiopia, which is dedicated to treating women who suffer from obstetric fistula — a malady that is directly related to early child-bearing.

of older wives — believed that their husbands were justified in using physical violence against them.[25]

Girls who try to escape early or abusive marriages risk retribution from their husbands as well as their natal families, including further abuse, imprisonment or even death. The Commission on the Status of Women in Pakistan, where honour killings are often linked to domestic violence, reported in 1989 that "men are constantly fighting to retrieve their women because they have run away."[26] Data from prisons in Afghanistan's capital city of Kabul in 2004 indicated that the majority of female inmates had been married before age 16, and that incarceration was highly correlated to child marriage. "Zabia" is one such case:

"When [Zabia] was 10 years old her parents sold her in marriage to a 50-year-old man who was deaf and dumb. She was raped on her wedding night. In the years that followed, [Zabia] ran away to her father's house some seven or eight times. Every time she returned, her father beat her and held her in chains until her husband came to retrieve her. She finally escaped to the city, where she met a kind woman who took her in. After some time, [Zabia] met a young male relative of the woman, became engaged and married him. She had been happily married for six months and was pregnant when she told her second husband her true history. The second husband, who accepted her past, went to meet [Zabia's] parents to tell them of her whereabouts and happy marriage and invited them to visit their daughter. Instead, [Zabia's] parents reported the couple to the police, who imprisoned them for illegal marriage."[27]

Husbands of young wives are often significantly older, and therefore more likely to die before their wives. While it may seem a reprieve in cases of violent marriages, lack of property or inheritance rights, as well as high rates of illiteracy among young brides, puts these widows at great risk for multiple forms of exploitation.[28] In certain parts of India, a girl

deceased husband. Any resulting children are given the name of the deceased husband, thus ensuring the continuation of his lineage. If a widow refuses to marry her brother-in-law, she not only risks being cast out of his family, but also losing custody of her children and any rights to her husband's property.[30] Widowed women also can be traded as commodities in dispute negotiations between families or communities — given as a wife, for example, from one family to another to reinstate the honour of an aggrieved man and his clan.[31]

The multiple health risks of child marriage

In addition to the physical dangers associated with domestic violence, child marriage poses many other health risks. Because of the greater permeability of their vaginal tissue and other biological factors like hormone fluctuations, girls are more vulnerable than mature women to sexually transmitted infections, including HIV. Their age, limited life experience and inferior status also make it difficult for young wives to negotiate safer sex.[32]

While marriage to girls is considered a protective measure for husbands, it may have the opposite effect on their wives, especially in polygynous societies. In a recent study undertaken in Rwanda and cited in a United Nations Children's Fund (UNICEF) report on child marriages, 25 percent of girls who became pregnant at 17 or younger were infected with HIV, even though many reported having sex only with their husbands. The study found that a higher incidence of HIV infection was directly correlated to a younger age of sexual intercourse and first pregnancy.[33] In findings from rural Uganda, girls aged 13 to 19 who were HIV-positive were twice as likely to be married as girls who were HIV-negative. For young wives, "abstinence is not an option — those who try to negotiate condom use commonly face violence and rejection."[34]

When [Zabia] was 10 years old, her parents sold her in marriage to a 50-year-old man who was deaf and dumb. She was raped on her wedding night. In the years that followed, [Zabia] ran back to her father's house some seven or eight times, but each time her father beat her and held her in chains until her husband came to retrieve her.

whose husband has died may be given in *nata* to a widower in the family. Although officially designated his wife, she may become "the common property of all the men in the family."[29] In parts of Africa, a widow is remarried, according to the practice of *levirate*, to a brother of her

The leading cause of death for 15- to 19-year-old girls worldwide is complications from pregnancy and child-bearing. According to public-health experts, for every girl that dies during pregnancy or childbirth, 30 more will suffer injuries, infections and disabilities. And the risks are not limited to the mother: If a girl is under the age of 18 when she gives birth, her baby's chance of dying in its first year of life is 60 percent higher than that of a baby born to an older mother.[35] Moreover, the extended reproductive span of a girl who is married early puts her and her children at risk due to a greater number of pregnancies and deliveries. According to one study, women who marry before age 19 will have two to four times more children than those who marry after age 25.[36]

The additional burden of obstetric fistula

One of the most physically and psychologically debilitating effects of early child-bearing is fistula, a rupture of tissue that results in an opening between the vagina and the bladder or the rectum, or both, which is reparable only with surgery. Primarily caused by obstructed labour, fistula is closely linked to marriage and child-bearing among girls between 10 and 15 years of age. In one 1995 study in Niger, for example, 88 percent of women with fistula were in this age group when they were married.[37] As with all pregnancy-related injuries, young married girls in resource-poor settings are least likely to get treatment for fistula.[38] With leaking urine or faeces, a malodorous girl suffering an untreated fistula is likely to be ostracised by her community and divorced by her husband.

Child marriage is so common in Ethiopia that doctors at the Fistula Hospital, based in the capital city of Addis Ababa, operate on approximately 1,200 girls a year.[39] Those who are aware of and manage to find transport to the hospital are probably only a small proportion of the young women needing treatment.

An urgent human rights concern

The Forum on Marriage and the Rights of Women and Girls, from which much of the information included in this chapter has been drawn, is a network of nongovernmental organizations with international affiliates that shares "a vision of marriage as a sphere in which women and girls have inalienable rights."[40] The early work of the Forum highlighted the fact that very little is being achieved at either the international or national level to address the global problem of child marriage.

The Forum's most recent report in 2003 emphasised that there is considerable work to be done to end the practice of child marriage. Much of this effort involves lobbying governments to adopt and enforce laws that both prohibit child marriage and ensure that girls have equal access to education. Just as important, however, is changing the attitude and behaviour of community and religious leaders, whose complicity

Their futures need not be preordained by customs that deprive them of their rights to mental, social and physical wellbeing.

allows child marriage to continue. Finally, the Forum asked for increased support to programmes that empower young girls, to help them realise that their futures need not be preordained by customs that deprive them of their rights to mental, social and physical wellbeing.

Agencies such as the United Nations Fund for Population Assistance and UNICEF have started to demand action to end child marriage, while international nongovernmental organizations, including Population Council and the International Center for Research on Women, have pioneered initiatives to research child marriage, raise awareness and inform policy discussion. Despite some of these gains, the magnitude of the problem requires greater effort, not only through prevention, but also through supporting girls who are already in child marriages. Policy makers, elected officials and community and religious leaders, as well as individuals, all have a critical role in making a difference in the lives of girls and young women. n

With leaking urine or faeces, young wives suffering from untreated fistula not only suffer the shame and pain associated with the condition but are often ostracised by their communities and abandoned by their husbands. Fistula is most prevalent in communities where child marriage and early child-bearing are common practices.

Image: Evelyn Hockstein/IRIN

"Jamillah", now 16, was forced into marriage two years ago. She has been staying at a fistula clinic in Niger while she recuperates from the injuries she suffered during the birth of her first child. From the clinic ward, she tearfully relates her story:

"My parents arranged the marriage. I had no choice. I was not even allowed to go to school. In rural areas it is thought, What is the need for formal education, especially for girls? Parents always say, 'No one knows the time we will die, so our girls must get married young so that we have lots of children — children who can take care of us.' I had to accept.

"I had my own feelings, of course, but they were not allowed to come out — they were destroyed by my parents. The culture has control. I was so influenced by my parents that I was not even allowed to go to a literacy programme.

"The delivery of the child I have just lost lasted for three days. It was during the delivery that the fistula occurred. I wept and wept. What shocked me most is that I didn't feel like other women. It is God's will that I have had fistula. All I want now is to recover. My father often comes to visit me — my mother died six years ago. My husband never comes to see me. I want to go home. I have been training here to make beaded necklaces and bracelets. I want to start a small business."

All over the world girls leave the relative security of their homes to attend school, where teachers take over from parents as daily caregivers. Too often, it appears, this trust is breached. Research in some settings shows high levels of sexual violence and harassment in schools, by teachers, headteachers and fellow students.

Unless indicated girls pictured in this chapter are not victims of sexual violence and/or harassment in schools.

Image: Brent Stirton

violence against girls in schools

"A teacher starts giving you more marks, invites you to his home and asks for [a] sexual favour. If you refuse ... you get to be a victim in class."[1]

"I left school because I was raped by two guys in my class who were supposedly my friends."[2]

"All the principal told him was, 'Stop — if you're beating girls already you'll grow up to beat your wife.' He didn't get detention. Nothing. I don't report anything anymore. I feel it's unnecessary. I'm just wasting my time."[3]

"All the touching at school — in class, in the corridors, all day everyday — bothers me. Boys touch your bum, your breasts."[4]

"They say 'You shagged the teacher,' but I didn't. He raped me."[5]

A hostile learning environment

Gender-based violence is one dimension of the broader problem of violence in schools, and it manifests itself in a variety of ways. Whatever form it takes, violence against female students and teachers creates an atmosphere of intimidation and danger in an environment that should nurture and inspire.

While both boys and girls can be victimised at school, there are specific forms of gender-based violence to which girls most often are subjected. It may be verbal harassment — in the form of so-called teasing — or it may be of a more physical nature, such as unwanted touching and contact. It can also be more overtly violent, as in cases where girls are sexually assaulted or raped on or near school premises. Research in schools in Ghana, Zimbabwe and Malawi has shown that violence against girls also includes sexual propositions to girls by older male students and teachers, as well as the use of sexually explicit language by teachers and students.[6] Overtly sexual graffiti also can intimidate young women and create a hostile school atmosphere.

Girls are more susceptible to violence because of inequities of power and status in society. Boys who are abused, however, usually are victimised by other boys as punishment for not conforming to the prevailing norms about what constitutes suitable male behaviour or appearance. Their perceived weakness lowers their standing in the school hierarchy, making them vulnerable to taunting, bullying and other forms of aggression. One boy in the United States was scared to admit to his male friends that he disagreed with their harassment of female students: "Some of the boys that I considered my friends even began to do it [sexually taunt girls]. It felt awful to watch, but if I said anything, it would not stop them and would only hurt me."[7] While it is difficult enough for girls to speak out about their experiences of violence, notions of appropriate masculine behaviour make it even harder for boys to admit that they, too, are targets of abuse.

Such oppressive control of sexuality in schools also pressures boys to follow certain models of masculine and heterosexual behaviour — which can result in greater acts of violence against girls. These notions are reinforced in many ways — formally through the curriculum and teaching materials, and informally, through the words and actions of teachers and other role models. Boys may feel the need to "prove" themselves, and one way of doing so is to sexually harass girls, either verbally or physically — and to do so publicly. In some circumstances this may go as far as gang rape. Human Rights Watch, for example, has documented cases in South Africa where girls as young as nine years of age were raped by two or more boys on the school campus.[8]

Girls, too, are under considerable peer pressure to conform to gender norms, such as making themselves physically attractive, tolerating harassment and allowing themselves to be the target of sexual jokes and innuendo. While there may be initiatives in place to make schools more "girl-friendly", the underlying dynamic is one of gendered power imbalances, with boys and men — and their perspectives — dominant. In much of South Asia and sub-Saharan Africa, for example, girls who attend upper primary and secondary schools are a very small minority. In countries such as India, Chad, Malawi and Mozambique, less than 50 percent of girls who start school remain until Grade 5.[9] Their institutions are dominated by male teachers and male students, and decision-making at all levels rests clearly in male hands. In Southern

Boys may feel the need to "prove" themselves, and one way of doing so is to sexually harass girls, either verbally or physically — and to do so publicly. In some circumstances this may go as far as gang rape.

Sudan, for example, less than 7 percent of teachers are women, and in Bolivia only 16 percent of all head teachers are women. Women hold only 30 percent or less of teaching posts in 16 countries of sub-Saharan Africa.[10] Female teachers usually are concentrated in urban settings, with far fewer in rural and remote areas.

Such male-dominated contexts make it very difficult for girls to assert themselves and to challenge male power. Doing so may mean ostracism and losing the support of friends and family. Reports from South Africa, for example, indicate that boys specifically target girls they perceive to

be arrogant or assertive, such as prefects, student leaders or girls who perform well at school.[11] Girls who are subjected to violence in school often have little recourse for complaint or even support — especially at the secondary level, where there are usually fewer girls compared with boys and very few female teachers. The majority of teachers are men, many of whom condone the behaviour of boys — or even worse, are perpetrators themselves. Girls may fear retaliation or negative consequences, such as exam failure or undue punishments, if they speak out and especially if they name the perpetrators.

A violation of trust

In many instances, the very people who are in positions of trust in a school and responsible for the well-being of students are the perpetrators of gender-based violence. A number of studies highlight the prevalence of sexual misconduct by teachers and the extent to which they neglect their duty to care.

A male teacher in Kenya was accused of grading girls based on their looks after making them parade in front of him at the head of the class while he studied their figures.[12] In a study in Botswana, 20 percent of girl students said that they had been propositioned for sex by teachers.[13] Ten out of 16 girls at a school in Ghana had been asked for sex by teachers, and five of them knew of a girl in their class who was having sex with a teacher.[14] In a similar study in Zimbabwe, 19 percent of the girls interviewed had been propositioned by a teacher, and a much larger number of them (63 percent) knew other girls who had been approached. Girls reported that teachers were quite open about their intentions, making advances on girls during class and sports activities. Some girls were thought to accept such propositions for financial benefit, to be favoured in class, to avoid punishment or to gain better marks.[15] In South Africa, one teacher who sexually abused a number of students offered a young woman high grades in exchange for sex:

"I went to his dorm and walked to the lounge. He gave me a hooch [an alcoholic drink]. I was lame. I knew what was happening to me, but I couldn't move. He picked me up and took me to his room and started taking my clothes off. He took his clothes off. He's twice my size and, like, five times my weight and has so many muscles. Then he penetrated me. When I came to, I got up and went to my dorm. ... I was scared to tell anyone because I was afraid no one would believe me. I had been

A young Rwandan girl attends HIV/AIDS awareness training in her school. The high incidence of sexual assault among school-aged girls has caused the Rwandan government to initiate these programmes as part of a nationwide campaign to sensitise the population about gender-based violence and the HIV/AIDS pandemic. Many women and girls in Rwanda suffered some form of violence during the 1994 genocide. It has been estimated that between 250,000 and 500,000 were raped.

Image: Julie Pudlowski

Statistics reveal that far fewer girls have access to education than boys. Getting more girls to school is already a global challenge – one further hindered by the threat of sexual violence or harassment facing girls in educational settings.

Image: Brent Stirton

raped before, and no one believed me then. … The next day he asked me to come back. I gave him back his key and said I didn't want to have anything to do with him. … About a week later he asked me if I would come do Afrikaans with him, and that he would give me good marks."[16]

Students who were the subjects of a study in Pakistan reported that teachers forced them to perform sexual acts by threatening them with or inflicting corporal punishment.[17] Physical punishment, with its sexual undertones, is another way in which male teachers assert their power over female students, and in which the sex-power-gender dynamics between men and women in society at large are played out in the school setting.

Where teachers are underpaid and lack access to professional support and development opportunities, sexual relations with students may be considered a "fringe benefit". This is especially true in remote areas, where there are rarely effective systems in place to supervise teacher conduct or prosecute incidences of violation. Girls and their families may think it is futile to seek justice. Furthermore, not all parents, teachers and students disapprove of such relationships. If a girl becomes pregnant by a teacher, parents may be reluctant to pursue prosecution. In some very poor communities — in Southern Sudan, for example — families actually may welcome the pregnancy, as it might compel the teacher to marry the girl or pay compensation. In other contexts, parents feel disempowered and are unaware of how to challenge a teacher's behaviour.

Leading by example

Even if they do not commit such acts against students personally, teachers who do nothing to combat verbal and physical harassment by other teachers and students (usually boys against girls) send out a clear message. Their failure to act is a tacit acceptance of the *status quo* and communicates to the students — especially boys — what behaviour is acceptable in school.

In the United States, a teacher refused to take action against a male student who was harassing a 14-year-old girl: "I was in class and the teacher was looking right at me when this guy grabbed my butt. The teacher saw it happen. I slapped the guy and told him not to do that. My teacher didn't say anything and looked away and went on with the lesson like nothing out of the ordinary had happened."[18]

One 13-year-old South African girl explained her disappointment with the inaction of her teachers after two male classmates raped her: "All the people who I thought were my friends had turned against me. And they [the rapists] were still there. I felt disappointed. … If they [the teachers] had made the boys leave, I wouldn't have felt so bad about it." The girl stopped attending school because of the incident.[19]

Such dynamics allow abuse to become an integral aspect of school life. Teachers who challenge the behaviour of colleagues — by opposing acts of violence or questioning the judgement of those who tolerate it — also risk professional ostracism. Although it is less well-documented, anecdotal evidence suggests that in South Asia and sub-Saharan Africa,

> "The [female] teachers themselves do not challenge sexual harassment in school but just choose to tolerate it, thereby giving [sic] a helpless situation to the girls."

female teachers also are intimidated by sexual violence and harassment. Female teachers in Pakistan who travel each day to work in villages away from their homes, for example, risk verbal harassment and even physical assault from men *en route*.[20]

The perception of risk to female teachers may be a significant factor in discouraging women from pursuing careers in education. Fathers or husbands may forbid their daughters or wives from teaching because of the threat of sexual violence against female teachers. This can have a negative impact in cultures where girls' access to education depends on the presence of female teachers. There is also evidence of sexual violence against young women in teacher-education colleges. In one study in Ghana, women said they were intimidated by college lecturers and pressured for sex in exchange for good grades, but this phenomenon warrants much further study in different country contexts.[21]

It would be wrong to assume that the presence of female teachers alone would prevent violence against girl students. If female teachers are marginalised and oppressed by the prevailing gender dynamics of an institution, they may not be able to prevent sexual harassment and abuse or provide the support girls need.

In a 2001 study in Uganda, girls felt that female teachers ignored the very real issue of sexual harassment by boys and male teachers in the school: "The [female] teachers themselves do not challenge sexual harassment in school but just choose to tolerate it, thereby giving [sic] a helpless situation to the girls." But when female teachers also are subject to sexual harassment by male teachers and students, there is little they can do to prevent it happening to their students.

A global problem

There is a correlation between a girl's age and the likelihood of her falling prey to violence at school. Adolescent girls are at greatest risk.[22] Such abuses, however, are not culture-specific. Girls of every ethnic, social and economic group can be targets. Although most recent research has concentrated on schools in sub-Saharan Africa, the problem is not unique to this region. Studies and interventions in North America, Europe, South Asia and Latin America suggest that violence against girls is a problem in schools around the world.

In the United States, a 2001 survey of more than 2,000 students between 13 and 17 years of age found that 83 percent of the girls and 79 percent of the boys had experienced harassment.[23] In the United Kingdom, research conducted with children aged 10 to 11 and 14 to 15 indicated that sexualised teasing of girls by boys in mixed secondary schools is common. Girls explained that boys called them names such as "prossie" [prostitute], flicked their bra straps, looked up their skirts and grabbed or fondled them.[24]

In refugee camps and other conflict-affected settings, abuse of power by men in positions of authority over vulnerable women and girls is also a major issue. Teachers may exploit their status within the community and use their economic power, however slight, to manipulate students, which can jeopardise the future of entire families. Refugee children see education as a critical means to improve their families' financial situation. Their desperation to succeed in school makes them all the more susceptible to abuse.

In a 2001 survey of 560 secondary-school girls in Botswana, 67 percent said that they had experienced unwanted touching, pressure for dates and other forms of sexual harassment. For 25 percent of them, this was a regular occurrence.[25] A report in 2002 found that girls at refugee schools in Sierra Leone, Guinea and Liberia were subjected to abuse and exploitation, often by their teachers.[26] The study revealed that in most cases good grades were exchanged for sex. The problem was widespread

and integrated into the culture of the schools, in part because there was no system of checks and balances to protect the girls.

Long-term losses

In addition to the immediate effects of intimidation, fear and physical suffering, violence against young women and girls in schools has some long-term ramifications, many of which are interconnected. Sexual violence in schools can deter parents from educating their daughters in the first place, or cause them to pull girls out of educational establishments when they reach adolescence. For parents who are concerned about protecting their daughters' — and their family's — honour, the perceived gains of attending school may not be as high as the perceived risks.

Girls who feel afraid of, intimidated and disrespected by their teachers and fellow students find it hard to concentrate in school and are unlikely to achieve high grades. South African girls who had been raped and sexually abused, for example, reported that after such incidents their concentration, motivation and school performance all declined significantly. Such feelings can lead to high drop-out rates among girl students, who leave school because of low self-esteem or a sense of not belonging — or because the violence has resulted in pregnancy. A 15-year-old South African girl who was raped by her teacher described how her experience had changed her opinion about school: "I feel less interested. I want to leave school. We were told that we could leave school after standard seven, so that's what I want to do. I want to leave and go. I just don't like it [school], the kids, the teachers."[27]

Sexual violence in schools can deter parents from educating their daughters in the first place, or cause them to pull girls out when they reach adolescence.

Girls who finish school with poor results have limited higher-education and career opportunities. If there are few girls who successfully and enjoyably complete their education, there will be a very small pool of potential female teachers. And, as discussed above, schools where there are few women in positions of responsibility are more likely to have problems with violence against girl students.

Sexual intercourse with older male students and teachers also puts girls at risk of unwanted pregnancy and increases the likelihood of contracting HIV and other sexually transmitted infections. Power imbalances in relationships, coercion and intimidation, as well as physical violence during sexual intercourse make it almost impossible for girls to protect themselves.

Three girls stand against the front wall of the school for the blind they attend
with boys and adult men in Sierra Leone. Studies suggest that girls with disabilities
may be at higher risk of sexual violence and harassment.

Image: Brent Stirton

Sibhale Puppeteers during a performance about HIV/AIDS and sexual abuse for children in Soweto, Johannesburg, in 2003. The risk of abuse in South Africa is so high that even primary-school children are targeted for programmes to raise their awareness.

Image: Mariella Furrer

The power to change

Schools have the power to either condone or condemn gender-based violence. There are many examples of promising work being carried out at international, national and local levels to protect girls and women in schools, create gender-safe learning environments and empower communities to be agents of change.

Two projects from South Africa focus on how teachers can make a difference. Part of a training programme at the School of Public Health at the University of the Western Cape asks primary school teachers to evaluate their own attitudes towards gender-based violence and reflect on the implicit messages conveyed through their words and actions.[28] Understanding the dynamics of gender-based violence in schools enables these teachers to incorporate activities to combat the problem into their daily routines. The manual "Opening Our Eyes: Addressing Gender-Based Violence in South African Schools" is also a tool for professional development and a starting point from which to develop whole-school approaches and policies. The module makes the very important link between gender-based violence and HIV/AIDS and also provides some very concrete strategies for creating safer schools.[29]

Following reports of sexual abuse and exploitation of refugee girls in West Africa, the International Rescue Committee implemented programmes to train women classroom assistants (CAs) for upper-primary classes. Working alongside male teachers, they serve as role models, monitor risks of exploitation of students by teachers and document cases of abuse. Boys and girls in these refugee schools said that their classrooms were more calm, organized and conducive to learning as a result of the initiative. Relations between teachers and students were more respectful, and because the CAs collected examination results directly from the teachers, there were fewer opportunities for exploitation related to grades. The girls especially appreciated having a "mother" or "big sister" figure in the classroom.

The work of the CAs is groundbreaking because they operate within the system to challenge entrenched gender patterns. Further development of the programme includes addressing some of the power imbalances between the CAs and the teachers and incorporating empowerment

Sexual intercourse with older male students and teachers also puts girls at risk of unwanted pregnancy and increases the likelihood of contracting HIV/AIDS and other sexually transmitted diseases.

strategies for women and girls. Another important issue being explored is how to equip students themselves to handle the threat of sexual abuse and exploitation. This multipronged approach will ensure the immediate protection of girls in today's classrooms and, in the long-term, empower them at school and in their communities.[30]

Schools play a very powerful role in the development of individual gender identities and reflect and shape the dynamics within communities. Attitudes and behaviours learned in school set in place patterns which can continue throughout a person's life. By addressing the problem of asymmetrical power relations, teachers and students have the capacity to break harmful cycles of discrimination and gender-based violence of all types.

"Rose", age 10, at her home in Nairobi, Kenya, just down the road from where she and her three girlfriends were raped in July 2005. It is Monday afternoon, and most children Rose's age are in class. But like many school-aged rape victims, Rose has refused to go to school since being assaulted two months earlier. "The teachers will beat me," she says. "They will beat me and laugh at me, and the other children will laugh at me. They know what happened.

"One afternoon, four of us were playing outside by the road, and a local vendor offered us some *mandazi* [fried dough]. We always saw him making and selling *mandazi*. He lives close to us, with his wife and kids. The man told us that he was not feeling well, that he was sick and couldn't eat any *mandazi* that day. He said that we could have them, and that we should go and eat them at his home.

"One of the girls went with him. Then he told us, 'I do not have any water in the house. Please go and get water for me.' We each took a Jerrican and went to get water. He asked us to take it into the house. When we were all inside, he locked the window and locked the door. Then he told us to take off our clothes. We started screaming. He went and got a knife. He said, 'Be quiet! Be quiet!' He said he would cut us if we did not stop screaming. We did not want to be killed, so we kept quiet. He undressed the first girl and told her to lay on the bed. He told us three to stand in front of the bed and watch. Then he slept with her. When he finished he picked the next girl, who refused to undress. When she refused, he told her he would stab her. So the man undressed her. He finished with the second girl, and she got dressed. I was the third person. … When my turn came I started feeling afraid. I refused to take off my clothes. When he said he would stab me I was scared. … He used force with the last girl. Afterwards, he opened the door and warned us that if he heard about what had happened from anyone in the community, he would kill us."

Rose did not return home until 9 p.m. that night, and her mother had been worried. When asked where she had been, Rose talked about the man, but was vague about what had occurred and reluctant to admit that she herself had been raped. At first, none of the girls disclosed exactly what had happened to them. When one of them was asked why she was walking funny, she said that she had been kicked in the leg. The mother of the fourth girl noticed some bleeding from her daughter, a result of the force the rapist used. Eventually, when their story was pieced together, the father of one of the girls took them to the police station to report the rapes and to identify the perpetrator, who admitted to "having the urge to have sex" but denied having penetrated the girls. The four girls were treated at Nairobi Women's Hospital, where they were underwent forensic examinations. The perpetrator was arrested and held in remand until the trial in October 2005.

In this photo, Rose holds the syringe she uses to take antiretroviral medication to reduce her chances of contracting HIV from the rape. The treatment will last four months. Before the assaults, one of the four girls already was enrolled in a community health programme for children who are HIV-positive.

Image: Leah Weinzimer

Now in a shelter for girls who have been rescued from trafficking, this Cambodian girl was trafficked internally and forced into prostitution at a young age. Since the early 1990s, Cambodia's sex industry has been growing exponentially, attracting foreign tourists who are drawn to the young age of many prostitutes. Surveys show that Cambodian men use prostitutes extensively, with up to 90 percent having their first sexual experience with a prostitute and many continuing to use them throughout their lives.

sex trafficking in women and girls

When a young trafficked girl in Kosovo was asked to define "trafficking", she replied, "It's something to do with cars, isn't it?"[1] For many people around the world — even its victims — human trafficking is at best an indistinct concept, yet it constitutes one of the most serious and, possibly, fastest growing global human rights violations. In the Rome Statute of the International Criminal Court, trafficking in persons is not only characterised as a form of enslavement but, in some circumstances, as a crime against humanity or a war crime.[2]

Defining trafficking

In November 2000 the United Nations Protocol to Prevent, Suppress and Punish Trafficking in Persons, Especially Women and Children, was added to the United Nations Convention against Transnational Organized Crime. The protocol offers the most universally acknowledged definition of trafficking:

"The recruitment, transportation, transfer, harbouring or receipt of persons, by means of threat or use of force or other forms of coercion, of abduction, of fraud, of deception, of the abuse of power or of a position of vulnerability or of the giving or receiving of payments or benefits to achieve the consent of a person having control over another person, for the purpose of exploitation. Exploitation shall include, at a minimum, the exploitation of the prostitution of others or other forms of sexual exploitation, forced labour or services, slavery or practices similar to

slavery, servitude or the removal of organs."[3]

Involuntary servitude is the essential feature of human trafficking. For this reason, trafficking is often synonymously referred to as "modern-day slavery". Men, women, boys and girls are bought and sold — sometimes many times over — to work in brothels and strip clubs, in sweatshops, in mines, on plantations, at construction sites, as beggars, brickmakers, domestic help, circus performers and even camel jockeys. Some of them are held in debt bondage and expected to pay off a balance due to win their freedom. Others have no debt, but as a result of threat or force live as virtual prisoners.

Closely linked to money laundering, drug trafficking, document forgery and human smuggling, trafficking in persons generates an estimated US $9.5 billion in annual revenue, much of which goes into the coffers of organized-crime networks.[4] Every country in the world is implicated in this slave trade, whether as a point of origin, transit or destination.[5]

Since 2000 the United States Department of State has issued the world's most comprehensive annual report on trafficking. The latest edition calculates that 600,000 to 800,000 human beings are trafficked across

... 600,000 to 800,000 human beings are trafficked across international borders each year ... 80 percent of transnational victims are women and girls, and most of them are trafficked into the commercial sex industry.

international borders each year — and these figures do not account for those who are trafficked "internally", from one destination to another within their own countries or communities. The report further estimates that 80 percent of transnational victims are women and girls, and most of them are trafficked into the commercial sex industry.[6] According to the International Labour Organization, this industry "has become highly diversified and global in recent years."[7]

Although exact numbers are difficult to obtain, available estimates give some indication of the scope of the problem. Approximately 100,000 Albanian women and girls are thought to have been sold into the sex trade in neighbouring Balkan countries and Western Europe.[8] Between 1990 and 1997, 200,000 Bangladeshi women were believed to have been trafficked.[9] Some 200,000 Nepali girls under the age of 14 may be working as sex slaves in India.[10] An estimated 600,000 Thai children have been sold into prostitution.[11] Israeli police speculate that 99 percent of women working as prostitutes in Israel are victims of trafficking.[12] In Belgium, between 10 percent and 15 percent of known foreign prostitutes are thought to have been trafficked from abroad.[13] As many as 130,000 women enter Japan on entertainer visas every year, but only about 10 percent of them actually perform in legitimate venues. The rest — many of whom are believed to have been trafficked — are most likely working in sex clubs or as prostitutes.[14] The Middle East, Northern and Latin America, and Africa are also points of origin, transit and/or destination. As with other forms of trafficking, no region in the world appears to be free from the trade of women and girls for sex.

The hazardous journey

Beyond the common denominator of exploitation, every woman's or girl's trafficking experience is unique. In Albania, where 13-year-old "Alma" is living with her family in a camp for Kosovar refugees, she is

convinced by her boyfriend of two weeks to run away to Italy. After they arrive, he forces her into prostitution and beats her repeatedly whenever she refuses.[15] In Nigeria, just before "Betty" is sent to Europe, her sex trafficker has a voodoo priest convince her that her soul will be held captive until she has paid back her debt to the trafficker — possibly as high as $50,000.[16] In Nepal, a familiar older woman in the community — perhaps one who was sent to an Indian brothel years earlier and has now returned as a "matchmaker" — approaches the house of "Kamala" and convinces her parents of the good life their daughter will have in Mumbai, India. As she reassures them about how much money Kamala will send home, she is liable to forego discussing the considerable dispensations to herself, the transport organizers and escorts, and the brothel owner.[17]

In Brazil, "Anita" is befriended by an older man and offered a promising job in a big city, far away from the remote rural community where she lives with her impoverished family. She later discovers that her would-be employer has sold her into prostitution.[18] "Karin", a single mother of two from Sri Lanka, is transported to Singapore by a man who agrees to find her a waitressing job. Shortly after her arrival, she is taken to an open market, where she and other women — from Indonesia, Thailand, India and China — are inspected and purchased by men from Pakistan, India, China, Indonesia and Africa.[19]

Health risks and consequences

As each trafficking incident unfolds, the victim experiences threats to her physical and mental health. These risks have been catalogued in detail in a multicountry study of trafficking covering Albania, Italy, the Netherlands, Thailand and the United Kingdom. From the predeparture stage, to the travel, transit and destination stages, through to detention, deportation and integration or return and reintegration, women and girls may experience repeated physical, sexual and psychological abuse or torture, including forced or coerced use of drugs and alcohol, lack of adequate food, withholding of medical treatment, forced unprotected sex, threats or intimidation of their loved ones, denial of privacy, frequent relocation, public discrimination and social exclusion.[20]

Acute and chronic physical and mental health problems are the frequent outcome. Beatings and/or rape initially may be used by traffickers to establish their authority, instil fear and discourage any attempts to

"Mary" a Nigerian prostitute, trafficked into Spain and working in the Casa de Campo in Madrid. Every year, thousands of Nigerian women are trafficked into Western Europe and forced to work in the sex industry to pay back debts of up to US $50,000. Having entered Europe illegally, the women are pushed onto the periphery of society. Ninety-five percent of the women who are trafficked from Nigeria come from Edo State in the south, where traffickers have set up their networks. The madams control the women through the practice of *juju* (voodoo), which is carried out before they are trafficked out of Nigeria. *Juju* is a strong spiritual tradition in southern Nigeria, based on the unbreakable bedrock of faith, and the psychological fear is very real for these women. During a *juju* ceremony, an oath of loyalty is signed between a god, the trafficker and the woman. The god keeps the woman's spirit until the debt is paid.

Image: Lorena Ros/Panos

Officers from the United Nations Mission in Kosovo and the Trafficking and Prostitution Investigation Unit question a dancer from a local nightclub. Many of the girls have been trafficked from Moldova, Romania and the Ukraine. Some say they came to Kosovo voluntarily and have not been forced to work as prostitutes.

Image: Teun Voeten/Panos

escape. Victims' failure to comply with traffickers' demands may result in further violence. Physical and sexual assault also occur in encounters with clients. Because many women and girls who are trafficked for prostitution are unlikely to be able to negotiate safer sex, they are also highly vulnerable to contracting sexually transmitted infections, including HIV. In all forms of prostitution, the links to HIV vulnerability are high, especially when clients are violent and/or refuse to use condoms.[21] In Nepal, HIV prevalence among prostitutes is estimated at 20 percent. In Cambodia, that figure climbs to 29 percent, and in Zambia to 31 percent. In South Africa, as many as 70 percent of prostitutes are infected with HIV.[22]

Other potential consequences of the abuse and torture suffered by trafficked women and girls include forced and/or unsafe abortions, malnutrition, tuberculosis, hepatitis, depression, self-harm, addiction and, ultimately, death.[23] "Neary" and "Svetlana" are among the incalculable number of women for whom trafficking proved fatal.

" 'Neary' grew up in rural Cambodia. Her parents died when she was a child, and — in an effort to give her a better life — her sister married her off when she was 17. Three months into the marriage, Neary went to a fishing village with her husband, who rented a room in what she thought was a guest house. But when she woke the next morning, her

"Karin" is transported to Singapore by a man who agrees to find her a waitressing job. Shortly after her arrival, she is taken to an open market, where she and other women — from Indonesia, Thailand, India and China — are inspected and purchased by men from Pakistan, India, China, Indonesia and Africa.

husband was gone. The owner of the house told her that she had been sold by her husband for $300 and that she was actually in a brothel. For five years, Neary was raped by five to seven men every day. In addition to brutal physical abuse, Neary was infected with HIV. The brothel owner threw her out when she became sick, and she eventually found her way to a local shelter. She died of HIV/AIDS at the age of 23."[24]

" 'Svetlana' was a young Belarusian looking for a job in Minskland when she met some Turkish men who promised her a well-paying job in Istanbul. Once Svetlana crossed the border, the men confiscated her passport, took away her money and imprisoned her. Svetlana and another foreign woman were sent to the apartment of two businessmen and forced into prostitution. In an attempt to escape, Svetlana jumped

out of a window and fell six stories to the street below. According to Turkish court documents, the customers called the traffickers instead of taking her to hospital. Svetlana died as a result of her injuries, and her body lay unclaimed in the morgue for two weeks until Turkish authorities learned her identity and sent her body to Belarus."[25]

The supply side of the sex-trafficking equation

Some victims of sex-trafficking are simply abducted and relocated internally or transnationally. Many others, however, choose to leave their homes in search of a brighter future. Deceived by traffickers' promises of the good life, they have no idea that they will be forced into prostitution. Even the few victims who understand and accept that they will be working in the commercial sex industry cannot anticipate the extent to which they will forfeit control over their health and welfare. They may believe they are choosing the best of possible options.

The supply side of the trafficking equation is made up of the conditions that cause individual women and girls to be vulnerable to trafficking. Researchers have described a convergence of "push" and "pull" factors. Push factors for an individual woman or girl might include domestic violence, child sexual abuse, single parenthood or inducement by impoverished parents or criminal husbands.[26] At the broader societal level, push factors might include poverty, lack of education and employment opportunities, economic crises or war.[27] HIV/AIDS is another push factor, to the extent that the pandemic is leaving an increasing number of the world's children orphaned and vulnerable. Pull factors might include the hope of a higher standard of living, shifting and/or increased migratory flows and, for many women and girls, "the timing and apparent quality of the offer to depart."[28]

According to one expert, "Traffickers are extremely clever and full of a lot of common sense."[29] In other words, they choose their targets carefully. The particular vulnerabilities of women and girls that make them the preferred mark of traffickers are fundamentally linked to gender-based discrimination, oppression and violence. Where women have little power, rights or opportunities, they are at greater risk of being trafficked. As such, trafficking is as much a product of violence against women and girls as it is a source. In a remote village in Nepal, for example, girls traditionally are afforded very few rights within their families or society. Their disempowerment is a boon for those who control their fate:

"In Chautara, a Tamang village north of the Kathmandu valley, Bhim Tamang is a relatively wealthy man. His cottage is roofed with tin, and his son's motorcycle is parked outside, next to the buffalo shed. Although he has no electricity, a television stands in the corner of the room, covered with a cloth. 'We will have electricity here in a few months,' he says. Bhim's prosperity is a result of his fortune to have fathered four daughters. Three are working in the brothels in Mumbai. The fourth, age 12, will go next year. 'Gurung and Magar families send their sons to the army. Their sons send money home. Why shouldn't we send our daughters to help us?' "[30]

The demand side of the sex-trafficking equation

For many individuals operating at the local level, such as Bhim Tamang, poverty alleviation is a driving force for engaging in trafficking. In countries including India, Pakistan, Burma, Nepal and Thailand, girls may be sold into prostitution to pay off money loaned to their parents.[31] Further along the chain of exploiters, all the way up to the organized-crime networks, commercial profit is the primary incentive in the escalation of human traffic around the world. Established routes used by drugs and weapons racketeers, especially in southeastern Europe, facilitate the illegal trade in humans.[32] Many of these routes pass through "transition countries". In these countries, which often are marked by war or steep economic decline, the forced sex industry is 10 times more lucrative for exploiters than other forms of forced labour.[33]

Regardless of the elements of poverty, greed and organized crime, no trafficker would be successful without market demand. The sex industry throughout the world is the most recognised source of demand for the trafficking of women and girls. In some settings, sex tourism further feeds the incentive for trafficking.[34]

It is not just the sex industry itself, however, that promotes sex trafficking. Racial and social discrimination within the sex industry figure prominently in the commercial sexual exploitation of women and girls. According to one expert, "Research shows that historically and cross-culturally, a large percentage of clients seek prostitutes whose racial, ethnic, caste or national identities are different from their own. Thus we find that women and children in prostitution serving local demand are often

migrants, and that men's prostitute use increases when they are abroad."[35]

By importing and exploiting foreign prostitutes, traffickers are better able to meet demand criteria, and at reduced cost. Hence, a sign outside of a sex club in Hong Kong reads: "Young fresh Hong Kong girls; White, clean, Malaysian girls; Beijing women; Luxurious ghost girls from Russia."[36] Mitko, a pimp working in Bulgaria, promises his customers, "Ten minutes and I can get you a girl — any girl — blond, brown, black or white."[37]

Another perceived attraction of a trafficked woman or girl is her powerlessness. She is significantly less likely to have authority in the sex transaction than a voluntary commercial sex worker who is legally or otherwise empowered to exercise some measure of control over her working conditions. If she is young, the added promise of virginity attracts men seeking to protect themselves from sexually transmitted infections.[38] Conversely, clients who already have sexually transmitted infections may believe, according to the myth of the "virgin cure", that sex with a virgin will heal their disease. In a study conducted in 2003 by the International Organization for Migration (IOM), three-quarters of the 185 clients surveyed expressed a preference for prostitutes under the age of 25, and 22 percent preferred those 18 years of age or under. For many of these clients, this predilection is related to the fact that younger women and girls will be more docile in the sex transaction.[39]

Yet another source of demand for trafficking is men seeking brides, domestic workers or sex slaves. While consensually arranged marriages do not fall within the trafficking rubric, the conditions in which a young bride may find herself once she has entered the marriage may amount to trafficking. The mail-order bride industry has come under scrutiny by trafficking experts for this very reason. The largely unregulated trade of mail-order brides follows traditional trafficking patterns. Brides from impoverished countries within the former Soviet Union, Asia and Latin America are sent to paying clients in the United States, Canada, Europe and Japan.[40] In the most extreme scenario, according to one expert, a mail-order bride client "may go so far as to undertake serial sponsorships of immigrant women to supply new recruits for prostitution rings. In this

> "Research shows that historically and cross-culturally, a large percentage of clients seek prostitutes whose racial, ethnic, caste or national identities are different from their own."

The body of a prostitute gunned down with her pimp in Albania. Every year, thousands of women and girls either are forced to leave their homelands or are deceived into doing so with promises of employment opportunities and a better life. Many end up working as prostitutes in virtual slavery to pimps and gangs. Stripped of passports and with minimal access to cash, they are invisible to the authorities and extremely vulnerable to violence.

Image: Francesco Cito/Panos

case, he will hold the bride in debt bondage because he paid for her to immigrate to North America, and then force her to participate in slavery-like practices in order to obtain her freedom."[41]

Responses to trafficking

A representative from the Protection Project, a United States-based organization that monitors global trafficking, noted in April 2005 that approximately 25 countries have implemented comprehensive antitrafficking laws, and bills are pending in another 15 countries. One hundred or so other countries do not have specific antitrafficking legislation, but nevertheless have criminal-law provisions that comply with the United Nations Protocol to Prevent, Suppress and Punish Trafficking in Persons. Fifty more countries, in the words of the Protection Project representative, "do not care."[42]

Even where legislation exists, it may not protect against all forms of trafficking. According to the State Department of the United States, "Many nations misunderstand the definition of trafficking."[43] They may limit their focus to cross-border movement, failing to recognise internal trafficking or other forms of involuntary servitude that do not involve relocation of the victim. Nor do laws criminalising trafficking necessarily signify a just response to victims. In many settings, trafficked women and girls are at risk of being treated as illegal migrants, as in the case of "Luisa", a 17-year-old orphan from Uzbekistan:

" 'Luisa's' aunt engineered her abduction to Dubai using a cousin's passport, because she wanted to take Luisa's apartment. In Dubai, Luisa was sold to a slavery and prostitution ring. When she was no longer useable in prostitution [from the pimp's point of view], the traffickers sent her to a psychiatric centre. An Uzbek [nongovernmental organization] located her in Dubai. The [agency] arranged to move her to a shelter, and they began working on her repatriation. Because she entered the UAE [United Arab Emirates] illegally, on a false passport, the UAE immigration service said she should serve a two-year prison sentence. Government officials and the Uzbek nongovernmental organization are currently advocating on Luisa's behalf to expedite her return to Uzbekistan."[44]

Unlike Luisa, many victims of trafficking never receive such assistance. Instead, they may be subject to criminal charges for engaging in prostitution. In August 2002, for example, 10 Vietnamese girls who had been trafficked into Cambodia for prostitution were arrested by Cambodian authorities and sentenced to three months in prison, after which they were deported.[45] Summary deportation not only makes it difficult to prosecute trafficking offenders, it may further endanger trafficking victims. In fact, rapid return without sufficient reintegration planning and assistance puts women and girls at risk of being trafficked yet again. Children may be returned to parents who first sold them, and women may be sent back to abusive households.[46]

In recent years, the importance of a victim-centred approach to trafficking — compassionate treatment focusing on "rescue, rehabilitation and reintegration" — has gained increased international attention.[47] The World Health Organization has produced ethical and safety recommendations for interviewing trafficked women.[48] The IOM, the Organization for Security and Cooperation in Europe, the Global Alliance Against Trafficking in Women, La Strada and many other international and local institutions are supporting victim-response

Summary deportation not only makes it difficult to prosecute trafficking offenders, it may further endanger trafficking victims.

programming in several parts of the world, as well as spearheading international advocacy efforts to highlight the scope of the problem and to promote cross-border cooperation and collaboration among governments as well as nongovernmental organizations.

Despite these efforts, many groups providing assistance to trafficking victims "remain relatively unrecognised and seriously underresourced," with funds going to law enforcement rather than to victim support.[49] In her first report from early 2005, the recently appointed United Nations Special Rapporteur on Trafficking in Persons noted that trafficking "continues to be treated mainly as a law and order problem."[50] One of her primary activities to redress this imbalance will involve drawing attention to victims' rights.

While increased services are critical to the care and recovery of those who have been trafficked, prevention is at the root of any efforts to protect potential victims. A number of countries where sex trafficking is prevalent have undertaken public-education campaigns to alert young women and girls to its dangers. Public education, however, does not address the core issues that make women and girls vulnerable, such as "the demand that exists virtually everywhere for children and young women to sexually exploit, and the grinding poverty that generates the supply of children and women, desperate to survive."[51] The United Nations Commission on the Status of Women has recently adopted the first United Nations resolution to focus on eliminating the demand for trafficking. A first step in this process will involve understanding and addressing the forces of racial, ethnic and social discrimination that propel the forced exploitation of women and girls in the sex industry.

Any lasting efforts to reduce sex trafficking also will require a long-term commitment to improving the rights and welfare of women and girls. In the words of one advocate, "Every provision to provide young girls with an education and with skills is an antitrafficking program."[52] Ending modern-day sexual slavery means exploiters — from the traffickers to the clients they serve — must be held criminally accountable, and women and girls must be emancipated from the enormous inequities that define their everyday existence. ∎

On one of their night raids, a South African police taskforce set up to fight the commercial sexual exploitation of children discovered a traumatised three-year-old boy locked in a room. Initially, the police believed he had been left behind as collateral for a drug loan. When his mother, "Maggie", was found later that night about 80 kilometres away, she told the authorities the full story.

Maggie was a sex worker in Pretoria and had worked for herself since her early teens. One evening, a friend who also worked as a prostitute invited her to join a group of people for a drink at an apartment in Johannesburg. Maggie went for a drink, after which she fell asleep, probably because the cocktail was laced with drugs. When she woke up in the apartment, her friend had disappeared. Maggie called her friend to ask what had happened, and the woman explained that a pimp had offered her money to bring Maggie to them. Maggie was then locked in a room and forced to work day and night as a prostitute. She was expected to service clients in the middle of the night if the pimp knocked on her door and told her to do so.

After Maggie managed to escape, she immediately fell under the control of another pimp, who refused to allow her to go and see her young son, who was living with Maggie's sister in Pretoria. Instead, he offered to collect the boy and bring him to her. Maggie agreed. Once the pimp had her

son, he made a bargain with Maggie: The boy would stay with him, and if Maggie brought in enough money each week she could see him on Sundays. Maggie was given R20 ($3) each day for food and several rocks of crack cocaine. She lived on bread and mayonnaise, and her pimp provided her with clothes. For the three months that her little boy was held hostage, Maggie worked so that she could see him and keep him safe. She would have liked to run away, but she was afraid the pimp would hurt her son. After they were rescued, the boy was put in a safe house and Maggie entered a drug-rehabilitation programme.

Doctors who examined the boy also suspected that he had been given drugs to keep quiet. After looking at his gums, they surmised that the child had been gagged almost constantly. They were unable to determine whether he had been sexually abused. Maggie did well in rehab and was determined to turn her life around. Unfortunately, because she did not have any vocational training at the facility, she had no means to support herself after she was released. Maggie is back on the streets, working for herself this time. Her son is in foster care.

Images: Mariella Furrer

"My name is 'Shaliba', and I am 15 years old. I was born into slavery and live with my master. My family members are all slaves to the master's family, and we live in the same compound. I have to work so hard, fetching water and firewood and doing domestic chores.

"My master's daughter is getting married in Nigeria, and she will need a slave girl, so I must go with her. At first, I refused to go and was badly beaten. My parents are not happy about my moving away. They asked the master to let me stay with them, but he said that because I am a slave I must do what I am told. I have no choice.

"In rural areas like this, teachers recruit children to go to school. A teacher came to my village and insisted that my master allow me to study. He refused, but when the teacher threatened to take him to court he relented. My master said that if I worked for him in the mornings and evenings I could go to school. I studied up to Class Five, but now he has forbidden me to continue. When my teachers in school would talk about the slave trade, they said slavery doesn't exist anymore. I was too afraid to say anything.

"My master has forced me to sleep with him so many times, starting when I was about seven years old. I used to refuse, but then he would beat me. He takes me into his room, unclothes me and rapes me. It makes me so sad. I reported it to my father, but he couldn't do anything because he, too, is a slave. I have been having problems with my periods. They have not been normal and I have had bad pains. The last time I had a period was about three or four months ago. My master raped me three months ago."

"Saymin" is 21 years old and comes from Bangladesh. She has five sisters and one brother, and her family is very poor. Saymin's father died when she was very young, and her mother did whatever work she could find to sustain the family, from picking up rubbish and selling it to doing domestic work.

When Saymin was 10 years old, a female "recruiting agent" came to the house and said she could find a job for her in India. Saymin's mother asked where her daughter would be taken, and the agent told her that once the girl was settled she would send the address. Desperate from poverty, Saymin's mother let her go, reasoning that the child would at least earn a living.

"I was terrified and crying a lot when we left. It was night-time and I didn't know the roads. We went through the jungle in the border areas — I don't know what route we took. It took us two days to reach Kolkata in India. The woman who brought me there sold me in Khidirpur, the red-light district. She said that the madam of the house was her sister. The madam explained to me that I had to entertain people, to take my clothes off and let them do whatever they wanted. When I protested, I was beaten. They played music really loud so no one could hear my screams. Another madam, who was a neighbour, told the woman I worked for to be careful because I was so young, and warned her that if the police came there would be trouble. So she put me to work as a domestic servant.

"When I turned 12, I was forced to have sex. It was very difficult. Because I was sexually and physically immature, I couldn't entertain too many people — but even then I had to have sex with two or three men every day. If I had a fever or fell ill they would bring me medicine but never take me to a doctor — I never had a check-up. The clients would pay me between 150 and 500 rupees ($3 and $11), but I saw none of it. I would get five rupees a day for food. They used to beat me and abuse me and say, 'We have spent money on you. You must entertain customers!'

"I continued to protest — this was even before I had reached puberty. We were never given condoms to use. I got pregnant once. I had a daughter who survived only seven days — she had chest problems. I was forced to have sex right up to my 9th month of pregnancy. I had to entertain even when I had my period or if my genitals were swollen. I ran away once, but they caught me. They said they would always find me. Once I became so desperate I did not want to continue living. I went down to the bridge to commit suicide, and met another girl."

The girl Saymin met was also a sex worker, and she brought Saymin to "Roya Bel", a madam who cared for prostitutes and tried to protect them. When Saymin's original madam tried to get Saymin to come back, claiming she was her sister, she was unsuccessful.

"'Roya Bel' said, 'I will break your legs if you come and try to harass this woman. If she wants, she can stay in her own room here and earn her own income independently. She is not going to live under anyone and go back to the slavery that you have subjected her to. I will call the police if you people don't go away from here.' "

Because she had worked as a prostitute, Saymin would not return to her family in Bangladesh — even if she could afford the transport. She worked for some time under Roya Bel's protection and married a client she met while working as a "flying sex worker", a prostitute who goes to various districts and takes a room for a couple of hours a day. When Saymin told her future husband her life story, he fell in love with her and said he wanted to save her from prostitution. They now have two children. He works in a hardware shop, and Saymin only does housework. Her husband likes her to stay at home.

"My dream is that my daughter does not have the same misfortunes that I have had and that both of my children go to school. Had I been educated, I would not have been in this state."

Image: Georgina Cranston/IRIN

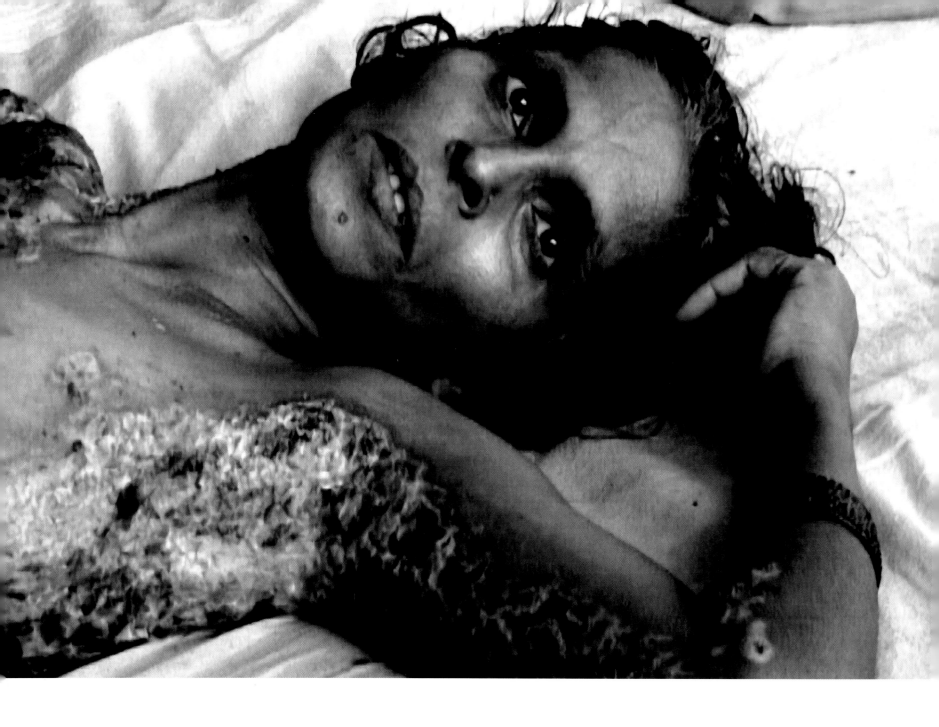

A survivor of a dowry burning recuperates in an Indian hospital. The truth behind such cases is often concealed. Many victims of dowry-related "accidents" fear repercussions from their husbands and in-laws, some of whom go so far as to bribe police officials to cover up their crimes.

Image: LC Visuals

dowry crimes and bride-price abuse

"Young Housewife Burnt Alive for Dowry" (27 May)

"Woman Ends Life Due to Dowry Harassment" (7 June)

"Body Found Floating" (7 June)[1]

These newspaper headlines, appearing within the span of 11 days in the *Times of India* in 2001, are from just three of thousands of articles published each year that catalogue the rising number of women who have lost their lives because of dowry crimes in India.

The persistence of dowry crimes

As many analysts and women's activists are quick to point out, femicide by husbands is not unique to India, nor is it more prevalent there than in many other parts of the world. The rate of intimate-partner violence in the United States, for example, is at least commensurate with that of India when compared on the basis of population.[2] The women's movement in India, however, has gone to great lengths to publicise this particular form of violence against women, shedding light on the combined forces — including the lack of basic human rights and the tolerance of violence against them — that put some women and girls in mortal danger at the hands of their partners.

Although India outlawed the modern dowry system in 1961, the practice has escalated among the expanding middle class, crossing religious, socioeconomic and ethnic boundaries. The National Crimes Record Bureau of the Government of India recorded 6,917 dowry-related deaths in 1998, a 15 percent increase over the number reported in 1997.[3] Because incidents are grossly underreported, these statistics probably represent only a small sampling of the violence occurring across India every day. In 1999, the founder of the International Society against Dowry and Bride Burning in India estimated that 25,000 brides are killed or maimed each year as a result of dowry disputes.[4] In 2000, a United Nations report estimated that on average five Indian women a day were killed in "accidental" kitchen fires by husbands whose demands for dowry payments had not been met.[5] "Mina" is one of these statistics:

Beaten and harassed by her husband for almost four years for not bringing in enough dowry, Mina eventually left him and filed a harassment case with the local police. Her husband convinced her to return to him, however, and shortly thereafter she suffered a fatal "accident". According to her husband and his family, Mina "fell on a chimney." As she lay dying from the burns that covered more than 94 percent her body, Mina was asked by police — as is customary — to make a declaration regarding the accident. She did so, absolving her husband and his family of any responsibility for her death.[6]

From empowerment to exploitation

A chief historic motivation for bestowing dowry, as practised in ancient Greece, Rome, India and medieval Europe, was to provide a degree of financial autonomy to a bride, who otherwise had little or no right to property after marriage.[7] According to various traditions, dowry might flow from the groom and/or his family to the bride — thus ensuring her economic wellbeing in the event of her husband's death or the dissolution of the marriage — or from the bride's parents to the bride and her new husband, as a form of a bequest, or premortem inheritance, for their daughter.[8]

Now practised primarily in Asian cultures, dowry payment in its current manifestation typically involves the transfer of wealth from the parents of the bride to the groom and his family.[9] Although women and girls are no longer the direct beneficiaries, some researchers maintain that the practice still confers benefits to the bride by enhancing her status in the marital home.[10] Evidence from India, however, indicates that the positive effects of dowry for wives have more than diminished. Once considered a beneficent and even spiritual act observed only by the wealthiest and holiest castes (with the lower castes practising the more

As she lay dying from the burns that covered more than 94 percent of her body, "Mina" was asked by police — as is customary — to make a declaration regarding the accident. She did so, absolving her husband and his family of any responsibility for her death.

pragmatic tradition of bride price, involving compensation by the groom's family to the bride's family for the loss of human capital), the dowry system today often functions more as a commercial transaction and has been resolutely embraced by the middle and lower classes.[11]

India's modern dowry: groom price

Several theories have been advanced to explain why the middle and lower classes in India replaced the custom of bride price with the dowry system. Some suggest that it was an attempt by lower castes to emulate higher castes. Dowry payment became a status symbol, one that bestowed greater respectability on the bride and her family and increased the likelihood of the bride "marrying up".[12] It continues today because of caste-related systems of wealth dispersion.[13] Another hypothesis contends that the interrelated influences of colonialism and the rise of a male-dominated market economy led to the devaluation of women, who lost their productive worth.[14]

Others cite demographic shifts in South Asia as a possible reason for the change. Reductions in overall mortality that began about 60 years ago have resulted in there being more young people than old in the region. Because women are likely to marry at a younger age than men, there is a surplus of marriageable women. Increasingly inflated dowry payments are sometimes six times the bride's family's annual income. These dowries now function as a groom price — a means for young women to compete for respectable husbands.[15] According to this hypothesis, recent declines in fertility and increases in sex-selective abortions should reverse the trend of escalating dowries over time and may even result in a return to bride price as the shortage of eligible women and girls results in men competing for wives.

Dowry as a form of violence

Although paying dowry may be a culturally specific practice, many of the circumstances that conspire to promote dowry-related violence against women in India are similar to those affecting women around the world: a lack of basic human rights, including education and property; an absence of support services for victims; and impunity for perpetrators. Indian tradition dictates that once a wedding is celebrated and a newly married bride has moved into her husband's home, she cannot request a divorce, nor may she return to her parent's home. In some marriages, the captive bride becomes a bargaining tool with which the groom and his family continue to extort dowry.[16]

Wife abuse actually may be higher when a husband and/or his family believe dowry payments are inadequate, as evidenced by one Indian study in which husbands were found to be more likely to beat wives with wealthy parents when the men thought their in-laws should be paying higher dowry. In the same study, it was documented that larger dowries reduced the risk of violence.[17] Thus, women whose families either refused or could not meet ongoing dowry demands appeared to

The body of a woman wrapped in cotton, on its way to be dumped into the Ganges. After four days of intensive care in hospital, this woman died of burns that were believed to have been sustained during a dowry dispute. No one was prosecuted for her murder, and no one claimed her body.

Image: LC Visuals [film still]

"Asha", from central India, was set on fire but managed to escape her tormentors and douse the flames. Shivering from fever and seriously burned, Asha huddled under a blanket in the corner of her hut, slipping into a semi-coma. When she regained consciousness three days later, the flesh of her charred arms had fused together.

Image: LC Visuals

be at greatest risk. Another study concluded that having in-laws who were dissatisfied with the amount of dowry put wives at four times greater risk of being beaten.[18]

Similar findings on the impact of dowry in neighbouring Bangladesh suggested that marriages without dowry arrangements had a reduced incidence of violence: "Paying no dowry is just as protective, if not more so, in terms of preventing abuse, as the largest dowry payments."[19] Whereas bride burning is common in India, acid attacks in Bangladesh are a cheap and easy way to disfigure women whose families fail to meet dowry demands.[20] In the most extreme circumstances, the groom and/or his family may decide that the promise of additional dowry in subsequent marriages is of greater value than a wife's life.

Dowry crime's cousin: bride-price abuse

The tradition of bride price, also referred to as "bride wealth", has been the global norm throughout history. In an ethnographic study of over 1,000 societies around the world, approximately two-thirds of the communities were found to have customs where wealth from the groom's kin was transferred to relatives of the bride.[21] While variations of bride price continue in a number of Asian countries, the negative impact of these practices on women and girls is arguably most pronounced in sub-Saharan Africa — or at least the relationship between bride price and violence against women is receiving increased attention there.

In African history, the payment of bride price — usually in the form of livestock, foodstuffs, cash or other resources — has served different functions among various tribes and ethnicities. At its most essential it is a social contract between families, one that not only bonds clans but, in many settings, also ensures that future children belong to the groom's lineage.[22] According to custom, all or a portion of the bride price is expected to be returned to the groom's family should a wife die prior to childbirth or should the marriage dissolve. If a husband has not paid bride price and his wife dies, tribal elders may permit the bride's family to take custody of any children produced during the marriage.

Bride price is a competitive practice that often favours the highest bidders, and a large payment is a mark of status for the bride and her family. Some theorists have argued that the custom generally implies greater social demand — and thus greater value — for women than does the practice of dowry, especially in its current manifestation as groom price.[23] Bride price, however, does not necessarily elevate the status or welfare of an African woman or girl. In fact, it can be as profoundly harmful as dowry is in other parts of the world.

Bride price as a form of violence

In the male-dominated and often polygynous societies in which bride price is perpetuated, African women are increasingly speaking out against the practice. Women's rights campaigners say that bride price objectifies women in the eyes of their natal families and their husbands. In 1999, for example, South African women testified at hearings on violence against women that bride price, especially when delivered in cash, constituted "buying a wife".[24] In instances where bride price is especially inflated relative to the local economy, husbands are much more likely to perceive the payment of bride price as a financial transaction, and hence more likely to consider it a right of ownership.

According to Miria Matembe, a Ugandan parliamentarian, "The girl's parents look at her as a source of income and demand too much from the groom's side. Once the groom has paid so much, he starts looking at his wife as property. … Bride price perpetuates the low status of women and keeps them in bondage."[25]

"We are going to shout about bride price across Africa, and we are going to say 'No' to the sale of women!" The words of Atuki Turner, the director of a nongovernmental organization in Uganda that works with victims of domestic violence, reflect the direct relationship that she and her staff see between marital violence and bride price.[26] Some women the agency serves are forced to have sex with their husbands — who claim to "own"

"The girl's parents look at her as a source of income and demand too much from the groom's side. Once the groom has paid so much, he starts looking at his wife as property. … Bride price perpetuates the low status of women and keeps them in bondage."

them — and beaten if they refuse. In the context of polygynous practices across sub-Saharan Africa, this disempowerment puts women at significant risk of HIV/AIDS, as well as other illnesses. In many traditional communities, wives are not allowed to place sexual demands on their husbands — including requesting that they use condoms — nor do they have a right to decide on birth control.[27]

In some settings, bride price also puts girls at risk of child marriages. Impoverished parents may seek to "sell" daughters as young as age 10 to considerably older men — who are more likely to be the highest bidders — to reap a high bride price (as is often the case in war-torn settings such as South Sudan, where poverty is endemic and sources of material wealth are few).[28] Child marriages also may be arranged to obtain the higher bride price paid for girls who have not been sexually active prior to marriage, a trend that has escalated due to the HIV/AIDS pandemic. Girls who marry young usually stop going to school because of their responsibilities in their new family, and consequent early sexual activity and child-bearing exposes them to myriad reproductive-health complications.[29]

Attempts by young girls to resist early marriage are often futile in traditional societies where females have few rights and where, according to custom, the wellbeing of the community is prioritised over that of an individual woman or girl. Once married, women and girls who try to leave abusive marriages may risk additional violence at the hands of their natal family, whose worries about paying back the bride price can take precedence over any concerns about the health and welfare of a daughter or sister. Reduced to the status of chattel, incalculable numbers of women across sub-Saharan Africa have no recourse from the violence that defines their everyday existence.[30]

Eradicating dowry and bride price

Just as the women's movement in India specifically targeted the issue of dowry abuse in the 1970s and 1980s, African women are now coming forward to denounce the custom of bride price.[31] At the first international conference on bride price in Africa in 2004, participants drafted a declaration calling for the abolition of the practice and sent it to all African presidents, the United Nations Secretary-General, the African Union and the Arab League of Nations.[32] In Uganda, a domestic-relations bill is pending in which bride price is redefined as an optional marriage gift that cannot be refunded.[33]

Legislating against bride price in Africa will not be a conclusive solution, just as prohibiting dowry has had a limited effect in India. An important lesson learned from India is the need for adequate resources for law enforcement and support services. The government shelters in India are reputedly "so horrible that a bride will prefer to die at the hands of her in-laws than to move to one."[34] In Delhi, where the population exceeds 14 million, the police response unit that deals with dowry crimes has one van to respond to all calls. By the time the team arrives at the scene of a reported bride-burning, it is often the case that the police already have recorded the death as a cooking-stove accident, having been "assisted towards this conclusion with a wad of rupees."[35] Even with widespread

> **"They are told it is only bride price that gives them value. Since many women believe this, it is no wonder that even today they don't support the abolition of ... bride price."**

corruption and limited resources, however, there are successful convictions — so much so that the main prison in Delhi has a cell block designated exclusively for mothers-in-law who have killed or harassed their daughters-in-law.[36]

According to one activist in Uganda, many women defend the practice of bride price because without it they consider themselves worthless, despite the work they perform in the household. "They are told it is only bride price that gives them value. Since many women believe this, it is no wonder that even today they don't support the abolition of ... bride price."[37]

Women's activists in Africa agree that lasting reform will require long-term strategies of community sensitisation and women's empowerment — something well-known to Indian women's groups that have struggled for the past 30 years to combat dowry crimes.[38] Often told by families to "back off" because one daughter's rescue might limit another daughter's prospects for marriage, victims' advocates in India have had to confront entrenched cultural and economic systems in which women are both victims and perpetrators of such crimes.[39] Activists have realised that addressing dowry crimes independently of other social and economic factors that undermine women's equality is short-sighted. Improving the condition of Indian women requires broad-based legal and cultural reforms in women's and girls' property and inheritance entitlements.[40] The same inevitably will be true in Africa, where any efforts to modify the tradition of bride price must include the promotion of women's basic social and economic rights, particularly among the victims themselves. ▪

A young Palestinian bride-to-be follows her mother past Israeli tanks on the way to her wedding. Her mother carries a suitcase crammed with cash — without which the marriage will not take place.

Image: Jaafar Ashtiyeh/AFP [newsprint photo]

While a documentary crew was at a hospital in India filming a report on dowry burnings, this woman was abandoned on the steps of the facility, burned from head to foot. In excruciating pain, she implored a member of the film team, "Please look after my baby girl." They were her last words.

Images: LC Visuals [film still]

"Jamilla" was born in Filimgue in Nigeria, which is around 155 kilometres north of the capital, Niamey.

"I have nine siblings. My parents treated us very well. When I was 13, my father told me it was time to marry. The husband he had chosen was my 30-year-old cousin. I told my father I was too young, but he said I had no choice. I resisted and cried so much. My father knew I was unhappy, but he had promised his brother that I would marry the man, whose first wife had run away. He had paid my father 120,000 CFA [US $220]. I tried to escape, but I was brought back home and forced to marry my cousin.

"When I went to live with my husband, his brothers and friends tied my arms and legs and dragged me to him, beating me. My husband just watched. He didn't touch me — but he didn't stop them, either. I cried so much — I still have scars from that time. We were living in the village where I was born, in a hut made of mud. The men took off my clothes and tied me to the bed. I screamed so loud that people came in. One of the people who came in was my father-in-law, who beat me and told me I must live with my husband. I told them all that even if they beat me I wouldn't sleep with him, and they said they would kill me if I didn't.

"My husband had some mental problems — I am not sure what they were. Maybe that is why he would just stand and watch. When they tied me naked to the bed, he didn't rape me. I think it was too humiliating for him to do it with everyone there. I would have preferred to live with an animal than this man. My legs were torn where they had tied me to the bed.

"I tried to forget what had happened and get on with work. One night, I told my husband I needed to go out to the toilet. I took a lamp with me and escaped. He didn't know that the day before I had sold my marriage clothes and hidden the money in my headscarf. I ran for two days with only water to drink along the way. When I arrived in Niamey, I was very sick and could not walk. I was taken to hospital. It took me two weeks to recover. My father came and was so angry — he said I had humiliated him. I told him it was better for me to humiliate my father than to stay with that man. My father said that if that was the case I must repay the dowry.

"There was a man who was a friend of mine before my marriage. I asked him to help me. He paid back the dowry, but as a result I had to marry him. I didn't love him.

"For the first year I lived happily with my new husband, who was a butcher. We lived in a small house made of mud in Niamey. But then he started taking drugs and drinking alcohol. He started to insult me and beat me. At first, I didn't do anything but then I started fighting back – but only when he was drunk and weaker than me. I was only 14 and he was around 30. He wouldn't even remember the beatings the next day.

"Sometimes I consented to have sex with him, but other times I said no. If I refused he would beat me and hold me around the neck and force me. He used to bite me — I still have scars. People tried to help, but my husband would beat them, too. I was so unhappy — I felt like I was always in a bad situation. I told my husband I wanted to divorce him. He said that if we divorced I would have to pay back the dowry.

"I didn't have my period for about two months, but then one day he punched me in the stomach and blood started pouring out of me. We have no children. I never used contraception — I am not sure why I never got pregnant. My husband used to sleep with prostitutes. He gave me a sexual disease, but there was nothing I could do to stop him.

"I lived patiently with my husband for four years. Two months ago, he went out and I ran away to my mother's house. I explained the situation to my family, but they have their own problems. I have refused to go back to my husband and am afraid that he may come and get me.

"My older sister is also suffering abuse from her husband. There are so many problems with forced marriage — it should be stopped. I want to be able to have a choice. The authorities should sensitise people. Why I should suffer like this, and twice over?"

Image: Georgina Cranston/IRIN

"Have you seen the burnt woman?" Nisha shouted from her doorway when we passed the slum on our way home. We hadn't, and asked the girl how bad it was. Nisha shrugged her shoulders. All she knew was that a young woman called Aleesha was lying badly injured in one of the illegal shacks near River Assi. She showed us to the hut and we decided to have a quick look before going home. Upon entering, we saw, in the dim light of a small electric bulb, a young woman lying on a bed, obviously in shock, most parts of her body grotesquely burned. Molten remnants of her synthetic sari stuck to loose patches of blackened skin, thick swollen blisters revealing raw flesh, infected wounds riddled with swarming flies.

Aleesha had been suffering in this hut alone and uncared for, but as soon as we arrived a group of men and several women appeared on the scene, each of them shouting their version of what they thought had happened and what should be done. Big-eyed children, some of them not older than three years, jostled one another in the doorway. Amidst this chaos, Aleesha lay staring at us, her blackened body in sickening contrast with the bright colours of her bedcover. We found out that she had laid helpless on this bed for six days, slowly slipping in and out of consciousness, refusing food and drink, softly crying because she was unable to breastfeed her youngest child. While the days wore on, her wounds got contaminated, attracting scores of flies. It was then, late in the afternoon of the sixth day, when young Nisha took us to the hut.

With the exception of Aleesha's mother and younger sisters, we made everybody leave the hut, and asked Aleesha if she could tell us what had happened. Even though it was obvious that speaking was virtually impossible for her, she bravely attempted to tell us what had happened to her. It

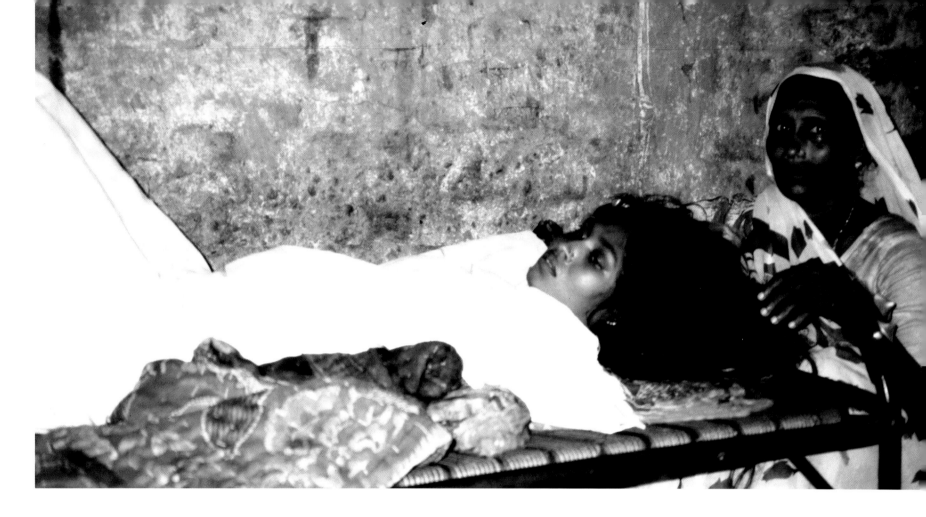

was in the house of her in-laws, at the other side of the city, her *bhabhi* (sister-in-law) and *saas* (mother-in-law) had doused her with kerosene and set her afire. Exhausted, Aleesha leaned back and closed her eyes. There was no time to lose; we had to have her hospitalised as soon as possible.

It took several days and as many conversations to piece together the story that led to the dreadful event which almost killed Aleesha. Today, she is about 26 years old but she was married off 13 years ago to Raj Kumar, an ice-cream vendor. Being the owner of a cart, he was regarded a good match. Aleesha's parents had to plunge deep into debts to cough up an enormous dowry: 6000 rupees [$135] in cash as well as several expensive gifts. On top of this, they had to pay for the wedding and feed scores of guests, most of whom were invited by Raj Kumar's parents.

After the festivities, as tradition dictates, Aleesha went to live with her parents-in-law, her husband, his brother and his wife. Being the youngest, and new to the extended family, she had to work very hard, her *saas* had stern demands. Aleesha was scolded by both her *saas* and her *bhabhi* and received no support from her husband whatsoever.

She felt increasingly lonely, a pain which was somewhat alleviated by motherhood: She gave birth to three sons, who give her a lot of happiness, and who are the reason for the one and only compliment ever given to her by her mother-in-law. As far as her marriage is concerned, she abhors being intimate with her husband. She hates having sex, she says it gives her no pleasure and her husband is aggressive in sex.

On the afternoon of July 5, Aleesha was preparing tea, squatting behind her stove, when suddenly *saas* and *bhabhi* came in and threw kerosene on her lower body. *Saas* put a match to it and in no time Aleesha, wearing a synthetic sari, was ablaze. From what she told us, we understood that she tried to extinguish the flames with her bare hands, whereupon both her arms caught fire. Next to her burning body, two of her sons screamed in terror. Aleesha managed to stagger to the street in front of the house, where *saas* and *bhabhi* were now pretending to rescue her. They threw a bucket of water on Aleesha, which only made matters worse, and rushed her on a barrow to the government hospital, where she was refused entry.

She was refused entry at other hospitals too and eventually left with her mother in the hut by the river. Hospitals refused to take her in before the police had made a report. Cases of burnt women were invariably linked to attempted killings and first had to be dealt with by the police, they said.

On the streets, selling his ice cream, her husband had known his wife would be set ablaze that very afternoon. He had known and didn't intervene and now after the burning Aleesha knew her husband had known of what awaited her that day. Nonetheless, she wanted him to stay with her in the hospital and look after her. She wanted to stay with him, for a life without husband would be worse. Life as a single mother would be impossible. Her mother also had made it very clear to Aleesha, when she was still in shock and long before we arrived on the scene, that Aleesha could not stay with her in her miserable hut. Where would she get the money from, to feed Aleesha and four extra children? It was impossible: Aleesha had to return to her in-laws. That was the only solution in their situation.

Later, while Aleesha was recuperating in the hospital, we had long talks with Aleesha's mother. It was clear that this woman, mother of seven and living in abject poverty, was incapable of ordering her thoughts, incapable of reflecting on her life. It felt as if this was the first time she was asked to tell about her life, her feelings, and her sadness. There was much sadness. She cried a lot and then, as if she remembered then and there, she revealed that one of her sons also set his wife ablaze. Her own son had done the exact same thing to his wife. The grief-stricken woman didn't condone the act, of course, but somehow she wanted us to understand that poverty was the main reason things like this could happen.

"They were poor, he was desperate and when he could not force his parents-in-law to give more dowry, he faked the kitchen accident and set his wife ablaze with kerosene. Yes, like many other men had done in this very city. She died, and he got remarried, managing yet a bigger dowry than the first one."

Excerpted from an account of Aleesha's story by a social worker from the Duniya Foundation (www.duniya.org) whose work includes helping victims of dowry burnings.

Aleesha today. Recovered from the terrible burns she suffered
at the hands of her husband and in-laws, she has returned to
her marital home. Aleesha feels she had no choice in a society
where a single woman with children would be lucky to survive
outside the relative protection of a family. "Life as a single
mother would be impossible," she said.

Images: LC Visuals

In Madrid in 2002, 150 women marched in the streets wearing their wedding dresses and holding thorns on cushions in protest of violence committed against women by their partners. Experts researching the full extent of domestic abuse worldwide consider they have only examined the "tip of the iceberg".

Image: Pierre-Philippe Marcou/AFP

intimate-partner violence

Chapter 9

On average, 36,000 women in the Russian Federation are beaten on a daily basis by their husbands or partners. In Pakistan, an estimated 90 percent of married women are abused by their husbands. According to a 2002 report approximately 1.8 million women were assaulted by an intimate partner in Spain, of which only 43,000 reported the assault to the police. Eighty-three percent of female homicide victims in the Dominican Republic in 2003 were killed by their current or past spouses or long-term partners. In the United States, a woman is battered, usually by her husband, every 15 seconds. In the United Kingdom, on average 120 women are murdered by their intimate partners each year.[1]

Defining intimate-partner violence

Intimate partner violence (IPV) is a phenomenon without cultural, racial or geographic boundaries. Occurring in every country around the globe, it is one of the most pervasive types of violence against women and girls worldwide.[2] Alternatively referred to as "domestic violence" or "spousal abuse", intimate-partner violence includes a broad spectrum of harmful behaviours, from physical and sexual violence to psychological cruelty and manipulation. Although some of its aspects are culturally specific — like the prevalence of gun use in intimate-partner homicide in Western countries as opposed to kerosene or acid in parts of Asia — many characteristics of this abuse are remarkably similar.

Physical violence can range from pushing, slapping, arm-twisting or hair-pulling to severe assault and battery. Sexual violence might include forced or coerced intercourse or other sex acts, as well as dictating reproductive-health decisions such as contraception and child-bearing. Psychological cruelty often entails threats and intimidation, humiliation and enforced isolation from friends and family. It can also consist of other controlling behaviours, such as restricting access to money and other resources.

While both men and women may suffer violence by a partner, the "single most powerful risk marker for becoming a victim of violence is to be a woman."[3] Findings from countries as disparate as the United States, India, Colombia, Zambia and China have confirmed that intimate-partner violence is distinctly gender-biased. The rates, the levels of violence and the negative health impacts associated with it are much more significant for women than for men.[4] According to the World Health Organization (WHO), women are most vulnerable to violence within intimate and familial relationships, whereas men are much more

intimate-partner violence   115

likely to be attacked by a stranger or acquaintance.[5] Moreover, women suffer the ill effects of IPV disproportionately when compared with men. Research from Canada has found that women are three times more likely than men to be injured as a result of abuse by a spouse or boyfriend, five times more likely to require medical attention or hospitalisation, and five times more likely to report fearing for their lives.[6]

Several triggers for violence that are notably consistent throughout the world include: perceived disobedience of a female partner, suspicions of a female partner's infidelity, failing to care "adequately" for children, questioning a man about money and refusing sex.[7] In other words, violence often results when a man believes his wife or girlfriend has contravened conventional gender roles. His violence serves to assert and maintain his authority and domination.

Religious doctrine and cultural practices that promote proprietary relationships of husbands to their wives reinforce beliefs that legitimise and perpetuate partner violence. According to one researcher, "Beating a wife to chastise or to discipline her is seen as culturally and religiously justified [in Pakistan]. ... Because men are perceived as the 'owners' of their wives, it is necessary to show them who is boss so that future transgressions are discouraged."[8]

In some settings, women have internalised these patriarchal social norms, as evidenced in a comment by a female research respondent in India: "If the woman makes a mistake or if she is unfaithful to him then the husband can beat her. He does have the right to do so because the woman has failed to carry out her work duties properly. Being a man he can get angry quickly and will slap, but then later he will be affectionate so we should not make a big issue of this."[9]

The global enormity of intimate-partner violence

The silence, stoicism and shame of its victims make it difficult to generate reliable estimates of just how prevalent intimate-partner violence is. Even so, a growing body of quantitative research — the majority of it undertaken within the last 10 to 15 years — has contributed to a better understanding of the extent of this problem around the world. Population-based data on domestic violence compiled from 55 countries indicate that in over half of these countries, at least one in every three female survey respondents acknowledged some form of physical violence in the context of an intimate relationship. In approximately 10 of these countries, on average one out of every two women reported physical abuse by a husband or boyfriend.[10]

Research further suggests that those who experience physical violence often suffer multiple acts of aggression that are perpetrated over time.[11] In some cases these incidents are followed by a period of contrition, or at least calm, in which the perpetrator may try to minimise or deny the severity of the violence, or remorsefully promise that it will not happen again. It most instances, the violence is repeated, with greater frequency

> **"After the blows, he always came back to court me, bought me clothes. And afterwards, he always said, 'Forgive me. I won't do it again.' But then he always did the same …"**

and intensity. The experience of survivor Ana Christina, from Nicaragua, illustrates the repetitive nature of partner violence: "After the blows, he always came back to court me, bought me clothes. And afterwards, he always said, 'Forgive me. I won't do it again.' But then he always did the same afterwards. And then my grandmother would say to me, 'Child, what are you going to do with candies in hell?' "[12]

At least two patterns of intimate-partner violence have been identified by the WHO: "Common couple violence", in which simmering frustrations sporadically manifest themselves through physical aggression; and "battering", which involves a spiralling escalation of physical violence and psychological terror.[13] Whereas common couple violence is usually a spontaneous expression of frustration or anger, battering is systematic. And although men figure prominently as perpetrators of both types of violence, they are overwhelmingly represented among those who batter.[14] Fear and intimidation are two hallmarks of battering, employed by the perpetrator to establish, re-establish and/or maintain power and control over his partner.

Physical battering may often be accompanied by sexual violence. While an increasing number of governments are adopting laws that recognise marital rape as a crime, forced sex in marriage is not considered a crime in most countries. Lack of legislation on marital rape both reflects and reinforces the presumption of many men, as well as some women, that it is a wife's obligation to comply with her husband's sexual demands. In Zimbabwe, for example, a woman who refuses to have sex with her husband risks being "hunted with bad luck" by his spirit after he dies.[15] As a result, and also because of the almost universal cultural prohibitions related to discussing intimate sexual behaviour, sexual violence is even more difficult to investigate than physical violence. Nevertheless,

An eight-year-old boy in the United States shouts at his father as police arrest him for attacking the child's mother, his wife. For many children, witnessing domestic violence is as traumatic as being victimised themselves. Intimate-partner abuse is a learned behaviour, and for some children it can become part of the vocabulary of relationships they take into adolescence and adulthood.

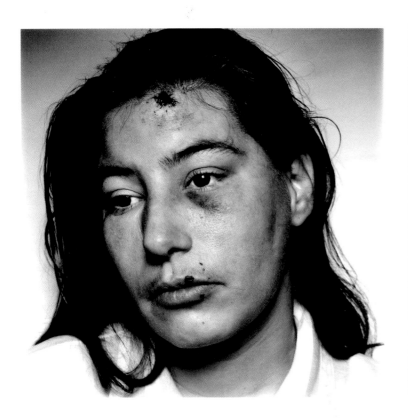

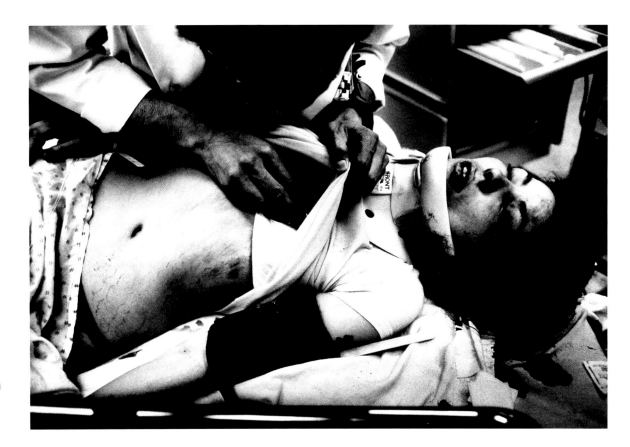

Images (facing): Annie Liebowitz (top left/bottom right) and Donna Ferrato/Network Photographers (top right/bottom left)

A woman in the United States [top] receives treatment for injuries sustained when her boyfriend ran over her with his truck. A doctor examines the tyre marks on her chest.

Image: Donna Ferrato/Network Photographers

In early 2005, Rania-al-Baz [right], a celebrated Saudi Arabian television presenter, was beaten unconscious by her husband during an argument. In an interview, she described the attack: "The next thing I knew he was strangling me. Then he threw me against the wall and banged my head down on the floor. He told me to say the *Shahadha* (the Muslim prayer of last rites) because I was going to die. I said it and I fainted. The next thing I remember, I was in the hospital." When al-Baz recovered, she did the unthinkable in Saudia Arabia: She spoke out.

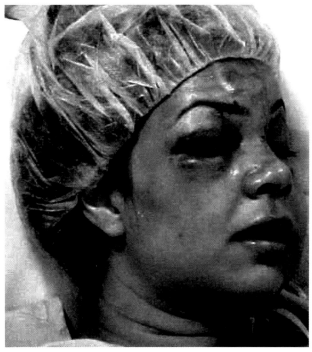

Images: AFP

A man arrested for domestic abuse remonstrates with the reporting officer at a police station in the United States. There are husbands and wives in cultures around the globe who consider male violence against women a normal part of married life.

Image: Donna Ferrato/Network Photographers

emerging data suggest that for women, "ironically, much non-consensual sex takes place within consensual unions."[16]

In research gathered from nine countries, on average one in five women acknowledged being forced to have sex by her partner.[17] Numbers can be significantly higher in select settings: Thirty percent of a sample of women in Bangkok, Thailand; 48 percent in Cusco, Peru; and 59 percent in Ethiopia reported being forced into sex by their partners.[18] Evidence from Papua New Guinea and India, where forced sex was reported by one-half to two-thirds of research respondents, indicates that it is often initiated or accompanied by beatings, as one woman in Uganda confirmed:

"My husband would beat me to the point that he was too ashamed to take me to the doctor. He forced me to have sex with him and beat me if I refused. ... Even when he was HIV-positive he still wanted sex. He refused to use a condom. He said he cannot eat sweets with the paper [wrapper] on."[19]

Perhaps the most invisible aspect of intimate-partner violence is psychological violence, though it is likely the most pervasive type of maltreatment that women in violent relationships are made to suffer. Psychological violence includes manipulative or threatening behaviours that are used to instil fear, such as punching walls, killing pets or stalking. It also includes verbal abuse, such as making comments that are derogatory, demeaning or embarrassing.[20] The impact of psychological violence can be as debilitating as physical or sexual violence, if not more so, as illustrated in the words of one woman from Nicaragua who suffered ongoing verbal abuse:

"He used to tell me, 'You're an animal, an idiot, you're worthless.' That made me feel even more stupid. I couldn't raise my head. I think I still have scars from this. ... I accepted it, because after a point, he had destroyed me by blows and psychologically."[21]

The implications for women

For several decades, women's rights activists and researchers around the world have described intimate-partner violence against women as a global human rights violation that undermines women's integrity, freedom, wellbeing and participation in family and society. It is only in the last 10 years, however, that its serious and pervasive public-health implications have begun to receive international attention. In a 1997 report, the United States Surgeon General concluded that domestic violence poses the single largest threat to all American women — more than rape, muggings and car accidents combined.[22] The Council of Europe similarly asserted that this type of violence accounts for more

"My husband would beat me to the point that he was too ashamed to take me to the doctor. He forced me to have sex with him and beat me if I refused. ... even when he was HIV-positive he still wanted sex."

deaths and health complications than cancer or traffic accidents: Violence by partners is the major cause of death and disability for European women aged 16 to 44.[23] A recent study of women aged 15 to 44 in Victoria, Australia, identified partner violence as the leading contributor to death, disability and illness, stating that it was "responsible for more of the disease burden than many well-known risk factors such as high blood pressure, smoking and obesity."[24]

Assault by a partner can result in a wide array of acute physical injuries. A 1998 report from the State Department of the United States indicated that 37 percent of all violence-related emergency-room visits by injured women were the result of physical abuse by a husband or boyfriend.[25] It is also a major contributor to chronic disabilities and illness, including a variety of reproductive-health problems.

A number of studies — from Canada, Chile, Egypt, Australia and Nicaragua, for example — have shown a high rate of partner abuse during pregnancy.[26] "Sharofat", a woman from Uzbekistan who eventually was abandoned by her husband, recalled the abuse she suffered during her marriage:

"He beat me so hard that I lost my teeth. The beatings happened at least one time each month. He used his fists to beat me. He beat me most severely when I was pregnant. ... The first time he beat me, and I lost the baby. I was in the hospital. The second time was only a few days before a baby was born, and my face was covered with bruises. He beat me and I went to my parents. My father refused to take me to a doctor. He said, 'What will I say, her husband beats her?' "[27]

Considering the association between physical violence and pregnancy, it is especially alarming that women who experience partner violence may be more likely to have higher numbers of children. Research in Nicaragua showed that violence was correlated with larger families, but in most cases its onset preceded the advent of child-bearing.[28] One hypothesis related to these findings is that women in violent partnerships may be less able to exercise control over contraception. A

Hadija Namaganda's HIV-positive husband raped and beat her viciously. During one brutal attack, he even bit off her ear. When he lay dying of AIDS and was too weak to beat her anymore, he ordered his younger brother to continue beating her.

study from India found that unplanned pregnancies occurred more than twice as often in abusive relationships, especially when the violence included sexual abuse.[29]

Physical and sexual violence by an intimate partner also increases the risk of sexually transmitted infections, including HIV. Findings from Rwanda, Tanzania and South Africa demonstrate that women in violent relationships are at up to three times greater risk of contracting HIV than those in nonviolent partnerships.[30] Research by Human Rights Watch in Uganda harshly illustrates this link:

"Hadija Namaganda's HIV-positive husband raped and beat her viciously during their marriage. During one brutal attack, he even bit off her ear. When he lay dying of AIDS and was too weak to beat her anymore, he ordered his younger brother to continue beating her. Now HIV-positive, Hadija recalled, 'He used to force me to have sex with him after he became ill. He would accuse me of having other men. He said he would cut me up and throw me out. I didn't know about condoms. We didn't use them.' "[31]

HIV infection can be both a cause and a consequence of violence. The husband of one woman from the Dominican Republic told her, "If you have something [a sexually transmitted disease], I will kill you."[32] Evidence from Africa, where women and girls are the largest and fastest growing risk group for HIV infection, indicates that women who fear reprisals from abusive husbands avoid or delay testing, disclosure and treatment for HIV/AIDS and other sexually transmitted infections.[33]

In its most severe form, intimate-partner violence ends in murder. Approximately 120 women in the United Kingdom are killed each year by a husband or boyfriend.[34] In Zambia, an estimated five women are killed by a male partner or family member each week.[35] Studies from Australia, Canada, Israel, South Africa and the United States have indicated that between 40 percent and 70 percent of women murder victims were killed by their husbands or boyfriends.[36] In the Dominican

Republic in 2003, the proportion of femicides committed by an intimate partner was as high as 83 percent.[37]

Even if a woman is not killed by her partner, the fear, helplessness and hopelessness that often accompany violent relationships may lead a woman to attempt suicide. According to the United Nations Children's Fund (UNICEF), multiple studies — from the United States, Fiji, Papua New Guinea, Peru, India, Bangladesh and Sri Lanka — have illustrated the causal link between suicide and partner violence. A woman who has been abused is up to 12 times more likely to try to kill herself than one who has not. In the United States, 35 percent to 40 percent of battered women attempt to end their lives.[38]

One of the most horrific demonstrations of suicidal behaviour among women victims of partner violence is self-immolation, or setting oneself on fire. Relative to other methods of suicide, self-immolation is unusual in that it is customarily limited to Middle Eastern and Central Asian countries. Like other forms of suicide, self-immolation is not solely or even primarily restricted to women suffering from partner abuse. But when it is related to intimate-partner violence, self-immolation is a very powerful representation of the desperation women feel.

Other repercussions

Women victimised by their partners are not alone in their misery, as their children usually suffer the consequences alongside them. Partner abuse has been shown to increase the risk of infant and early-child mortality and can further contribute to a host of emotional and behavioural problems for children who survive to witness the violence.[39] Studies from Ireland, Mexico and Eritrea indicate that children living in abusive households regularly observe violence.[40] The impact of bearing witness to such acts, according to findings from research in the United States, can be as damaging to a child as direct abuse.[41]

The fallout of domestic violence extends well beyond the households in which the abuse occurs. Providing public health, social welfare and protective services to victims and their children places an enormous financial strain on communities and nations. The indirect and long-term costs associated with increased morbidity and mortality, behavioural problems of children, transgenerational perpetuation of violence, work-related absenteeism and job loss also take their toll on societies.[42] For

"Carolina" is a street prostitute in Granada, Nicaragua. She met her husband at a party when she was 15, and they dated for about eight months before getting married. "When I met him he was working as a carpenter. After I had our first son, Brian, he started changing. His friends started hanging out at the house; they were drinking. They brought him into a gang."

After joining the gang, Carolina's husband became more abusive: "He hit me, he kicked me. He would leave me half-dead. I almost lost our first baby two times. He would take me to hospital and then he would apologise. I tried to leave a couple of times, but he threatened to kill me. He only hit me when I was pregnant — so I feel his intention was for me to miscarry. He would throw me against the wall, pull my hair. Sometimes he was sober, sometimes he was high. I was pregnant with our second son when I finally left him. I came to Granada when I was eight months pregnant. I couldn't find work because I had to care for my first baby. Prostitution was the only thing I could do. I had to choose this life. I have been doing this for a year. My mind is blank, and I don't think about my future."

Image: Evelyn Hockstein/IRIN

some developed countries such as Canada and the United States, the annual costs associated with IPV have been estimated in the billions of dollars.[43] For developing countries, the measurable costs may be significantly lower, simply because services are not as established or widespread. Even in settings where costs are more difficult to measure, partner abuse has far-reaching consequences. It drains precious existing resources while at the same time handicapping the ability of women and children to contribute to social and economic progress.

Responding to intimate-partner violence

In a study in Eritrea, women who had been beaten and abused by their partners were asked why they did not leave their relationships. Many responses expressed sentiments of powerlessness and futility:

"He wouldn't accept no. He wouldn't accept that I was leaving."
"Would I walk away alive?"
"Just the kids — he'll take them. That's it, really."
"Where would I live?"
"I was pregnant, and I thought he would hurt the baby and my family."[44]

These women, like others around the world, felt they had no escape from abuse. Their responses reflect some of the dynamics that reinforce intimate-partner violence: fear, poverty, and the lack of legal protection and social support.

Addressing the problem requires an understanding of its basic ecology: the interplay of individual and cultural factors that foster abuse in homes, communities and societies.[45] For this reason, much work has been done in recent years to improve local and international research capacity. In particular, the WHO has spearheaded multicountry studies

efforts, in addition to the work undertaken by independent researchers and women's activists, have produced an emerging portrait of the global magnitude of the problem, which in turn has provided an important basis for local, national and international advocacy. Most experts agree that the research conducted thus far has revealed only the tip of an iceberg, especially in developing countries. A considerable amount of work remains, particularly in terms of standardising research methods to improve comparability; investigating what puts women at risk, as well as what protects them from it; and understanding its impact.[46]

The last 20 years of activism on the part of women's and human rights groups has laid firm the foundation to combat intimate-partner violence. Evidence suggests that in the majority of countries across the globe, there are at least some small efforts being made to identify and address the issue. In some settings, those endeavours are widespread. While strategies vary according to culture, commitment and the availability of resources, almost all involve legislative and policy reform, as well as grassroots initiatives that support women's rights.[47]

Strategies also seek to build the capacity of health, social-welfare and legal-justice systems to recognise, monitor and respond to IPV and ensure rapid and respectful care of women who have been abused. In addition, international, national and local media campaigns and education programmes have been developed to highlight the impact of intimate-partner violence.

As a result of community mobilisation, education and advocacy efforts, many countries have made progress in introducing legislation against intimate-partner violence, though less so against marital rape. The number of projects that enhance responses to victims, especially in the areas of healthcare and police training, have grown. In some countries, support services include hotlines, safe houses and community centres.

These women, like others around the world, felt they had no escape from abuse. Their responses reflect some of the dynamics that reinforce intimate-partner violence: fear, poverty, and the lack of legal protection and social support.

Still, too many countries fall short in terms of law enforcement, governmental involvement and access to care. Research repeatedly shows that many victims do not use support services. Whether this is because of lack of access, lack of confidence in services, shame, resignation or fear of retribution, the end result is that many women around the world "suffer abuse silently".[48] This should act as a clarion call to service providers and activists to evaluate the accessibility and value of victim-support activities. To date, very few programmes have been assessed for their effectiveness. In fact,

on intimate-partner violence and, in the process, established global standards for ethical and methodologically sound approaches to investigating violence against women. International demographic and health survey experts also have devised methods to include standardised questions about intimate-partner violence in national-level research around the world. During the last 10 years, the outcomes of these

monitoring and appraising interventions is one of the crucial steps towards improving local, national and international capacity to address the problem.

In addition, comparatively little attention has been paid to improving prevention efforts. Many of the limited resources dedicated to intimate-partner violence have naturally gone to ensuring the safety and welfare of victims, at both the individual and policy levels. The unfortunate side effect of this approach is that partner abuse "has largely been regarded as a woman's problem."[49] While it is critical that women survive and recover from the violence they have suffered, significant additional resources must be earmarked for prevention if societies around the world are to reach the long-term goal of eradicating the problem.

Developing prevention strategies is an area of great promise, particularly with regard to reducing the factors that lead men to act violently towards women. Model programmes for "male involvement" have been initiated in many countries, but their reach and impact is sorely inadequate when compared with the number of men who abuse their partners. And while programmes to engage men are crucial in the fight against intimate-partner violence, effective prevention requires the active engagement of all members of the community — men, women, boys and girls.

The WHO has said the basis for change is the province of future generations, who "should come of age with better skills than their parents generally had for managing their relationships and resolving the conflicts within them, with greater opportunities for their future, and with more appropriate notions of how men and women can relate to each other and share power."[50]

Winning the worldwide fight against partner abuse requires fundamental social change that supports women's human rights as well as their equal participation in all relationships, especially those that are most intimate. n

"Clementine" is 22 years old and lives in the Democratic Republic of Congo.

"I got married in 2001, when I was 18 years old. I was pregnant, but it was our choice to get married. We had known each other for four years. We went to live with his parents. For me, our time there swung from good to bad. It was hardest with my mother-in-law and sister-in-law, which can be a common problem. Then we moved house. We lived well. My husband was a casual worker for the International Committee of the Red Cross. He lost that job and is now employed as a casual worker for another organization, but he doesn't work every day. I don't work — I look after things in the house. We were happy until things changed recently.

"The start of our problems was when he changed friends. He started spending time with boys who go to hotels and bars. When he is spending time in hotels, it makes me angry. The problem is that I have kept quiet about it, and doing so has made me suffer psychologically. I would get hypertension. It made me worry that because of these friends, he may slide into drinking alcohol or being in the hands of women. A friend told me that I shouldn't let the problem fester, I should open up and talk about it. So I looked for an opportunity.

"On Sunday, 20 February 2005, when we were on the way back from visiting my family, he lied to me and told me he had been called to work. I told him I would continue home. As he went I became suspicious that it wasn't true. A man later told me he had seen my husband going with friends to a hotel. He told me, 'They are in there, but don't go to find him. When your husband comes home, don't tell him I told you.' I went home and fell asleep on the sofa.

"My husband came home with a friend at 8 p.m. and asked me what the problem was, why I was sleeping on the sofa. I told him I was feeling bad. I went into the bedroom, and he followed me and locked the door. He held my arms from behind me and said, 'Now you are getting really familiar with me, and you are following me wherever I go.' Then he started beating me. He beat me so hard. He pulled me from the bed to the floor and started trampling on me. I tried to hide my face. He used his hands to beat me, his fists and his feet. He beat me for about 20 minutes. I was screaming and screamed so loud when he trampled on my abdomen that his older brother who lives nearby heard me and tried to come in. My husband's friend who had come back with him told my brother-in-law to leave us alone and let us sort out our problems.

"When my husband heard his brother's voice, he said, 'Leave. I will not do anything to my wife.' I got the strength and managed to open the door. His brother took him outside, and I stayed with my sister-in-law and the friend. I fainted and fell to the ground, hitting my head on the window. The glass smashed, and my husband thought I had broken it. He came back in and said, 'You have destroyed everything in the house.' He took a piece of wood and hit me on the head and in the lower stomach. It broke in two pieces. He beat me again so badly. The others were trying to hold him back but it didn't work. Eventually they managed to hold him off and his brother's wife took me to her house.

"My husband sometimes forces me to do things. Many times he has forced me to have sex when I haven't wanted too. He told me the fact that he beat me should not prevent us from having sex. He says it is in the past. He never apologised. He said he didn't know why he was so angry to the point of beating me, but he also didn't understand why I had followed him. I am so afraid of him since this happened. His family were angry with him and told him what he did was wrong, but this was when I was there so I am not sure if it was genuine. They told me not to keep grudges. His older brother told me never to tell anyone. He said, 'This is a common story, so don't tell it to others. … What one man does to his wife is no one else's business.' "

Image: Georgina Cranston/IRIN

"Maria", age 27, came to the police station with a black eye after her husband had hit her with a stick. The vision in her left eye is already damaged from previous beatings. "Last night he was drunk. He is a driver for a construction business. Every few weeks he beats me, but every day he verbally abuses me."

Maria's husband also beats the two children she has from a prior relationship. At the police station, the officer says, "If you don't leave him, he will kill you. You have to find a way to get away from him."

"He threatens to take my children away," Maria says. "So I am always with my children. What kind of education will he give my children?"

The police captain tells Maria, "You cannot keep bearing that much violence — even if you are a Christian. You are a human being. You need protection. You need your rights to be respected."

"Last night I told my husband I would go [to the police]," Maria says. "I called the police patrol. They said they would come, but they didn't."

Images: Evelyn Hockstein/IRIN

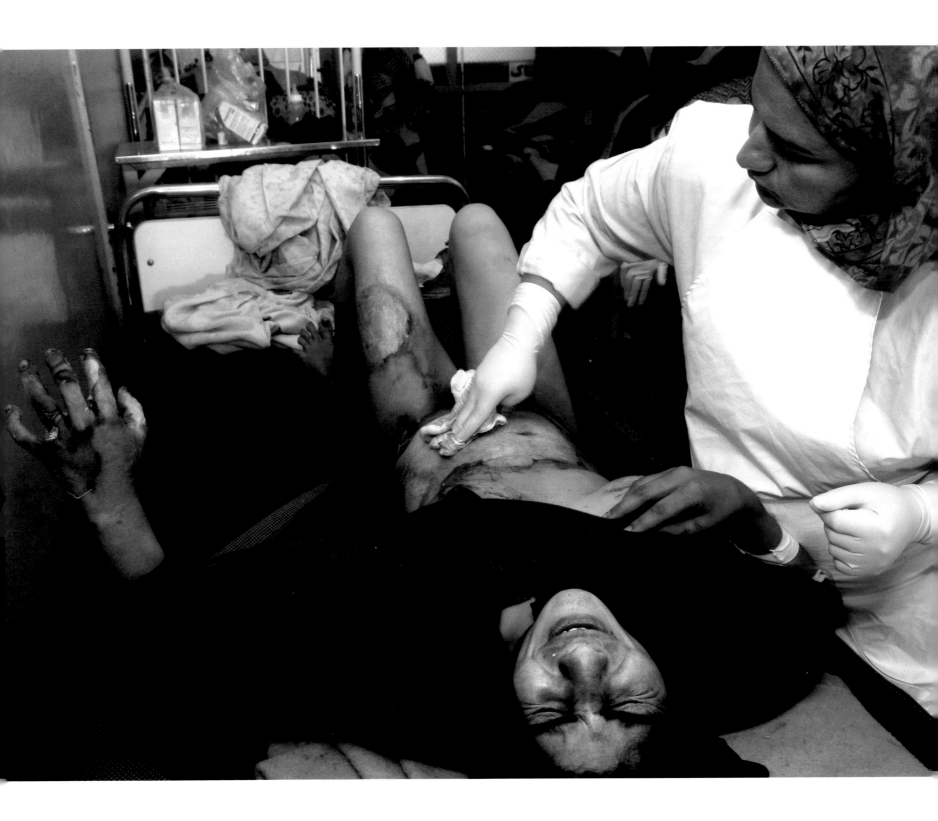

An 18-year-old wife and mother of a four-month-old baby, "Rizufa" lives in Herat, Afghanistan, where many of the oppressions previously suffered by women under the Taliban regime persist. She has been married for a year to a man who beats her regularly. He has hit her with a wooden stick, kicked her and thrown objects at her. One night when she did not prepare dinner on time, he threw something that cut her eye.

When Rizufa was pregnant, her husband bought some meat for her to eat. Her father-in-law heard about it and challenged Rizufa, asking her why they were eating expensive meat when the whole family was so poor. She tried to explain, but her husband was angry that she had answered back and argued with his father. She was beaten for her insolence.

After the beating, Rizufa went to her mother's house to explain her predicament. Her brother said that he wanted to kill Rizufa's husband. The family went to the *shura*, a traditional court, which sentenced the husband as well as the father-in-law to one month in jail. During this time, she stayed at her mother's house.

When her husband was released from jail, Rizufa had to return to their home. He forbade Rizufa to see her family again, and she did not see them for five months. The separation upset her, and she would sometimes look at family photos as a substitute. One day her husband came home while she was looking at the pictures. He said, "Give me the photo. I will tear it up. I don't like your mother, and you shouldn't either." He grabbed the photo and tore it up. When Rizufa started to cry, he threatened to kill her if she did not stop. She replied, "You don't have to. I will kill myself."

When her husband left the room, Rizufa doused herself in kitchen fuel and lit a match. She ran outside in flames, screaming, and he tore off her shirt. He brought her inside and sent for her mother. Her parents took her to hospital.

Later, lying in a hospital bed and covered with burns, Rizufa said she intended to return to her husband. "I have to stay married because of my son. Divorce is a bad thing in our culture, we would rather die."

Image: Evelyn Hockstein/IRIN

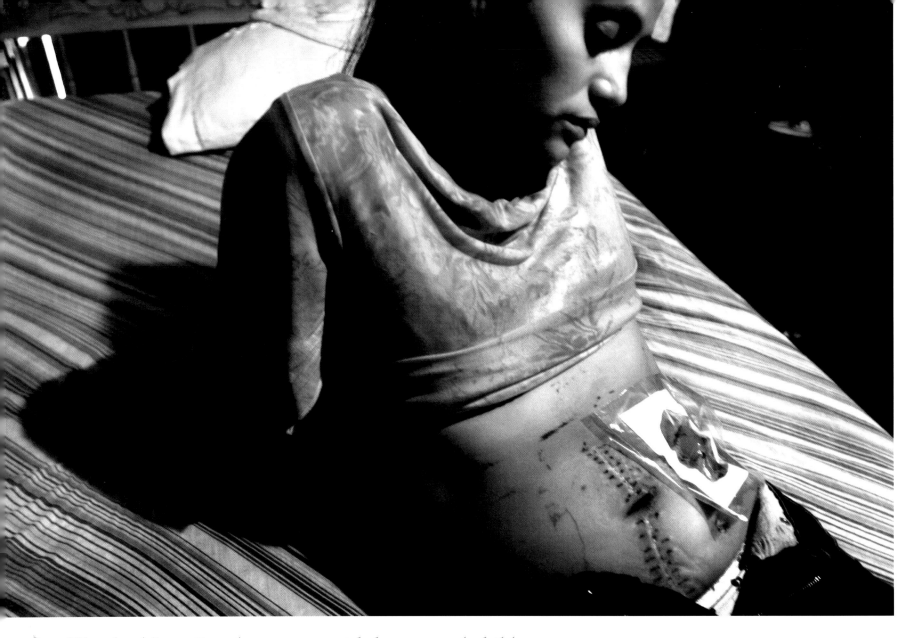

"Elizabeth" is 17 and pregnant with her second child. She and her husband live with Elizabeth's mother and have been married for eight months. Her husband hits her when he is drunk, and the beatings usually coincide with the arrival of his monthly paycheck. She is worried that he will kill her someday — he almost did the last time he attacked her.

"I came home from work, and my husband was drunk. Later that evening, he started to insult me. He hit me, and I asked him to respect my mother's home. My husband said he didn't care and continued to hit me — on my arms, not my face. Then he grabbed my shirt and punched me twice. I put his clothes in a box, left them outside, and told him he had to leave.

"He stabbed me and ran away. The neighbours caught him — the guy who did almost got stabbed as well. My mother was shouting, 'He killed my daughter!' There was a lot of blood — he had perforated my intestines and I had to hold my hand on the wound. When I walked out of the house,

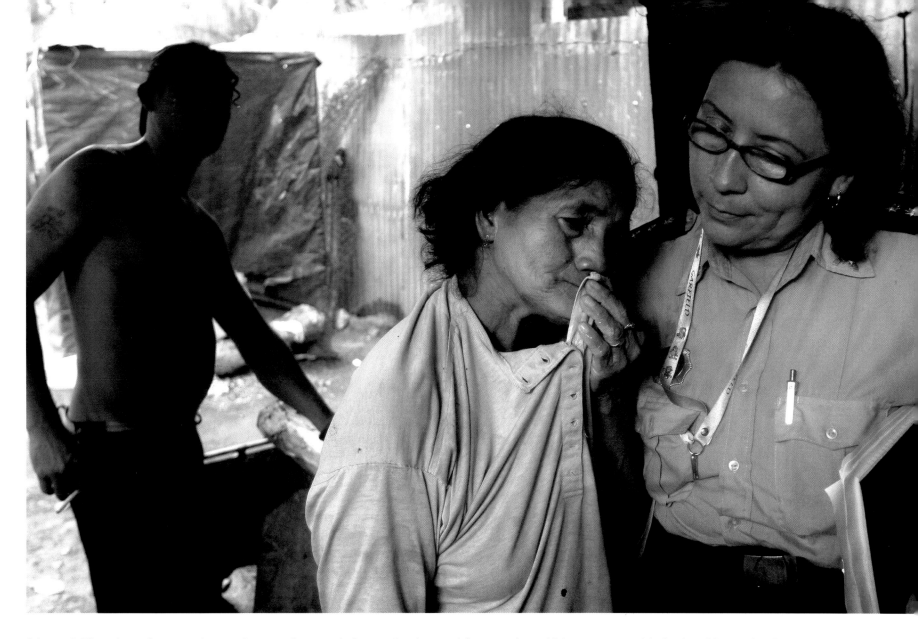

I fainted. They brought me to hospital in a pickup truck. I stayed in hospital for a week, and I lost an ovary. My husband knew that I was pregnant when he attacked me.

"I want the police to keep him under arrest for a while. There is going to be a trial. I feel threatened because if he didn't kill me this time he will kill me the next time. I am worried he will come after the baby and me. We women are alone. There is no one to protect us."

Elizabeth's mother, pictured above with a policewoman and a neighbour, witnessed the attack. "Some of us women take these men to the police station. But then the men's families try to convince us to stop the process."

Three victims of acid attacks in Bangladesh, where visual aesthetics are highly prized and facial disfigurement can be used by husbands as legal grounds for divorce. Rejection of romantic advances or dissatisfaction with dowry are the main motivation behind these crimes, which are especially prevalent in South Asia.

crimes of "honour"

In many societies around the globe, women and girls are the repository of family and community honour and held liable for infractions against that reputation regardless of their guilt or innocence. Unsubstantiated rumours of a woman or girl acting "inappropriately" can lead to — and then be used to justify — extreme punitive measures. Even in cases of rape, codes of honour very often dictate that the victim be punished.

A culturally condoned atrocity

A young Bangladeshi woman was flogged to death by order of village clerics for "immoral behaviour".[1] An Egyptian man paraded the head of his daughter on a stick through the streets of his neighbourhood after he killed her for besmirching his name.[2] A teenager's throat was slit in Turkey because a love ballad was dedicated to her over the radio.[3] A Pakistani woman was gunned down by her own family in the presence of her human rights lawyer for pursuing a divorce from her abusive husband.[4] A 13-year-old Turkish girl's husband slit her throat in a public square after pulling her out of a cinema and accusing her of being a prostitute.[5] A 35-year-old Jordanian man shot and killed his sister for reporting to the police that she had been raped.[6] A Turkish girl was killed by her father for telling the authorities that she had been raped and then refusing his demand that she marry the rapist.[7] A 29-year-old woman was dragged from her house in Afghanistan by her husband and

local officials and stoned to death for committing adultery, while the man with whom she was alleged to have had an affair was whipped and then freed.[8]

Each of these executions was committed within the past five years in the name of "honour". Many of the perpetrators received no criminal penalties; others served only short sentences. Considered justifiable punishment for a wide range of perceived offences, contemporary honour crimes are based on archaic codes of social conduct that severely circumscribe female behaviour while at the same time legitimising male violence against women.

Honour crimes are typically engineered by male family members but are often tacitly or explicitly condoned by the community and/or the state. In many countries the responsibility for the murder itself is assigned to an underage male, thus ensuring a (reduced) juvenile sentence in the event the case is prosecuted. In most instances, the murderer is hailed as a "true man".[9] It is also not unheard of for female family members to act as accomplices to the killing or even to carry out the murder itself.

Global prevalence

In recent reports, both the United Nations Special Rapporteur for Violence Against Women and the Special Rapporteur for Extrajudicial and Summary Executions have highlighted this egregious type of violence against women, citing incidents in Bangladesh, Turkey, Jordan, Israel, India, Italy, Pakistan, Brazil, Ecuador, Uganda, Morocco, Syria, Egypt, Lebanon, Iran and Yemen, as well as among migrant communities in Germany, France, Sweden and the United Kingdom.[10] Honour crimes also have been reported in Afghanistan and Iraq.[11]

The actual scale of the problem is impossible to determine. In many cases deaths are not registered; in others murders are made to look like suicides, or women are forced or induced by their families to kill themselves.[12] Burns or acid attacks not resulting in death often are attributed to accidents, a claim which victims may not refute for fear of further reprisals. In societies where these crimes occur, protection and support are often extended to the perpetrator rather than to the victim.

Despite the lack of reliable statistical data, estimates based on reviews of police reports and court dockets, newspaper articles and other sources in

> "Women are considered the property of the males and their family irrespective of their class, ethnic or religious group. The owner of the property has the right to decide its fate. The concept of ownership has turned women into a commodity which can be exchanged, bought and sold."

a variety of countries suggest that thousands of women and girls are murdered each year in the name of honour. Anecdotal evidence from Pakistan, for example, suggests that more than 1,000 women are victims of honour crimes annually.[13] Over one-third of femicides in Jordan are thought to be such killings.[14] In Turkey, an annual report of the Human Rights Association concluded that more than half of women killed by family members in 2003 were victims of honour crimes.[15]

In 1997, the former attorney general of the Palestinian National Authority suggested that 70 percent of all murders of women in Gaza

and the West Bank were honour crimes.[16] In the same year, as many as 400 honour killings took place in Yemen, and 57 were reported in Egypt.[17] In late 2004, 117 murders in the United Kingdom were being investigated as possible honour killings.[18] In Lebanon, 36 honour crimes were reported between 1996 and 1998.[19]

According to the Special Rapporteur on Violence Against Women, the number of honour killings "is on the rise as the perception of what constitutes honour and what damages it widens."[20] Its global prevalence suggests that honour crimes are not unique to specific cultures, religions or classes. In fact, the justification for these crimes has it roots in various social and legal systems around the world.

Honour or subjugation?

In the broadest sense, honour crimes involve the murder or maiming of a woman or girl whose behaviour is at odds (whether in fact or by perception) with the norms of the society in which she lives. In many cases the cause of the woman's actions — even if she is under extreme duress or in fear of her life — is immaterial if her family feels that she has compromised their supposed honour. The inherent subjectivity of such notions of honour opens these codes to wide and convenient interpretation. At the most basic level, "what masquerades as honour is really men's need to control women's sexuality and freedom."[21]

According to Thaira Shahid Khan, the author of *Chained to Custom*, "Women are considered the property of the males and their family irrespective of their class, ethnic or religious group. The owner of the property has the right to decide its fate. The concept of ownership has turned women into a commodity which can be exchanged, bought and sold."[22] That perception also means that women are expendable when their actions, real or imagined, threaten a family's sense of honour.

While honour crimes are most prevalent in Muslim and some Mediterranean cultures, the popular conflation of Islam with such acts is misguided: Islamic scholars and clerics alike have publicly decried the practice, confirming that it has no basis in Islamic scripture or teachings.[23] Nevertheless, in traditional Muslim societies, concerns about shame and honour may take precedence over individual human rights and freedoms. One contention is that honour crimes have their

Young women share a dormitory-style room at a women's prison in Herat, Afghanistan. Many of them have run away from forced marriages or been accused of committing adultery. One of the girls at the facility, "Ramia", had been sent there for tarnishing the honour of her family, who claimed that they had not given consent for their 15-year-old to marry — even though Ramia's father had chosen his son-in-law two years before the marriage. To separate the couple and punish his daughter, Ramia's father arranged for the police to arrest her and put her in prison. "Halima", another 15-year-old girl at the facility, was accused by her brother-in-law of killing the 60-year-old husband she had been forced to marry.

Image: Evelyn Hockstein/IRIN

Sixty percent of "Rabisa's" body was severely burned in punishment for challenging the authority of her husband, who had forbidden her to go to her mother's house to take an overseas call from her uncle. When Rabisa and her mother insisted she be allowed to speak with her uncle, Rabisa's husband threw his mother-in-law out of his house and knocked his wife against a wall, breaking her nose. He then poured kerosene over Rabisa and set her alight.

Rescued by her mother, Rabisa survived an excruciating recovery process. She continues to have trouble breathing through her nose, and her vision has deteriorated because her burned eyelids can no longer protect her eyes. Rabisa cannot wear glasses to correct this: Her ears melted away while her body was on fire.

origins in the Arabic expression "A man's honour lies between the legs of a woman."[24] In Turkish, the term *namus* is used to describe honour. A woman's *namus* is primarily defined through her sexuality, her physical appearance and her behaviour, a man's *namus* is achieved through the sexual purity of his wife, daughters or sisters.[25]

Others contend that current justifications for crimes of honour are the result of colonial influences, including both Napoleonic and British codes that cite provocation as an exonerating or mitigating factor in criminal assault.[26] Indeed, the concept of provocation in "crimes of passion" between men and women — where women are held accountable for inciting men to violence — has tenacious roots in many societies across the world. As recently as 1999, an American man was sentenced to only four months in prison for murdering his wife and wounding her lover in the presence of their 10-year-old son.[27]

In Sindh, Pakistan, honour crimes take the form of *karo-kari* killings. *Karo* literally means a "black man" and *kari* means a "black woman". Having brought dishonour to their families through adultery or other "inappropriate" behaviour, the customary punishment for both *karo* and *kari* is death. In practice, however, the *kari* woman is usually killed first, giving the *karo* man an opportunity to flee. Following the woman's punishment, the man may be able to negotiate a truce with the dishonoured family by paying financial compensation and/or by replacing the woman who was killed with a woman from his own family.[28]

In some instances, reputed *karo-kari* killings can serve as pretence for economic gain. In fact, evidence suggests that faked honour killings often conceal other crimes: Men murder other men for reasons not associated with honour and then execute a woman of their own family to camouflage the initial killing. Some experts believe that honour crimes also are used to cover up misdeeds such as rape, incest, adultery, unlawful or undesired pregnancies and for inheritance purposes.[29] In Jordan, for example, investigators surmise that a substantial portion of the 20 to 35 honour killings documented each year are the result of other motives.[30]

An ever-present threat

In settings where honour killings are prevalent, the constant threat against women and girls is yet another form of violence, aptly described

in the Pakistani poet Attiya Dawood's rendering of the daily experience of a young Pakistani girl: "My brother's eyes forever follow me. My father's gaze guards me all the time, stern, angry ... We stand accused and condemned to be declared *kari* and murdered."[31]

For some women, this threat leads to suicide, whether or not a family orders it. One young woman in Pakistan, for example, laid herself across a train track after being pressured by her parents to marry a man she did not choose.[32] Other women and girls may be forced to undergo virginity exams — an often painful and degrading process — and are still killed despite medical verification of their chastity.[33]

Whether or not the threat of violence actually results in murder, the risk of being killed results in the virtual death of many women, whose only option, in the absence of adequate protective services, is to enter prisons or other custodial facilities. In Jordan, for example, police imprison potential victims to protect them from being killed by their male relatives. While those who threaten them remain free, victims languish in custody for years on end. In some societies, women are not released from custody until a relative signs for their discharge. Too often, a

"My father's gaze guards me all the time, stern, angry ... We stand accused and condemned to be declared *kari* and murdered."

woman or girl who is handed over to relatives who promise to protect her is immediately killed by them. In one instance, Jordanian police returned a 36-year-old woman to her father's home after he had consented not to hurt her. He shot her while the police were still downstairs, and his punishment was one month in prison.[34]

Evidence suggests that there is a great demand for services, including shelters, for abused women. But even where shelters are available, there is often little they can provide in terms of concrete assistance because of the limited rights and opportunities afforded to women by the prevailing culture. Moreover, shelter workers, human rights activists, journalists and lawyers are at risk of being targeted by angry families and communities.[35]

Police rarely investigate honour crimes, and the handful of perpetrators who are arrested often receive only token punishments. In some settings police may overtly or covertly champion the killers as vindicated men. Elsewhere, police act within a network of conspirators who benefit economically from honour killings.[36] Many countries where such crimes are commonplace have retained legislation allowing reduced sentences or exemption from prosecution for those who commit honour crimes.[37]

In Pakistan, for example, an ordinance gives the heirs of a murder victim the right to pardon the murderer. Since family members most often are complicit in honour killings, many perpetrators go free.[38] Specific articles in the Jordanian penal code offer similar protection.[39] In Brazil, men alleging adultery may also go free. In one such case, a man stabbed his wife and her lover to death after catching them in a hotel room. The case was appealed three times, and each time the jury acquitted the defendant. Such defences are found to varying degrees in the penal codes of Peru, Bangladesh, Argentina, Ecuador, Egypt, Guatemala, Iran, Israel, Syria, Lebanon, Turkey, the West Bank and Venezuela.[40]

Taking action against honour crimes

The work of local and international activists is bringing gradual pressure to bear in many of the countries where honour crimes are most prevalent. Turkey, for example, has taken steps to conform its legislation to international standards. In 2003 and 2004, three defendants were sentenced to life imprisonment for crimes of honour. Real change, however, takes time. In another case in 2004, the 24-year sentence of a man convicted of killing his wife was commuted to two years after he presented to the court pictures of his wife with another man.[41] In Pakistan, intensive pressure on the government has resulted in the drafting of legislation against honour crimes, which has yet to be formally presented to parliament.[42]

A grassroots campaign against honour killing in Jordan gathered some 15,000 signatures on a petition to repeal an article in the penal code that pardons honour crimes that are the result of a wife committing adultery. In 2001, a temporary amendment was passed precluding exoneration based on adultery, although it retained adultery as a mitigating circumstance. To date, ratification of the amendment is still pending, and parliamentary resistance to the legislation is apparently strong in some conservative quarters.

One Jordanian member of parliament who opposed repealing the law on honour crimes opined, "Women adulterers cause a great threat to our society because they are the main reasons that such acts take place. ... If men do not find women with whom to commit adultery, then they will become good on their own."[43]

There are differing opinions about the best ways to address the problem of honour crimes. Some argue that any local efforts must be supported by the international community, while others express concern that intensive media coverage by the international press — Western press, in particular — may generate a backlash that undermines the important work of local activists.[44] Similarly, education programmes in some local communities about the tenets of Islam that proscribe honour crimes have

> "Women adulterers cause a great threat to our society because they are the main reasons that such acts take place. ... If men do not find women with whom to commit adultery, they will become good on their own."

been valuable in mobilising against the practice. Project workers elsewhere, however, have found that invoking the Qur'an has not proven useful in denouncing violence. They favour promoting traditional preventive practices of family dialogue to support mediation and reconciliation.[45]

Most parties agree, however, that eradication strategies must support the implementation of protective laws. Tunisia is an example where legislative reform has had considerable success. Historically, several provisions in Tunisian law reduced criminal penalties for perpetrators of honour killings. Derived from the Napoleonic code and influenced by colonial history, these provisions held wives, but not husbands, criminally liable for adulterous behaviour and stipulated significantly reduced penalties for murderous husbands who caught their wives in an act of adultery. Reforms in both these provisions were accomplished in the last three decades with little debate or dissent from the Muslim leaders or populace.[46] Notably, there have been no documented cases of honour crimes in Tunisia in the last twenty years.[47]

Most activists also agree that efforts must be vastly but incrementally increased to promote shifts in community perceptions about gender roles, rights and responsibilities. Such initiatives may be slow-paced, but the goals are nonetheless radical: "In the end, honour killings will only be eradicated when power over women is not seen as central to a man's self-respect, and domination of women and girls is not seen as reassuring social glue."[48] At that point, there will be no more "honour" in killing wives, sisters and mothers. n

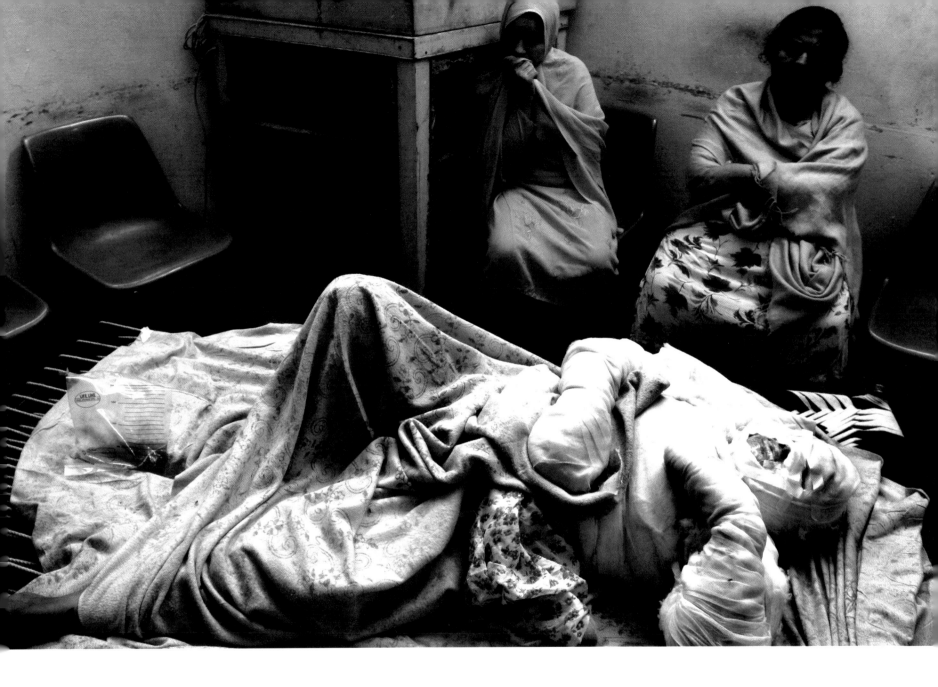

Hospitals in Asia treat a disproportionately high number of female burn victims. Whether the burns are caused by acid attacks, deliberate immolation (often called "kitchen-stove accidents") or self-immolation, they are often linked to issues of honour — and the perpetrators are usually the victims' in-laws or husbands. The nurse who cared for the patient in this photo suspected that the woman's burns were related to the fact that she is unable to have children.

Image: Evelyn Hockstein/IRIN

These images are from the funeral of Zubeda Bibi, age 60, who was murdered by her son-in-law and his friend. Zubeda's daughter, Shenaz, was married at age 14 to Adil Kamal, a considerably older man. After having two children with him, Shenaz discovered that her husband already had a wife and six other children in another part of the country. Upon learning that Adil had another family, Shenaz asked him for a divorce. He refused. Zubeda tried to pressure her son-in-law to at least give more support to her daughter and share some of his property with Shenaz's children. Adil's response to her questioning his authority — thus bringing shame on him — was to return from work one night in March 2005 and slit his mother-in-law's throat.

Images: Evelyn Hockstein/IRIN

"Sadia" lives in one of the few protective shelters available to women in Pakistan. Her story is not unlike that of many other young women who resort to protective confinement under the threat of honour killing. Sadia, who ran away from her parents after they forbade her to marry the boy of her choosing, was arrested along with her boyfriend and put in jail. Sadia's father bribed the police with 20,000 rupees to beat his daughter into submitting a statement against her boyfriend, which in turn would pre-serve the family honour. Sadia continually refused to make a statement and finally was released into her aunt's care. Her boyfriend remained in jail. Eight days after Sadia's release, her parents persuaded her to marry another man — the only way she would be assured that her boyfriend, who remained in jail, would be freed. Three months into her marriage, Sadia ran away to her boyfriend's house. Fearing for her life, she entered the shelter. Sadia intends to remain there until she and her boyfriend can devise a safe escape from her family.

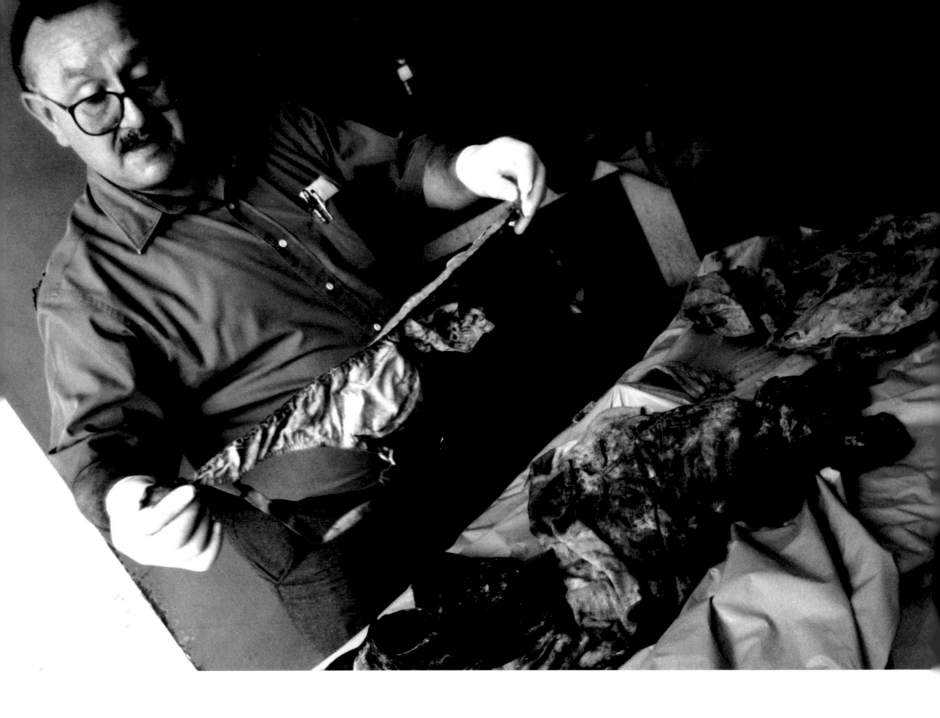

Dr Enrique Silva, who is in charge of autopsies in Ciudad Juarez in northern Mexico, examines the clothing of recent rape and murder victims. Mexican police have been baffled by the number of young women found brutally raped and murdered in the outskirts of the industrial town that borders the United States. In some cases, the victims have been mutilated and horribly disfigured: Objects have been inserted into their vaginas or anuses and/or their left breasts have been cut off.

sexual assault and harassment

A young South African man participating in a recent ethnographic study of perceptions regarding sexual violence offered researchers his definition of rape: "What rape is, it is dragging a person forcefully and force [sic] her to have sex with you without her consent, totally, and she is not your girlfriend." According to another young man from the same study, "If you think about rape, you should notice the place. ... You hardly ever hear that a person was raped in her own room ... it happens there in the *veldt*. ... Even the cherry [girl] doesn't think you raped her." One young female research subject, who told a story of being forced by her boyfriend to have sex and then being beaten by him for responding (in his words) "like a corpse", claimed that her experience was "different from rape in that I didn't want sex but I loved him and in the case of rape I don't love the person at all."[1]

Debunking the rape myth

Common myths and assumptions related to sexual violence are shared the world over. They often reflect and reinforce social attitudes and customs that aggrandise male aggression while at the same time purporting female passivity. In many settings, sexual activity is popularly represented as a "battle of the sexes", in which sexually driven men are expected to compel sexually hesitant women.[2] The implicit message is that it is socially acceptable for sexual transactions between men and women to involve some degree of force.[3] The explicit outcome is that the majority of victims of sexual violence around the world are female, and the majority of perpetrators are male.

Ideas about what constitutes "unacceptable" sexual behaviour between men and women more often serve to protect the *status quo* of male dominance, such that "the volition, perceptions, and feelings of the woman or girl" are "amazingly absent from most cultural definitions of violence."[4] Determinations of the moral, legal or social permissibility of a given sex act are more likely to focus on the context in which it occurs — "who did it to whom and under what circumstance" — rather than on "the act itself or its impact on the woman."[5] This failure to consider the rights and wellbeing of women and girls is vividly demonstrated in nearly universal attitudes towards rape.

According to conventional assumptions prevalent across cultures, rape primarily happens in dark alleys or other remote locations, is committed by strangers and involves physical brutality. The act of rape is a social aberration and, therefore, a rare event. Following this logic is the notion that the majority of rapists are sociopaths — mentally ill men who have uncontrollable sexual urges. If they are not part of the "lunatic fringe", then they are men who have been unnaturally provoked by sexually promiscuous women.[6] In the latter model, responsibility to prevent rape falls to the potential victim, a sentiment illustrated in the recommendations of a Malaysian parliamentarian who argued, "Women should wear *purdah* [head-to-toe covering] to ensure that innocent men do not get unnecessarily excited by women's bodies and are not unconsciously forced into becoming rapists. If women do not want to fall prey to such men, they should take the necessary precautions instead of forever blaming the men."[7]

Such delimiting characterisations of sexual violence support impunity for the average rapist, not only because they blame the victim, but also because they disguise the global reality: that sexual assault, including

> "Women should wear *purdah* [head-to-toe covering] to ensure that innocent men do not get unnecessarily excited by women's bodies and are not unconsciously forced into becoming rapists."

rape, is more often perpetrated by someone known to the victim and occurs in her own home or in another familiar environment. Rape does not necessarily involve physical force, and the perpetrator need not be pathological.[8] Evidence from countries around the world confirms that while the classic "stranger" rape does exist, it represents only the "tip of the iceberg" of sexual assault.[9] Understanding the true extent of sexual violence is fraught with a number of challenges, not least of which is defining exactly what it entails.

Coercion, consent and choice

In the last 20 to 30 years, women's right activists have emphasised the basic human rights of women and girls — and the accountability of men and boys in respecting those rights — when differentiating between acceptable sexual contact and sexual violence. They suggest that force is not inevitable in sexual relations, but rather a reflection of male ideologies of control over women. Their work has informed contemporary definitions of sexual violence, which increasingly challenge conventional stereotypes that interpret "real" sexual violence only in the context of stranger rape.

In a 2002 global report on violence and health the World Health Organization (WHO) defined sexual violence as "any sexual act, attempt to obtain a sexual act, unwanted sexual comments or advances, or acts to traffic, or otherwise directed, against a person's sexuality using coercion by any person regardless of their relationship to the victim, in any

setting, including but not limited to home and work."* Sexual assault is a form of sexual violence involving bodily contact. Rape is a further delineated form of sexual assault that entails "physically forced or otherwise coerced penetration — even if slight — of the vulva or anus, using a penis, other body parts or an object."[10]

A key determinant of sexual violence within this definition is the issue of coercion — which may involve physical force but also can involve "psychological intimidation, blackmail or threats — for instance the threat of physical harm, of being dismissed from a job or of not obtaining a job that is sought. It may also occur when the person aggressed is unable to give consent — for instance, while drunk, drugged, asleep, or mentally incapable of understanding the situation."[11]

By emphasising the concept of coercion rather than physical force, the WHO definition of sexual violence calls attention to the potentially wide range of behaviours that violate the rights of the victim. A definition based solely or even primarily on coercion presents challenges, however, because what amounts to coercion may be contested by those involved: A victim may experience behaviours as highly coercive when the perpetrator does not. To overcome ambiguities inherent in interpretations of coercion, many women's rights activists have stressed the primacy of consent.[12]

The United Nations Special Rapporteur on Violence Against Women has described consent as the "legal dividing line between rape and sexual intercourse."[13] Another expert explained that a definition of sexual violence based on consent "recognizes and ratifies a simple principle ... [which is] our personal sovereignty. We have the right not to be acted upon unless we wish to be acted upon and communicate that wish to the actor. Our silence is not our permission."[14]

Other feminist theorists prefer the concept of choice to that of consent

*According to the World Health Organization definitions broad ambit, sexual violence can be perpetrated by a wide range of actors and can include an equally wide range of acts and practices, such as sexual harassment, forced prostitution and trafficking, child sexual abuse, forced marriage, female genital mutilation, forced sex in intimate partnerships and rape by strangers. Although many of these forms of sexual violence have overlapping features, several have been covered more explicitly in other chapters of this book. The primary focus in this chapter is rape and sexual coercion committed outside the context of war and, to a lesser extent, sexual harassment in the workplace.

"Carolina" grew up on a farm in the northern province of Sucre, Colombia. When armed militias terrorised her village in 2001, Carolina and her family were forced to flee. They relocated to Nelson Mandela, a ramshackle *barrio* for internally displaced persons on the outskirts of the port city of Cartagena. Carolina, then 14, was often left alone to watch her younger siblings while her mother worked. She was seduced by a neighbour in his sixties, who wooed her with pocket money and treats. He raped her three times over a period of several months. Carolina told her parents about the rapes only after she realised that she was pregnant, having previously feared the neighbour's threat to kill her family if she told them anything. With her family's support, she reported the rapes to the authorities — who declined to investigate. With the help of a lawyer, Carolina is currently seeking justice through the Inter-American Commission on Human Rights in Washington, D.C.

Image: Jennifer Szymaszek

because "it does not implicitly assume that men initiate all sexual overtures."[15] The language of choice, even more so than consent, underscores and promotes female autonomy in sexual relations.

Choice is the exception, rather than the rule, however, for many women and girls around the world. A teenage girl in South Africa observed, "Forced sex is the norm. It is the way people interact sexually."[16] In

"A woman can refuse, but then this woman will run the risk that she will be forced into sex. I would like to change it, but it cannot be done because a woman needs to follow the man."

qualitative research in Zimbabwe, young women acknowledged their powerlessness in sexual relationships: "A woman can refuse, but then this woman will run the risk that she will be forced into sex. I would like to change it, but it cannot be done because a woman needs to follow the man."[17]

Even when choice is clearly absent, many women and girls who suffer sexual assault still may not view their victimisation as rape because their experience is not represented in hegemonic definitions of sexual violence. Based on encounters reported by a national sample of college women in the United States, researchers concluded that from one-fifth to one-quarter of all college women are at risk of an attempted or completed rape during their college years. However, for those respondents whose experiences were categorised as completed rape according to the standard definition used by the researchers, only 46.5 percent believed the incident to be rape. Forty-nine percent said it wasn't rape, and 4.7 percent said they didn't know.[18]

Any attempts to study sexual violence must understand this important distinction. As one women's rights advocate noted, "Just because a woman doesn't call it rape, doesn't mean she doesn't feel violated."[19]

Generating reliable data on sexual violence

According to a sexual violence expert from the United States, "rape appears in many guises" and, as such, requires careful investigative methods that capture the range of women's and girl's experiences.[20] When researchers use narrow definitions of sexual violence, the reported rates of sexual crimes are likely to be relatively low. Crime-victim surveys reflect this: While they are useful because of their broad scope and comparable methodology, questions on sexual violence may

not discriminate between different types of sexual assaults and/or perpetrators. In data presented by the WHO on a select number of crime-victim surveys, rates of reported sexual victimisation (recorded in the five years prior to each survey) range from less than 2 percent in Bolivia, Botswana, China and the Philippines to 5 percent or more in Albania, Argentina, Brazil and Colombia.[21]

Although still scarce and somewhat difficult to compare because of differences in data-collection techniques and definitions used, more targeted sexual violence surveys typically generate higher rates of reporting among participants. A variety of such surveys from the United States, for example, suggest that between 14 percent and 20 percent of the general population of women in that country will be raped at least once in their lifetime.[22] In the Czech Republic, 11.6 percent of women responding to a national survey reported that they had experienced forced sexual contact, most commonly in the form of vaginal intercourse.[23] Forty percent of a random sample of 420 women in Toronto, Canada, reported at least one episode of forced sexual intercourse since the age of 16.[24] Specific subgroups are at even greater risk. Research from the United States on women with disabilities, for example, indicates they are at one-and-a-half times greater risk of sexual victimisation than women without disabilities.[25]

The use of explicit questions in these surveys helps to overcome underreporting related to biases or preconceptions associated with the semantics of rape. Even employing the language of forced or coerced sex, rather than rape, can produce more accurate estimates of women's and girl's exposure to sexual violence. In a South African study, 11 percent of the adolescents surveyed said they had been raped, but a further 72 percent reported being subject to forced sex.[26] A survey of unmarried adolescents seeking abortions in 17 hospitals in China found that 48 percent had experienced sexual coercion at least once.[27]

An increasing number of studies have focused on the issue of coerced or forced sexual initiation among adolescent girls. Average estimates of coerced first sex among adolescents around the world range from 10 percent to 30 percent, but in some settings, such as Cameroon and Peru, the number is closer to 40 percent.[28] In a survey of high school students in Korea, 39 percent of sexually active females reported that their first experience of sex was the result of force or pressure from their partner.[29] Studies of nine countries in the Caribbean estimated that incidents of forced first intercourse were as high as 48 percent.[30]

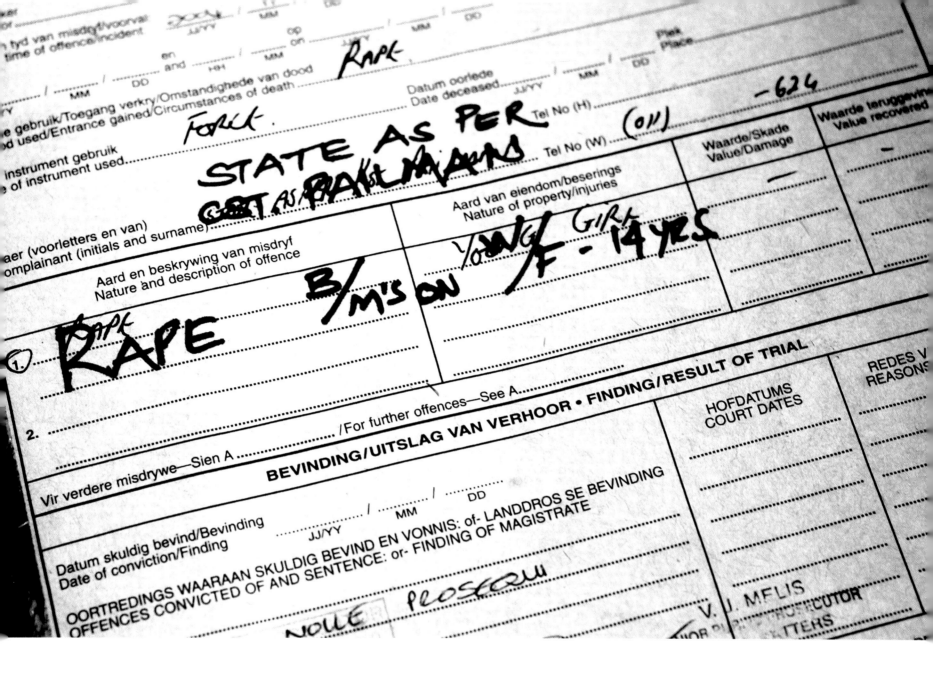

An example of a police docket from Durban, South Africa. In this case a 14-year-old girl was raped by multiple perpetrators but the findings of the magistrate were *"nolle prosequi"*, a legal term indicating that the prosecutor will proceed no further.

Image: Mariella Furrer

Crosses mark the graves of women who were killed in Ciudad Juarez, Mexico. Local women's rights groups believe that at least 187 women have met violent deaths in the border town since 1993. Many of the dead were murdered by pimps, drug dealers, husbands and boyfriends. At least one-third of the deaths are unexplained, however, and police have no suspects. Authorities believe that about 30 of the cases have the common elements of torture and rape and may be the work of one or several serial killers. Most of these victims were slender, dark-haired girls between 14 and 18 years of age who worked in one of the numerous United States-owned *maquiladora* factories. Many were killed on their way to or from work.

Identifying the perpetrators

Many studies have confirmed that most perpetrators of sexual violence are known to the victim. In fact, according to the WHO, "One of the most common forms of sexual violence around the world is that which is perpetrated by an intimate partner."[31] In a recent study of a representative sample of married and unmarried young men and women in Kenya, more than one in five sexually experienced young women had been subjected to nonconsensual sex. Those who had been married were at greater risk of coercion than respondents who had never been married, and husbands were often identified as perpetrators.[32] Other studies from around the world that have specifically investigated intimate-partner violence suggest that on average one in five women has been forced to have sex by her partner — in some settings those numbers are much higher.[33] In general, sexual assaults by intimate partners are reported two to eight times more often than assaults by strangers.[34]

One sexual violence expert concluded, "The most important lesson learned about interpersonal violence in the past 20 years is how frequently it is perpetrated by apparently normal individuals."[35] Rather than verifying assumptions that rape is committed by a small number of disturbed men, research suggests that many men around the world share the attitudes and beliefs necessary to commit an act of sexual violence.[36] In other words, the "high prevalence of rape largely reflects a high level of social tolerance of the crime."[37]

Social acceptability of sexual violence

The United States has been called one of the "most rape-prone of all modern societies."[38] Regardless of whether this is true in absolute terms or more a reflection of the relative preponderance of research conducted among men there, studies from across the United States have shed light on the intersection of male entitlement, sexual aggression and the perpetration of sexual violence. In one study, 85 percent of a sample of men from the midwestern United States who were defined by researchers as highly sexually aggressive had victimised women with whom they had had relationships.[39]

In other studies, one-third to one-half of college males indicated that they would rape if they knew they would not be punished.[40] Similar percentages of high school males interviewed in yet another study from the United States agreed that it was acceptable for a man to force sex on a woman if she " 'led him on', changed her mind, or sexually aroused him."[41] One young man who raped his date after she had voluntarily touched his penis but then declined intercourse reported, "I felt as if I had gotten something that I was entitled to. And I felt I was repaying her for sexually arousing me." For him, committing rape was "very powerful and titillating. ... It made me feel as if I was in control."[42]

These attitudes are not restricted to the United States. A recent study conducted by Australia's National Crime Prevention Authority highlighted the connection between young men's presumptions of sexual entitlement and the high prevalence of forced sex reported by young Australian women.[43] The same link has been illustrated in research from other parts of the world, where men insist on their right to sexual access of women, regardless of the feelings and desires of the women themselves. In Kenya, for example, adolescent boys admitted to drugging and even gagging girls to obtain sex, claiming, "We seduce them at first, but if they remain adamant we force them."[44] The reflections of one incarcerated rapist from the United States illustrate male entitlement in the extreme: "Rape is a man's right. If a woman doesn't want to give it, the man should take it. Women have no right to say no. Women are made to have sex. It's all they're good for. Some women would rather take a beating, but they always give in."[45]

Perceptions like this have led feminist theorists to conclude that in the vast majority of cases of sexual violence, sex is the mechanism through which men express their control over and objectification of women. In her 1975 book *Against Our Will*, Susan Brownmiller argued that throughout history rape has been employed to generate and reinforce female subordination to males. According to the theories of Brownmiller and many others, sexual violence is less the expression of an individual man's unrestrained sex drive than it is a reiteration of patriarchal social structures and norms. Rape is primarily motivated by power, not sex.[46]

Sexual violence as both a reflection of and an exercise in control of women is most unambiguous when it is used as an overt method of punishment. Such practices are evident in the history of cultures around the world. Among the Cheyenne Indians of the United States, for example, a wife suspected of adultery was "put on the prairie" as

> "One of the most common forms of sexual violence around the world is that which is perpetrated by an intimate partner."

punishment by her husband, and men were invited "to feast" on her through gang rape.[47] In a modern example of rape as retribution, teenage girls in Kenya reported that appearing "haughty" and "in need of a lesson" by failing to respond to the attentions of boys might result in punishment through rape.[48]

In some instances, the target for punishment is not only — or even primarily — the woman herself. In cultures where women are considered the property of men, rape may be used to avenge male family members. Mukhtaran Bibi, for example, was recently sentenced to gang rape by a Pakistani tribal council as punishment for a crime allegedly committed by her brother. After being raped by four men, she was forced to walk home nearly naked while being jeered at by approximately 300 onlookers. Bibi took the extraordinary step in her conservative community of fighting back against her attackers, six of whom were convicted. But after becoming a "ferocious spokesperson" against violence against women in Pakistan, Bibi was punished again. The Pakistani government put her under house arrest and held her passport to prevent her from travelling to the United States at the invitation of Pakistani-Americans. As yet, her documents have not been returned to her and she remains unable to travel outside her country unless she complies with her government's requirement that she be accompanied by an escort.[49]

Silencing the victim

Unlike Bibi, the majority of rape victims never speak out about their experiences. In the United States, rape is more likely than any other form of victimisation to be kept secret.[50] Data from Canada suggest that rape is four times less likely to be reported than domestic violence.[51] A 1999 demographic and health survey from South Africa found that only 15 percent of women who had experienced an incident of forced sex had reported it to the police.[52] Criminologists in Taiwan estimate that 10 percent of rapes committed there are reported, a rate that some emergency room doctors who treat rape victims believe to be optimistic.[53] Seven percent of the young women and girls surveyed in 2001 in Nigeria acknowledged being raped, but only 1 percent had reported the incident to the police. The case of a 15-year-old from Lagos illustrates some of the reasons why:

"Adeola" blamed herself when she was raped by the lodger, a friend of her father, and became pregnant. After he found out about the rape, her

father accused Adeola of being a prostitute. Instead of protecting her from further violence, her parents ostracised her. She fled the house, eventually finding her way to the only shelter for women in Lagos, which is run by a women's human rights organization. She hoped to continue her studies after the delivery of her baby. She did not want to press charges against the lodger.[54]

Shame, blame, social ostracism — these are powerful inhibitors to seeking assistance, let alone justice. A 17-year-old girl from Zambia who was raped by the priest of her local church told researchers, "I'm scared to tell the police. They won't believe me because he's a priest. ... I feel

After being raped by four men, she was made to walk home nearly naked while being jeered at by approximately 300 onlookers. Bibi took the extraordinary step in her conservative community of fighting back against her attackers.

ashamed. ... Others think you want it to happen."[55] A survivor courageous enough to report her rape runs the risk of being revictimised by the very same beliefs that facilitated the rape. One sexual assault victim in India who filed a complaint was asked by a police officer if she knew "the meaning of the word rape." Another was told, "A woman like you will never get raped. Don't try to tell us that you did not enjoy it."[56]

In conservative Islamic cultures, a woman who cannot produce four Muslim witnesses to prove that she was raped may be imprisoned or publicly stoned to death for having committed adultery.[57] Afia Bibi, a blind Pakistani girl who was sentenced to three years imprisonment after being unable to produce the requisite number of witnesses to support her claims of rape, was lucky enough to have her case overturned by the federal court due to the national mobilisation of women's organizations.[58] Many other rape victims in Pakistan and elsewhere do not receive such support. If they are not killed by order of Islamic law, they may be murdered by a relative for tainting the family honour.

Creating a blanket of impunity

However draconian, such traditions reflect attitudes prevalent in many cultures that essentially hold women accountable for sexual violations on the grounds that they are responsible for protecting their own chastity — and, by relation, their family's reputation. Particularly in situations where a woman knows her rapist, the assumption is that she asked for and even wanted sex, and it is often her responsibility to prove otherwise. Evidentiary rules in a number of countries place the victim at

This woman, who is the representative of a labour union in Nicaragua, was sexually harassed by an accountant in the factory where she works. "One day as I left work, the man in charge of accounting told me that he wanted to talk to me. He asked for my address and kept on visiting me uninvited. I had told him that I wasn't interested in a relationship. Still, the next time I went to his office, he touched me on my arm and face. He tried to grab me in the dining hall and the corridors. I talked to the CEO several times, but he didn't do anything. The harassment only stopped after I threatened to go to the labour ministry and report it to the judiciary."

Images: Evelyn Hockstein/IRIN

A factory worker in one of Nicaragua's export-production zones told this photographer, "It is very delicate. We know there are cases [of bosses trying to sleep with workers], but we don't know the women's names. They are afraid that they will lose their jobs or that people won't believe them. We don't know for sure, but rumours go around." Workplace sexual harassment is widespread and particularly pervasive in the export-production zones, where Nicaragua's national laws do not apply. Women who do report such incidents to senior management risk losing their jobs — in a place where there are few options for employment.

a disadvantage. They not only require independent corroboration of a rape allegation, they also allow for testimony about the victim's sexual history — i.e., whether or not she was a virgin before the attack.[59] In some settings, a rape survivor may be required to undergo a virginity test, established by whether a doctor can easily insert two or more fingers in her vagina.[60] Such requirements imply a woman who is not a virgin is a less credible victim, and less deserving of protection.

Even when evidence proves a victim's innocence, rape can nevertheless decrease her value in the eyes of society. The stigma of rape attaches itself to the victim rather than to the rapist in a variety of ways. In Southeast Asian culture, a husband may abandon his wife if she has been raped because he perceives that she has "been used or left over."[61] Even in modern Taiwan, a survivor of acquaintance rape may be encouraged to marry her rapist to protect her reputation as a virtuous woman.[62] The same is true in other parts of the world: Among some tribes in sub-Saharan Africa, a girl's bride price will decrease if she has been raped. If the rapist refuses to marry the girl, he may be subject to fines to make up the difference of the reduced bride price.

Given few alternatives, the majority of sexual violence victims are forced into silence. A woman's subordinate status ensures many perpetrators a blanket of impunity. Around the world, as more and more women enter the public sphere through low-paying jobs that are supervised by men, the playing field for this vicious cycle of violence and impunity gets even larger.

Sexual harassment in the workplace

Like other forms of sexual violence, sexual harassment of women and girls is a manifestation of unequal power relations between the sexes. Because harassment refers primarily to nonphysical forms of abuse — such as threats and intimidation, verbal slander, unwanted sexual advances, intentional stalking and sexual humiliation — it is often considered a lesser form of sexual violence and has therefore received significantly less attention from researchers.[63]

The pervasiveness of sexual harassment, however, constitutes an ever-present threat. It can occur anywhere — on the street, at school and at home — "instilling fear and violating a woman's right to bodily integrity, education, and freedom of movement."[64] Moreover, the essential dynamics that drive sexual harassment are the same as those that lead to rape. According to one researcher, "Men who verbally harass women on the street say they do so to alleviate boredom, to gain a sense of youthful camaraderie and because it's fun — the same reasons men who rape give for their behaviour."[65]

One of the "more pernicious" forms of sexual harassment, in the opinion of the United Nations Special Rapporteur on Violence Against Women, is that which occurs in the workplace. Around the world, many women labour in climates of fear and degradation. One 22-year-old woman from Poland who worked as an assistant said that her boss "smacked her bottom ... and told her that he wanted to have sex with her." On one

The offence of sexual harassment in the workplace is further compounded by the fact that it "strikes at the heart of a woman's self-sufficiency."

occasion, he "came up behind her, and ... he fondled her breasts and genitalia and put his fingers into her pants. She was in shock and started to cry." Another Polish woman, who was working as a nurse, remembered when her director "grabbed my breasts from behind and started to kiss my neck. I was shocked but managed to get away. Then, in very rude words, he said, 'What are you afraid of? Nothing will happen to your pussy.'"[66]

The offence of sexual harassment in the workplace is further compounded by the fact that it "strikes at the heart of women's economic self-sufficiency."[67] Those who complain about sexual harassment risk losing their jobs. An 18-year-old Thai woman who had been molested frequently by her supervisor, for example, was encouraged by other colleagues who had experienced the same thing to take the case to the police. When an investigation was mounted, however, these same colleagues were reluctant to act as witnesses for fear of losing their jobs. The young woman was forced to resign.[68]

Raising global awareness

Over the last 20 years, based on a movement that has its origins in the United States, a growing number of governments have recognised sexual harassment in the workplace as a form of sex discrimination and a violation of basic human rights.[69] Even so, there is no widely accepted international definition of workplace sexual harassment, nor is there any international convention that specifically prohibits it. Instead, various national laws have defined workplace sexual harassment generally to include sexual advances or propositions to which an employee may be explicitly or implicitly expected to submit as a condition of employment (*quid pro quo* harassment), or offensive behaviour, questions or comments that create an intimidating or hostile working environment.

While data on the scope of the problem is limited, the rate of sexual harassment experienced by working women in the United States and Western Europe is estimated at 50 percent.[70] Research from countries as culturally dissimilar as Nepal, Bulgaria and the Czech Republic indicates similar numbers.[71] In Asia, where women are moving into the workforce in unprecedented numbers but often occupy the lowest paying

"Laws against sexual harassment might be okay, but sex is natural. It involves natural forces that move men to do things that are against morality. This is millions of years of human behaviour. You can't change this."

positions, the rates of sexual harassment are on the rise. Seventy percent of a survey of public officers in Korea acknowledged experiencing sexual harassment.[72] Eighty-four percent of Chinese women participating in research conducted by the Chinese Academy of Social Sciences confirmed their exposure, and in one sample of women from Malaysia, 88 percent reported sexual harassment.[73]

In many countries, sexual harassment is a relatively new legal and social concept. The attitudes that promulgate sexual violence in the larger community are reiterated within the workplace. One manager from Bulgaria, for example, stated, "Laws against sexual harassment might be okay, but sex is natural. It involves natural forces that move men to do things that are against morality. This is millions of years of human behaviour. You can't change this."[74] A Russian women's rights lawyer dismissed the problem of workplace sexual harassment by insisting women "like compliments".[75]

At the same time that the perpetrator's responsibility for his actions is minimised, the victim is blamed. A social worker in Poland commented that one woman exposed to sexual harassment "did not set up the right distance between herself and her boss in the beginning. ... She did not recognise the signs of the situation. Often women who are victims do not recognise the signs until it is too late."[76] Attitudes that blame the victim and the threat of losing a job force women to silently endure workplace abuse until it becomes intolerable, at which point they may choose to quit rather than fight an unresponsive system. According to the Special Rapporteur, women are nine times more likely than men to leave their job as a result of sexual harassment.[77]

The Ciudad Juarez example

The volatile combination of sexual harassment in the workplace and sexual violence in the community is perhaps most glaringly evident in Ciudad Juarez, Mexico. Since 1993, hundreds of women have been brutally killed and hundreds more have disappeared in the small border city. Most of the victims are young and poor migrants who have left their families in other parts of the country to work in one of Ciudad Juarez's many *maquiladoras* (assembly factories), where the salaries are meagre and labour rights violations are rampant. Sexual violence is commonplace, both inside the factories and in the community, and the government has taken little action to stem the tide of violence. Instead, culpability falls to the victim. In 1999, one government official said, "Women who have a night life, go out late and come in contact with drinkers are at risk. It's hard to go out on the street when it's raining and not get wet."[78] In Ciudad Juarez, as in other parts of the world, "to strive to live and work outside the watchful gaze of the family and community is to risk becoming a target for male violence."[79]

Breaking the silence

Rape and other forms of sexual violence cause a variety of short- and long-term physical and psychological afflictions, including chronic pelvic and other pain syndromes, unwanted pregnancies, negative pregnancy outcomes, gastrointestinal problems, headaches, chronic fatigue, sleep disturbances, eating disorders, substance abuse, suicidal tendencies and self-harm, depression, anxiety and difficulties in sexual and interpersonal relationships.[80] The risk of HIV/AIDS — increased in instances of sexual violence because of physical trauma such as cuts and abrasions — adds another element of fear and anxiety.[81]

The majority of survivors of sexual violence never receive medical treatment or psychosocial support. Those who are willing or able to report the crime are much more likely to have access to healthcare. In research from the United States, more than half the women who reported being raped received medical treatment, compared to less than one-fifth of those who did not come forward.[82] Clearly, one of the most crucial strategies for mitigating the effects of sexual violence is to create environments that are conducive to reporting.

Such environments would include, at minimum, a rapid and compassionate response by health professionals trained to not "look for signs of rape", but rather to collect forensic evidence and provide testimony during court cases.[83] Health workers also need to be able to provide emergency contraception, as well as antiretrovirals that can reduce the risk of HIV transmission. Supportive counselling and advocacy services also should be available to survivors to address their psychological needs and, if necessary, to assist them through the judicial process. Survivors also must be able to count on respectful and responsive police who are specially qualified to investigate sexual assaults.

The current low levels of prosecution for sexual crimes reinforce attitudes that explicitly or implicitly condone violence against women.

Improving reporting and prosecution, while important, cannot be the end goals if the objective is long-term prevention of sexual violence. The final frontier of prevention must focus on changing the beliefs and

The current low levels of prosecution for sexual crimes reinforce attitudes that explicitly or implicitly condone violence against women.

Legislation that only defines rape in terms of penile penetration of the vagina — still the case in many countries of the world — should be expanded to include anal or oral penetration or penetration with an object, and judiciaries need to be trained in applying these expanded definitions.[84] Laws also need to account for marital rape, as well as for rapes by other known assailants, so that a woman is not discouraged from reporting an experience that falls outside the stereotype of stranger rape. According to the WHO, several countries in Asia with recent legislation that significantly broadens the definition of rape and mandates state assistance have seen a substantial increase in reporting.[85]

Perhaps the most important way to encourage victims to come forward is to ensure that perpetrators are prosecuted. Globally, rape is among the least convicted of all crimes. On average, only 10 percent of all rapists will ever serve a jail sentence, and in many settings that number is likely to be even lower.[86] The response of the legal-justice system to rape "is a yardstick against which the seriousness of the crime is measured."[87]

behaviours that promote sexual abuse. The line between acceptable and unacceptable sexual conduct must be shifted, and with it, social assumptions and values regarding men's and women's behaviour.

Where male aggression and control is emphasised, sexual violence is likely to be more common. Where women are disempowered — economically, socially and politically — they are unlikely to step beyond the veil of silence that conceals the crimes against them and, in turn, protects their perpetrators. In an increasing number of countries, men are taking a stand against violence against women by developing advocacy campaigns and community-based education about gender and nonviolence. Just as crucial, however, are initiatives that improve the lives of women and girls, including increased access to education and economic empowerment. The ultimate aim is mutual respect, where power is shared equitably between the sexes, rather than monopolised by men and expressed in acts of violence against women's bodies. n

"My name is 'Azara' and I am 25 years old. I was born into slavery — my whole family were slaves. My parents and I served the same master. I have two children, both from when my master raped me. My daughter, Khdiza, is eight years old and my son, Mahamout, is three years old. I had three children, but one died. I feel very bitter about having my master's children, but all I can do is accept it. It is very hard to accept.

"As a slave I had to labour so hard, pounding millet and fetching water all the time. I worked day and night. I had to do whatever my master told me to do. It was out of the question to say no. If I ever said no, I was beaten so hard. I tried once to resist but he beat me with his hands.

"Both of my sisters are still slaves to him. We were three women serving one man. I can't count the number of times he raped me. As far back as I can remember he sexually abused me — I was probably the age of my daughter. He used to take me to his tent, often tie my legs to the bed and rape me. His wife left him when she found out he was sleeping with a slave. If I ever tried to resist, he used to beat me. I had to give in. He never gave me any reason. He didn't consider me to be worth anything.

"He considered me as his own property. I was considered as his animal. I escaped one and a half years ago when I couldn't bear anymore."

Azara made her way to a major city in Niger where she was directed to Timidria, a human rights agency that helps slaves. When Azara arrived she was wearing no shoes and a rag round her upper body. She looked disturbed and was very thin; filthy and with pimples over her body. It took a long time for her to tell her story.

Representatives from Timidria went to the house of Azara's master with the local police to rescue her daughter. With a court case pending against him, he was afraid to do anything against Azara. The master is being charged with owning a slave and rape. The agency currently is pursuing 30 similar cases, of which they have won only a single case to date. They know their fight is difficult. "Poverty is a big factor, when slaves escape they are faced with the difficulty of finding food and survival necessities. Many have to return to their masters."

Images: Georgina Cranston/IRIN

Halima's story

"I am a Tuareg but I am a slave. My master forced me to get married, and I now have three children. We are all slaves — he sees my children as his slaves as well.

"My master treated me so badly and often raped me. He would take me to his farm and sexually abuse me there in secrecy. He would not take me into his house, as I am a slave. Instead, he would put a headscarf on me to make me look like a proper Tuareg, because it's not good for him to be seen sleeping with a slave like me. It made him think I was not a slave during the time he raped me. He used to tell me that his traditional doctor said that if he slept with a slave he would be cured from illness. I had no choice but to accept. The way my master treated me made me feel valueless."

"Halima" didn't want to admit that one of her children was from the master, but someone sitting nearby said to her, "Why don't you tell the truth, that your son is a child of the master?" It was too humiliating for Halima to say it herself.

At the time of this interview, Halima's master, afraid of the Niger law that forbids slavery, was treating her better and allowing her more freedom. A local human rights organization recently reported that with their help, Halima had lodged a complaint against her master. Shortly thereafter she was liberated by her master, who suggested they make a peaceful out-of-court agreement. Her children, however, are still his slaves.

Images: Georgina Cranston/IRIN

"Joyce," who does not know her exact age but is between 65 years and 70 years old, was raped repeatedly last year when four men broke into her house in Kinyezire, Democratic Republic of Congo (DRC), and murdered her husband and one of her children. Joyce described her powerlessness against the attackers: "Three of them raped me, one after the other. They said nothing. They just raped me — there was nothing I could do. I couldn't resist."

The men who attacked Joyce were *Interhamwe* soldiers. During wartime, when traditional social-support networks break down, women of all ages are especially vulnerable to sexual assault. Anecdotal evidence from clinics and community groups that deal with sexual violence in war zones indicates that many older women have been raped in the DRC, Liberia, Sierra Leone and Rwanda. Unlike the majority of older victims who feel particular shame about disclosing their experience of abuse, Joyce came forward with an account of her ordeal. She is now being treated for malnourishment, and when she is stronger, she will undergo an operation to repair the fistula she suffered as a result of the violent rape.

Image: Georgina Cranston/IRIN

abuse of older women

"The public at large is generally unaware of the incidences of sexual assaults against the elderly. It is an unsavory thing to think of, yet it occurs and possibly with more frequency than we previously imagined. ... What we don't know, we turn our backs on."[1]

"Taboo and inconceivable"

There has been slow but increasing awareness of elderly abuse over the past 20 years. As challenging as it is for the population at large to acknowledge, it is even harder for older people to admit that they have been victimised. As a result, statistical evidence on the extent of elderly abuse is scarce.

A 2002 World Health Organization (WHO) study on the abuse of older adults in Germany, France, Sweden, Thailand, Kenya and Columbia reinforced "how difficult elder abuse is for some older adults to discuss."[2] Even when research participants do acknowledge sexual abuse, they tend to deny its extent or impact. Older people are often reluctant to reveal incidents of sexual violence because discussion of any sexual activity is often deemed inappropriate, "rendering the disclosure of abusive situations even more taboo and inconceivable."[3]

The global proportion of people aged 60 years and older is projected to double between 2000 and 2050 from 10 percent to 21 percent.[4] Because women make up the majority of older adults in almost all countries around the world — and because the proportion of women to men increases with age — it is important to understand the forms of violence against older women and the cultural traditions that place them in peril.[5]

Older women are more vulnerable to abuse than older men and are burdened with a lifetime of experiences and beliefs that may increase their susceptibility. What holds true in youth remains so in age: In most instances, "Those who are victims are female; those who abuse are male."[6] Violence and abuse against older women can be sexual, physical or psychological and also can include material or financial abuse and neglect. It can occur in the home, in institutions or as a result of harmful cultural practices that specifically target older women.

Abuse in the home

Researchers have identified domestic violence as the most common form of abuse against elderly females, and many women who suffer at the hands of their partners when they are young continue to be abused in their old age.[7] In a South Korean study, 21.5 percent of elderly married couples admitted to experiencing intimate-partner violence. The research showed that many older men with a history of domestic violence abused their wives throughout their relationships. In some cases, the abuse did not begin until later in the marriage, when a husband's frustrations with domestic changes that accompany older age, such as retirement, caused him to act out physically against his wife.[8] In a 2003 study in the United States, 38 older women between 55 years and 90 years of age discussed their experiences with domestic violence.[9] Many of the women admitted that they had stayed in violent relationships because societal expectations at the time of their marriage required them to "submit to the physical and sexual wishes of their husbands."[10]

Older women without intimate partners may be particularly vulnerable to abuse by other family members. Sons, for example, have been implicated as perpetrators of sexual violence against their mothers. In research in the Cape Flats township in South Africa, "Older people identified sexual abuse as the most common form of violence, including adult sons forcing their mothers to have sex with them."[11] One older woman explained the indignity of such abuse:

"When you are a mother … left behind with children who are boys, there is one amongst your children … he wants to sleep with you and wants that you must not talk about it. … You are afraid because you do not have the strength. He does that thing as he pleases."[12]

In a British study, more than half of the older women who had been sexually assaulted were abused by their adult sons, and most of the abuse was vaginal rape.[13] One theory suggests that adult sons who sexually assault their elderly mothers are assuming the roles of their abusive fathers. Another reason for this kind of abuse is the misconception in some communities that sex with older people can cure HIV/AIDS, a counterpart to the myth of the "virgin cure".[14]

Although studies have shown that sexual abuse at home usually is perpetrated by a relative, it also can be inflicted by unrelated domestic caregivers or by random assailants. While many people think that rape is a "sexually motivated crime" that affects only younger women, it is also, in fact, perpetrated against older women, whose perceived or actual vulnerability makes them likely victims.[15] In one case in the United States, a 19-year-old male broke into the apartment of a 76-year-old woman, "ripped off her clothing, raped her vaginally, then anally, and finally assaulted her vaginally with an umbrella lying nearby. He used a

> Researchers have identified domestic violence as the most common form of abuse against elderly females, and many women who suffer at the hands of their partners when they are young continue to be abused in their old age.

piece of glass from the broken window to cut her throat."[16] In another case, a 20-year-old offender assaulted and murdered a 77-year-old woman. He "repeatedly stabbed her in the face, chest, and vagina with a butcher knife."[17]

In Eastern Europe and Russia, older women are becoming more frequent targets for criminal attacks.[18] In the Caribbean, where many older women have been sexually abused, one woman expressed her concern about being raped by youth gangs: "I am afraid to go out alone, even on the beach or for a little walk."[19] Latin America has been identified as a region with particular social conditions that exacerbate violence against the elderly, including civil war, crime and drug-related violence.[20] In Zimbabwe, 30 percent of the respondents to a study on violence against the elderly said that the threat of being attacked was severe enough to prevent them from participating in their own communities.[21]

Abuse in institutional settings

While institutions such as adult-care facilities and hospitals can provide elderly people with support and security, residents are still at risk of sexual abuse by staff, other residents and visitors. One study of sexual crimes against the elderly in the state of Virginia in the United States revealed that 71 percent of assaults against older people took place in nursing homes.[22] Many incidents are difficult to investigate, however, because the age and health of the victim and/or perpetrator may compromise his or her ability to recollect important details of the assault.[23]

There are no national or crossnational studies that focus specifically on sexual abuse in institutions, but the cases that are reported illustrate the types of crimes that are being perpetrated. For example, an 84-year-old male resident of a nursing home in the United States committed

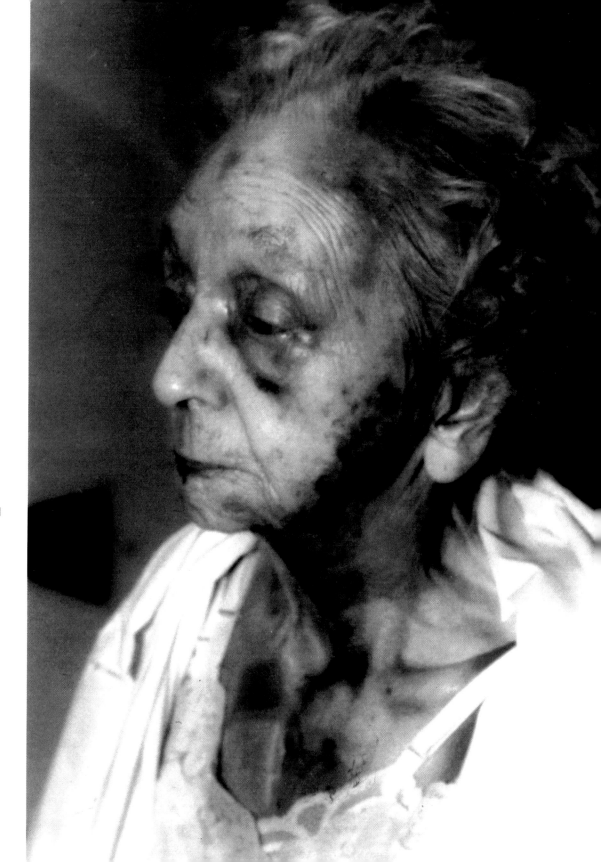

Bessie Shippey, now deceased, was removed from Valeries' Residential Care Home for the Elderly in the United States at age 98, after living there for one year. Her granddaughter and doctor grew concerned after discovering severe bruises covering her body. Although the home's caregiver explained that Bessie's bruises were from falling, the doctor believed otherwise: "When I saw this lady, I knew that it could not have been from falling. … [The bruises] were in all stages – they were not all recent. And there was the imprint of a hand on her face."

Despite her initial reluctance, Bessie eventually admitted to her granddaughter that the caregiver had started beating her soon after she arrived at the home. She did not speak out immediately because she did not want to burden her granddaughter, who was unwell. Deaf and almost blind, Bessie was particularly vulnerable. After leaving the home, she had nightmares and cowered, trembled and begged for forgiveness whenever she had an accident.

Image: National Center on Elder Abuse, Washington D.C.

This stone depicts the total union of a husband and wife according to the Indian tradition of *sati*, in which a woman immolates herself on her husband's funeral pyre. Widows who commit suicide in this manner are often worshipped as goddesses capable of performing miracles. Pilgrims visit *sati* shrines to bless the monuments with coloured powder or make an offering of marigolds. Feminists in India currently are lobbying for a ban on *sati* worship, which would include the destruction or closure of *sati* temples and public condemnation of the practice by the government. There are political and religious leaders today who publicly favour the practice, which encourages widows – who face ostracism in a society where women without husbands are considered incomplete – to follow this deadly custom. Women's advocates hope that by ending the glorification of *sati* widows will be less inclined to succumb to the tradition.

Image: Mirjam Letsch

numerous abuses: "One aide saw him rubbing an elderly woman through her adult diaper, another caught him on top of a resident, her pyjamas pushed up around her neck. He was found in one woman's room as she cowered behind a chair, naked."[24] In another case, also in the United States, police found an elderly woman who had run away from her nursing home wandering near a major highway. She did not want to return: "'I want to die. Please hit me with your car,' she begged. Several weeks later a nursing assistant walked into the woman's room and found a frequent male visitor with his hands between the woman's legs."[25]

While the number of older adults living in care facilities is low — between 4 percent and 7 percent in developed countries, between 1 percent and 4 percent in Latin America and even lower in other developing regions — lack of regulation or enforcement of rules at hospitals and nursing homes can create environments that are unsafe for older females.[26] In developing countries, elderly patients are frequently mistreated in institutions, many of which lack the necessary structural capacity and personnel. In Kenya, for example, the head of one hospital admitted, "Older people are a big headache and a waste of scarce resources. The biggest favour you could do to me as an older people's organization is to get them out of my hospital."[27]

Deadly traditions

All over the world, women live longer than their partners. Some forms of violence against older women are based on cultural practices that specifically target widows, who are often regarded as insignificant without their husbands. While widows of all ages are subjected to mistreatment, older widows can be particularly vulnerable when their age lowers their status in the community and makes caring for themselves more difficult.

In many countries, including Azerbaijan, Burundi, China, Ethiopia, India, Lithuania, Malaysia, Russia, South Africa and Sudan, over half of the women over age 60 are widowed. In 15 out of 16 countries listed in a 2002 report on the state of the world's older people, between 5 percent and 25 percent of men over age 60 are widowers, whereas 35 percent to 65 percent of women over age 60 in the same countries are widowed, a huge discrepancy.[28] The same is reflected throughout Asia: More than 50 percent of older women and only 13 percent of older men are widowed.[29]

> "Older people are a big headache and a waste of scarce resources. The biggest favour you could do to me as an older people's organization is to get them out of my hospital."

The *sati* tradition in India, where women immolate themselves on their husbands' funeral pyres, dates back thousands of years.[30] Early accounts describe tens of thousands of widow queens practising group *sati* after the death of their king, while others recount individual acts of *sati*. Even though the custom was abolished officially in 1829, rare but reported incidents continue, and many shrines still exist to honour thousands of these widows.[31]

There are different explanations for the motivation behind the custom, ranging from a widow's desire to join her husband in the afterlife — since traditional Indian culture dictates that a woman without a man is incomplete — to her relatives' desire to preserve family inheritance, as property is divided amongst male heirs after a widow has died.[32] Recent reports suggest that not all widows who follow the tradition do so willingly: In 2002, a 65-year-old widow from Madhya Pradesh died from immolation on her husband's funeral pyre. Authorities suspected that the woman, who had separated from her husband, did not commit *sati* of her own free will because she "did not have good relations with her husband" and "the grown-up sons did not make any attempt to discourage their mother from sitting on their father's pyre."[33]

Today, in parts of India where popular *sati* shrines exist, communities may encourage widows to follow the practice, as they stand to earn money from donations by visitors to the shrines.[34] Many people in India, however, are speaking out against the tradition. According to one activist, regardless of whether the motivation for a widow to commit *sati* is forced or voluntary, "no virtuosity of semantics can justify or condone such an act of nihilism. … It is totally unacceptable to distinguish between forced *sati* as being criminal and voluntary *sati* as being cultural tradition. There never was and never can be a cultural tradition that sanctifies the death of a human being."[35]

The tradition of wife inheritance in parts of Africa is rationalised by some as being essential to keeping widows integrated in their communities. In many countries, including Rwanda, Uganda, Kenya and Zimbabwe, a widow becomes the property of another man from her village, usually a brother or close male relative of her late husband. It has been argued that the custom benefits widows by offering them security, but because the practice is obligatory, it should be considered a form of gender-based discrimination that results in sexual abuse.

A deadly implication of wife inheritance is the degree to which the custom can transmit HIV. A widow who is HIV-negative faces the risk of contracting the virus from the man who inherits her. In other cases, a widow who has contracted HIV from her late husband — who may have died from an AIDS-related illness — will transmit the disease to her inheritor when she is forced to have sex with him. In the context of polygynous practices, this can set off a chain of events in which the man transmits the virus to his other wives, who may in turn infect others if they are widowed and inherited, and so on.

Notably, in western Kenya, the tradition of wife inheritance is practised by a number of communities — which not coincidentally also have the highest rate of HIV infection in the country. In 2000, the HIV-prevalence rate in Nyanza province, for example, was 22 percent,

In many countries, including Rwanda, Uganda, Kenya and Zimbabwe, a widow becomes the property of another man from her village, usually a brother or a close male relative of her late husband.

compared to the national HIV-infection rate, which was 13 percent.[36] Despite the risks, the tradition of wife inheritance continues because most widows have no alternative. If they refuse, they risk rejection by their communities.[37]

Widow cleansing is another custom that denies women their basic rights and increases their risk of HIV infection. According to the practice, a woman is required to have sex with a village cleanser after her husband dies in order to be reaccepted into her community. The tradition exists in Zambia, Kenya, Malawi, Uganda, Tanzania, Ghana, Senegal, Angola, Ivory Coast, Congo and Nigeria, among other countries. Widow cleansing "dates back centuries and is rooted in a belief that a woman is haunted by spirits after her husband dies. She is also thought to be unholy and 'disturbed' if she is unmarried and abstains from sex."[38] Another traditional belief holds that a widow who has not been cleansed can cause the whole community to be haunted.[39] In many instances a widow must undergo the ritual before she can be inherited.[40]

A widow cleanser in Malawi explained that the "tradition dictates that he sleep with the widow, then with each of his own wives, and then again with the widow, all in one night."[41] He admitted that he never uses condoms and acknowledged that he may be infecting hundreds of women, or even himself. A Kenyan widow cleanser expressed equal disregard for condom use. He said that the widows "wouldn't really be cleansed if the condom was there."[42]

Even women who are aware of the risk of HIV infection may submit to cleansing rituals because of community pressure. One woman from Malawi described her feelings of resignation and shame: "I was hiding my private parts. ... You want to have a liking for a man to have sex, not to have someone force you. But I had no choice, knowing the whole village was against me."[43]

Another Malawian woman, Paulina Bubala, who is now the leader of a community group for people living with HIV/AIDS, first participated in an alternative rite but was ultimately forced to undergo a widow-cleansing ritual. For the first step of the cleansing rite, Paulina and her co-wife "covered themselves in mud for three days. Then they each bathed, stripped naked with their dead husband's nephew and rubbed their bodies against his. Weeks later, the village headman told them this cleansing ritual would not suffice. Even the stools they sat on would be considered unclean, he warned, unless they had sex with the nephew. 'We felt humiliated,' she said, 'but there was nothing we could do to resist, because we wanted to be clean in the land of the headman.'"[44]

Witchcraft accusations also result in violence against older women in some African countries. In Tanzania, an estimated 500 older women are murdered each year because of witchcraft claims.[45] In Mozambique, more than 90 older women were victims of violence in one month, the majority a result of witchcraft allegations.[46] When communities cannot find logical explanations for events, "such as a death or crop failure," they may accuse older women in their village of witchcraft.[47]

Such accusations might be used to justify driving an older woman from her home, stealing her possessions or killing her for her property.[48] Ntombama Mlalazi, a 62-year-old widow, was accused of being a witch in her village in Zimbabwe and ordered to submit to an exorcism by her local chief. "People were dying, and *tsikamutanda* [witch hunters] said I was responsible. They made me crouch over a bucket with boiling water and covered me with a blanket. When I cried out that the steam was hurting me I could hear the *tsikamutanda* saying the demon was leaving me."[49]

Addressing elderly abuse

Underreporting and underinvestigation are major challenges to addressing the issue of violence against elderly women in the home, in institutions and in communities. In one community in Chile, of the nearly 30 percent of women experiencing abuse by family members, 61 percent of the victims did not seek support. They cited "fear, shame and lack of economic resources and information" as reasons for maintaining their silence.[50] In a study of 90 indigenous Australian women who were victims of intimate-partner violence, participants identified a number of barriers to reporting, including lack of access to services because of the women's remote location, language difficulty, guilt and fear of exposing family problems.

Cases of sexual violence against elderly women that are reported may not be properly investigated because embarrassment prevents some victims from providing crucial details, as was the case in Pennsylvania in the United States, where a 62-year-old woman was forced to perform oral sex on a stranger. She was so ashamed that she did not disclose to anyone the true nature of the assault. When the vaginal examination showed no signs of rape, the case was dropped. Months later, during a counselling session, the woman broke down and admitted that she was forced to perform fellatio.[51]

The strategies employed to help battered women — empowerment, education and support in assessing their options — transcend the age issue.[52] Still, many older victims of violence complain that most support services cater specifically to younger women. Older women seeking refuge from domestic abuse said that they would prefer taking shelter with their peers. When grouped together with younger victims, "They were expected to take on the 'grandma' role and felt unable to decline, even though they needed to deal with their own issues."[53] Older women who contract HIV from sexual violence — which is not unlikely during forced sex because their bodies are more susceptible to tearing, thus facilitating transmission — also may have difficulty finding appropriate support. Although HIV/AIDS affects older women, most programmes that deal with prevention and treatment of HIV are targeted at younger women.[54] Experts suggest that information about resources for older women should be available in places where they congregate.[55]

Concerns that are age-specific need to be incorporated into professional training programmes to establish appropriate ways to handle cases of elderly sexual abuse. Medical personnel are among the best people to identify cases of violence against members of any age group and are especially useful for recognising signs of abuse in older women, who are more likely to be seeing doctors for other health-related reasons, at least in developed countries.

Detecting evidence of abuse, however, is only the first step in a series of measures necessary to support older women who have been victims of sexual violence. "Even the most compassionate and experienced of service providers in aging, including those most directly involved in abuse issues, typically lack specific training in this area."[56] One researcher of elderly sexual abuse emphasised the lack of shared, professional knowledge:

"The problem is that when you need a specialised rape-crisis counsellor to deal with your 82-year-old victim, they're just not there. They don't exist. That's why we need to do some cross-training. Let's get the rape-crisis centre people, the battered women's centre people, and the elder-abuse people all together. If we give the rape-crisis treatment people some training in elder abuse, they'll be there when we need them. And the people who know elder abuse need to be talking to the people who know domestic violence. We need all three pieces."[57]

Peer support to older victims should be a major component of prevention and response.[58] In some communities, people already have started to address the problem. One peer-support initiative in Poland encourages older women who live alone to "buddy up" when walking outside.[59] In Peru, women's groups offer members a support network in which they can share their concerns. An older woman in Lima explained that she felt less isolated after she established a peer-support network:

"Once I got older and started not feeling so well I had to withdraw from my activities. It really hit me hard and I got very depressed. I saw myself getting worse because I wasn't participating anymore, so I decided to form my own group of older women like me — a group for older people."[60]

In Kenya, local women's groups teach their peers how to reject harmful cultural practices like widow cleansing and wife inheritance. Such

"The problem is that when you need a specialised rape-crisis counsellor to deal with your 82-year-old victim, they're just not there. They don't exist."

grassroots initiatives have been successful in convincing male community members that these customs can endanger an entire society, as evidenced by the reflections of one man: "We used to say we would die for our traditions. I used to say cleansing was good. But I think this attitude helps nothing. We all may die if we don't stop this one."[61]

Community responses should be complemented by public-awareness initiatives and governmental prevention strategies. In India, women's rights activists have lobbied the government to prohibit the worship of widows who have committed *sati*. Their work resulted in a government ban on celebrations of *sati* in 1988. A slew of pro-*sati* lobbies to the supreme court followed in an effort to undermine their progress.[62] One anti-*sati* activist remarked that lobbying the government is not enough to eradicate the practice: "It is clear that what is required is a multipronged strategy consisting of legal measures, effective state intervention, rehabilitation and public education."[63] On the African continent,

community activists have lobbied government officials to legislate against wife inheritance and widow cleansing, as these customs increase the risk of HIV transmission. In both Zambia and Malawi, national authorities "have spoken out against forcing widows into sex or marriage," illustrating significant progress by local female activists.[64]

Addressing the abuse of older women requires coordinating the efforts of researchers, healthcare providers, government authorities and community organizations. When a victim is courageous enough to come forward, she should be secure in the knowledge that she will have access to adequate support services by trained professionals and that her complaint will be properly investigated. For many women, being victimised in old age is yet another battle in a lifelong struggle against discrimination and abuse. The greatest challenge to stopping violence against older women lies in reforming the societies that tolerate or perpetuate the abuse of all women, regardless of their age. n

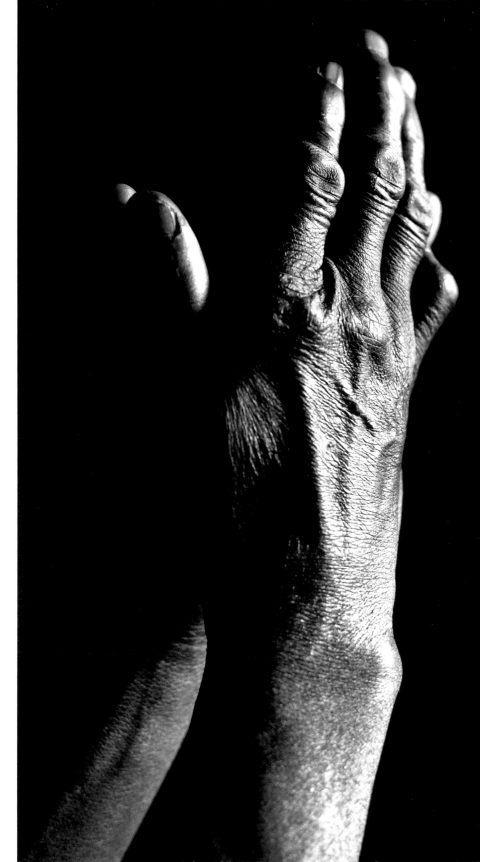

"It was at midnight when the attackers came. I was asleep, and my husband was visiting his sister in the village, so I was alone. There were five military men. They came in and removed all my clothes. They stabbed me in the head and on the top of my arms with a machete, as they forced my hands back behind my head. I was screaming all the time as they raped me, all five of them, one by one. As one was raping me another would say, 'Get out so I can enter.' They took me by force, causing my leg to be hit against something. They hit my hand with a stick and it is now damaged. My husband heard my screaming and came to find me. He was beaten with a gun — they beat him in the knees. I was aching so much, I felt great pains. When they left I crawled out of the house. They were burning a house in the village and then burned mine.

"They left me with fistula but I was cured by DOCS [Doctors on Call Services, in the Democratic Republic of Congo]. I couldn't stay long with fistula — the smell was so bad from the urine. I went to DOCS and returned in August 2004.

"I am very, very happy today to receive the goat, beans and hoe [from DOCS]. I have nothing. Look at the house [a mud house with tiny dusty room for cooking and a piece of cloth separating the bedroom from the kitchen, so dark]. When the goat gives birth, I will give the first baby to DOCS. Because of the famine it will not be possible to sell the beans at the first harvest, but in the future I plan to sell them. I want to give part of my first harvest to DOCS, the rest I will use to feed my family. I am strong to cultivate."

Image: Georgina Cranston/IRIN

Varanasi, India, is also called Kashi, or "City of Light". As the home of thousands of widows who have been ostracised by their families after rejecting the *sati* tradition – in which a widow immolates herself on her husband's funeral pyre — Varanasi has come to be known as the "City of Ten Thousand Widows". Its inhabitants, or *kashi-vas*, bide their time there, practising a variety of purification rituals in the hope that they will achieve *moksha*, or redemption. Before sunrise, the *kashi-vas* gather at the riverbank for their daily ritual bath. The rest of the day is punctuated by visits to temples, a single meal and prayer and sacrifice, or *puja*. While the exact number of widows living in *Kashi* is unknown, there are numerous old women in the city, alone or in small groups, begging for their existence. Most of the *kashi-vas* live on the streets in makeshift shelters of wood or plastic sheeting. A lucky few live in small rented rooms, supported financially by the family members who have sent them away. Rejected by both their family and society, the *kashi-vas* are highly vulnerable to random acts of physical and sexual violence. Some of the widows endure this meagre existence for more than 25 years, hoping that by the end of their lives they will have paid the price of outliving their husbands.

Images: Zana Briski (facing) and Mirjam Letsch (below)

Bemguema in Sierra Leone, 2002. A young girl, followed by women from her village, passes a group of soldiers from the national army on break from training. The war in Sierra Leone gained notoriety for the level of atrocities committed on civilians by gangs of young men and boys, who often were high on drugs and alcohol. The gangs were linked to different militias or rebel factions, and they raped, mutilated and killed thousands of civilians.

Image: Jan Dago

sexual violence in times of war

By 1993, the Zenica Centre for the Registration of War and Genocide Crime in Bosnia-Herzegovina had documented 40,000 cases of war-related rape.[1] Of a sample of Rwandan women surveyed in 1999, 39 percent reported being raped during the 1994 genocide, and 72 percent said they knew someone who had been raped.[2] An estimated 23,200 to 45,600 Kosovar Albanian women are believed to have been raped between August 1998 and August 1999, the height of the conflict with Serbia.[3] In 2003, 74 percent of a random sample of 388 Liberian refugee women living in camps in Sierra Leone reported being sexually abused prior to being displaced from their homes in Liberia. Fifty-five percent of them experienced sexual violence during displacement.[4] Of a sample of 410 internally displaced Colombian women in Cartagena who were surveyed in 2003, 8 percent reported some form of sexual violence prior to being displaced, and 11 percent reported being abused since their displacement.[5]

The changing face of war

A growing body of data from the wars of the last decade is finally bringing to light "one of history's great silences": the sexual violation and torture of civilian women and girls during periods of armed conflict.[6] Until recently, the evidence — along with the issue — had been generally ignored by historians, politicians and the world at large, yet it is hardly new. The licence of victors to "rape and pillage" the vanquished dates back to Ancient Greek, Roman and Hebrew wars.[7] In examples from the last century alone, Jewish women were raped by Cossacks during the 1919 pogroms in Russia; the Japanese military trafficked thousands of "comfort women" from countries across Asia and sexually enslaved them during World War II; over 100,000 women were raped in the Berlin area directly following World War II; and hundreds of thousands of Bengali women were raped by Pakistani soldiers during the 1971 Bangladeshi war of secession.[8]

Despite the history of sexual violence committed against women and girls by men in times of war, what is especially disturbing about the statistics from the past 10 years is how rife the phenomenon appears to have become. It might be argued that the current data simply reflect greater international attention to the issue — provoked in part by the media coverage of the sexual atrocities committed during the conflicts in the former Yugoslavia and Rwanda, and even more importantly by the decades of intensive awareness-raising by women's activists around the world — rather than a significant rise in absolute numbers of victims. A more likely explanation, however, is that the nature of warfare is changing, in ways that increasingly endanger women and girls.

Since the latter half of the last century, combat primarily limited to military engagements between national armies has been largely supplanted by civil wars and regional conflicts that pit communities along racial, religious and/or ethnic lines. The result is that civilian populations are victimised on a massive scale. Between 1989 and 1997, an estimated 103 armed conflicts were launched in 69 countries across the world.[9] Civilian casualties during these more recent conflicts are estimated to be as high as 75 percent, a stunning contrast to the 5 percent estimate from the start of the last century.[10] Although overall more men than women continue to die as a result of conflict, women and girls suffer myriad debilitating consequences of war.[11] So much so, according to a 2002 report of the Secretary-General of the United Nations, that "women and children are disproportionately targets" and "constitute the majority of all victims" of contemporary armed conflicts.[12]

What the current data conceal

However disturbing the current statistics are, they probably conceal more than they reveal in terms of the true extent of sexual violence against women and girls during armed conflict. For a number of reasons, data on rape in war are exceedingly difficult to capture — as seen in the sometimes dramatic variance in estimates from any given country, such as those from Bosnia that range from 14,000 to 50,000, and from Rwanda that range from 15,700 to a half million.[13] Sometimes the discrepancies reflect political interests, where a government or armed group may seek to downplay the extent of crimes committed by its members, while others are working to highlight those crimes. Yet even when research is undertaken by nonaligned human rights or other groups, obtaining an accurate representation of the scope of sexual violence presents tremendous challenges.

Research on sexual violence against women during war is in its relative infancy. Investigators have only just begun to develop and test methodologies for collecting representative data. In addition, substantial underreporting of rape is commonplace even in times of peace; in times of war and its aftermath, when constraining factors such as stigma and shame are compounded by political instability and threats to personal safety, rates of reporting are likely to be even lower. Exposing violence in the context of active conflict can represent a security risk for all involved — as evidenced by the May 2005 arrest of the Médecins Sans Frontières (MSF) head of mission in Khartoum, Sudan, who was charged by the Sudanese government with crimes against the state after publishing a report on women seeking rape-related medical treatment in MSF facilities throughout Darfur.[14]

In many more instances, there is simply no insitutional authority or organization to whom a woman can recount her experience. Even where services do exist, pervasive impunity for perpetrators of war-related sexual violence means that many survivors may accurately reason that

> However disturbing the current statistics are, they probably conceal more than they reveal in terms of the true extent of sexual violence against women and girls during armed conflict.

no justice — and thus no purpose — will be served by reporting their victimisation. Notably, in a 2001 study from Timor Leste (East Timor), only 7 percent of women who had experienced physical or sexual violence during the crisis of 1999 ever reported their victimisation to a local authority.[15] In a survey from Rwanda, only 6 percent of respondents who had been raped during the genocide ever sought medical treatment.[16]

The current statistics — detached as they are from the nature of the crimes — also do not reveal the depths of violence to which women and girls have been exposed, or the terror they are forced to endure when their bodies become the ways and means of war. It is only the personal accounts that do this — accounts that most of the world will likely never hear.

Three personal stories

Since the 1996 outbreak of hostilities among multiple armed factions in the eastern part of the Democratic Republic of Congo (DRC), atrocities against women have been so horrific and extensive that the violence has been referred to colloquially as the "war within a war" and the "war against women".[17] Although a peace process was initiated at the end of 2002, the prevailing lawlessness in the eastern part of the country continues to put many women and girls at risk. In recent research in South Kivu, 492 women — 79 percent of whom had been sexually assaulted by between two and 20 attackers — shared their experiences of rape, mutilation and torture.[18] One incident was related by a victim still confined to a hospital bed:

"A few moments after the *Interahamwe* [Rwandan militia] arrived in the village I heard my neighbour screaming. I looked out of the window and I saw some men, all holding rifles. Immediately, I wanted to run away and hide but three of them turned up at our house. My husband pretended to be asleep ... they grabbed me roughly. One of them

Young girls and adolescents may be particularly vulnerable to sexual violence during war and civil unrest. In eastern Democratic Republic of Congo, where this photograph was taken, the prevalence of rape is extremely high. Noncombatants – in addition to militiamen and soldiers – are also perpetrators. United Nations peacekeepers have been implicated in cases of sexual exploitation and coercion as well.

Image: Evelyn Hockstein

A mother in Darfur, western Sudan, looks down at her newborn son — the child of a rape she survived in 2004. Rape in Darfur has been a common weapon of the *Janjawid* militias. Women and girls have been assaulted in their villages, while looking for firewood outside camps for the internally displaced and even inside neighbouring Chad. The rapists commit their crimes in a climate of complete impunity while their victims often suffer the additional indignity of marginalisation by society and, at times, their own families.

Image: Evelyn Hockstein

restrained me, while another took my *pili pili* pestle and pushed it several times into my vagina, as if he was pounding. This agony seemed to be a

... they grabbed me roughly. One of them restrained me, while another took my *pili pili* pestle and pushed it several times into my vagina, as if he was pounding. This agony seemed to be a neverending hell ...

neverending hell ... then they suddenly left. For two weeks my vagina was discharging. I was operated on ... I have to relieve myself into a bag tied to an opening in the side of my belly. They also killed my husband and my son."[19]

In another instance, a Congolese woman described the brutality she endured at the hands of militia:

"I was busy cutting wood, when four armed men suddenly appeared at the other end of the field. They told me to undress and to volunteer myself to one of them. I refused. Then they took me, spreading my legs out and tying them, one to the bottom of a tree, the other to another tree trunk. They stuck my head between two sticks held diagonally, so that I couldn't sit up without hurting myself. I stayed in this position and one of the attackers penetrated me forcefully from behind in the vagina, and the other pushed his penis into my mouth, right into my throat ... I was retrieved by neighbours who watched my ordeal from a distance. When they found me I had fainted and was covered in blood."[20]

Similar atrocities were committed by all parties to Sierra Leone's 10-year civil war. The primary perpetrators of the most egregious abuses, however, were among the rebel forces, particularly the Revolutionary United Front. They raped as a matter of course, often in gangs, often in front of family members. They forced boys and men to rape their mothers and wives. They sexually assaulted and then disembowelled pregnant women. They mutilated women's genitals with knives, burning wood and gun barrels. One particularly violent rebel incursion, on the capital city of Freetown in January 1999, let loose a "hellish cycle of rape, sexual assault, and mutilation."[21] A 13-year-old girl, abducted during the incursion and forced into sexual slavery by rebels, already had given birth to a baby girl born of rape by the time she told her story to researchers in 2001. She remembered how her captivity began:

"We were taken to a house with about 200 people in it. My older cousin was sent to go and select 25 men and 25 women to have their hands chopped off. Then she was told to cut off the first man's hand. She refused to do it, saying she was afraid. I was then told to do it. I said I'd never done such a thing before and that I was afraid. We were told to sit on the side and watch. So we sat. They chopped off two men's hands. My cousin couldn't watch and bowed her head down to avoid the sight. Because she did that, they shot her in the foot. They bandaged her foot and then forced her to walk. We left the two men whose hands had been cut off behind. We were then taken to a mosque in Kissy. They killed everyone in there. ... They were snatching babies and infants from their mother's arms and tossing them in the air. The babies would free fall to their deaths. At other times they would also chop them from the back of their heads to kill them, you know, like you do when you slaughter chickens. One girl with us tried to escape. They made her take off her slippers and give them to me and then killed her. ... One time we came across two pregnant women. They tied the women down with their legs eagle spread and took a sharpened stick and jabbed them inside their wombs until the babies came out on the stick."[22]

The "murderous madness" of sexual violence in conflict

The motivation for rape committed during armed conflict varies. The violence can be a by-product of the collapse in social and moral order that accompanies war. In DRC, rape has become so indiscriminate as to be referred to as "murderous madness".[23] In one example, a Congolese mother walked into her house to find a paramilitary raping her 10-month-old baby.[24] Such incidents are not only limited to combatants. Men from the local community may exploit the chaos of conflict to commit sexual violence against women without fear of punishment. Under the volatile and disorganized rule of the *Mujahideen*, for instance, rape and sexual assault in Afghanistan's capital city of Kabul were reportedly so commonplace that the oppressive police state established after the Taliban takeover in 1996 was initially perceived by some women as a welcome reprieve.[25]

Sexual violence may also be systematic, carried out by fighting forces for the explicit purpose of destabilising populations and destroying bonds within communities and families. In these instances, rape is often a public act, aimed to maximise humiliation and shame. In Timor Leste, Indonesian military reportedly raped women in front of their families and forced Timorese men to rape Timorese women. Researchers on a 2004 fact-finding mission to Northern Uganda, where an 18-year insurgency by the Lord's Resistance Army (LRA) continues, spoke with one man who was commanded by members of the LRA to have sex with his daughter:

"I refused. ... They ordered my son ... for the fear of a cocked gun he complied. ... I was then forced to have sex with a hole they had dug in the floor using a knife. ... They forced my private part in the hole several times — the skin was totally destroyed. ... It was impossible to fight someone who is armed. ... This was all done in front of my wife, son, and the daughter. ... My wife went mad."[26]

A Sudanese man recounted to researchers his family's similar degradation in Darfur: "In February 2004, I abandoned my house

Particularly in conflicts defined by racial, tribal, religious and other divisions, violence may be used to advance the goal of ethnic cleansing. Public rapes in Bosnia, for example, were used to instigate the flight or expulsion of entire Muslim communities.

because of the conflict. I met six Arabs in the bush. I wanted to take my spear and defend my family, but they threatened me with a weapon and I had to stop. The six men raped my daughter, who is 25 years old, in front of me, my wife and young children."[27]

Sexual violence also can serve to quell resistance by instilling fear in local communities or in opposing armed groups. In such cases, women's bodies are "used as an envelope to send messages to the perceived enemy."[28] In the Shan Province of Myanmar, where the government has been trying to violently suppress a local rebellion since the mid-1990s, hundreds of women have been systematically raped.[29] In one example, an army major approached a young girl and "asked her about her parent's [whereabouts] and ordered his soldiers to wait at the edge of the farm and arrest anyone who came to the farm. He then raped [the girl] in a hut several times during the day and at about 4 a.m. burned [her alive] in the hut, and left the place with his troops."[30]

Comparable violations by Russian soldiers in Chechnya have been reported during "mop up" operations that ensue after rebel Chechen fighters have decamped a town. Of four Chechen women vaginally and orally assaulted by Russian military in February 2000, one purportedly suffocated to death while a soldier sat on her head.[31] In Colombia, paramilitary control of some regions often includes sexual violence and torture of women and girls. Intimidation campaigns are carried out on

their bodies, as in one of many cases reported in 2001 to the United Nations Special Rapporteur on Violence Against Women, where a Colombian girl was raped and killed, her eyes and nails then removed, and her breasts cut off.[32]

Particularly in conflicts defined by racial, tribal, religious and other divisions, violence may be used to advance the goal of ethnic cleansing. Public rapes in Bosnia, for example, were used to instigate the flight or expulsion of entire Muslim communities. Forced impregnation, mutilation of genitals and intentional HIV transmission are other techniques of ethnic cleansing. Women in Rwanda were taunted by their genocidal rapists, who promised to infect them with HIV. In Bosnia, Muslim women impregnated by Serbs reportedly were held captive until late term to prevent them from aborting.[33] In Kosovo, an estimated 100 babies conceived in rape were born in January 2000 alone — the International Committee of the Red Cross speculated at the time that the real number of rape-related pregnancies was likely to be much higher.[34] Sometimes attacks on women's bodies — particularly their reproductive capacities — specifically target perceived rival progeny. One woman from Darfur reported in 2004, "I was with another woman, Aziza, aged 18, who had her stomach slit on the night we were abducted. She was pregnant and was killed and they said, 'It is the child of an enemy.' "[35]

Sexual slaves to armed combatants

Many other instances have been identified where women and girls are abducted for the purposes of supplying combatants with sexual services. According to one soldier from DRC, "Our combatants don't get paid. Therefore they can't use prostitutes. If we politely ask women to come with us, they are not going to accept. So, we have to make them obey us so we can get what we want."[36] An elderly victim from Liberia, thought to be around 80 years old at the time she related her story to investigators, acknowledged being held by rebels in the town of Voinjama, where "at night, the men would come, usually more than one. They would rape me. They said they would help me. If I was lucky, they gave me 10 Liberian dollars (US 20 cents)."[37]

More often the victims of sexual slavery are younger, and in many cases their victimisation comes under the terms of military duty. An estimated 40 percent of child soldiers around the world are girls, the majority of

The decomposing bodies of a woman and girl, victims of the 1994 genocide in Rwanda.
"… if you looked, you could see the evidence, even in the whitened skeletons. The legs bent and apart. A broken bottle, a rough branch, even a knife between them. Where the bodies were fresh, we saw what must have been semen pooled on and near the dead women and girls. There was always a lot of blood. Some male corpses had their genitals cut off, but many women and young girls had their breasts chopped off and their genitals crudely cut apart. They died in a position of total vulnerability, flat on their backs, with their legs bent and knees wide apart. It was the expressions on their dead faces that assaulted me the most, a frieze of shock, pain and humiliation. For many years after I came back home, I banished the memories of those faces from my mind, but they have come back, all too clearly." (Excerpted from *Shake Hands with the Devil*, by Lt Gen Roméo Dallaire, Force Commander of the United Nations Assistance Mission to Rwanda, 1993-1994.)

Image: Mariella Furrer

Bosnian government troops reach out towards a Muslim woman who sits mute with shock by a roadside in Travnick, central Bosnia, in the summer of 1993. The woman was part of a group of Muslim detainees held captive by Bosnian Serbs. They had been deported across the frontline to the government-controlled area only minutes before this photograph was taken. Detainees who were with her said she had been raped.

Image: Anthony Lloyd

whom are forcibly or coercively conscripted.[38] Their responsibilities may range from portering to active combat, with the additional expectation that they will provide sexual services to their superiors or fellow combatants. Much of the violence reportedly committed against women and girls by guerrilla groups in Colombia, for example, is in the context of forced recruitment.[39]

Even those women and girls who "voluntarily" join fighting forces are unlikely to anticipate the extent to which they will suffer sexual exploitation. Data collected in 2004 from women participating in Liberia's disarmament and demobilisation programme indicated that 73 percent of the women and girls experienced some form of sexual violence.[40] In Uganda, a former child soldier of the National Resistance Army remembers:

"We collected firewood; we carried weapons. For girls it was worse because ... we were girlfriends to many different officers. ... At the end it became, like, I don't own my own body, it's their body. It was so hard to stay the 24 hours a day thinking, Which officer am I going to sleep with today?"[41] In a similar account from a 19-year-old woman voluntarily associated with the Maoists in Nepal, "Sometimes we are forced to satisfy about a dozen [militia] per night. When I had gone to another region for party work, I had to have sex with seven militia and this was the worst day of my life."[42]

Some girls who are forced or coerced into sexual slavery may succeed in escaping their captors only to be seized again. Such was the experience of 16-year-old "Hawa", from Sierra Leone:

"There were about 20 men. We ran to the bush, but I got separated from my family. I was with other people from the village, and we were captured by the rebels and taken to Liberia. ... At first I refused to be a

"Sometimes we are forced to satisfy about a dozen [militia] per night. When I had gone to another region for party work, I had to have sex with seven militia and this was the worst day of my life."

'wife', but I had to agree because there was nobody to speak up for me, and nobody gave me food except the rebels. I was a wife for about eight months. ... I had not even started my periods."

Hawa eventually escaped and walked for three days in the bush until she got to a town where she found her parents. When they returned

together to their remote village, Hawa recalled, "It was very sad when I ... met my sisters because I felt I was somehow discriminated against because I had been raped." Two years later, Hawa recaptured: "It was a different group: This time I was always with them at night as their wife."[43]

Hawa escaped a second time and was reunited with her family. For too many other women and girls who attempt to escape the perils of war, the threat of sexual violence follows them — from flight, to displacement in camps or other settings, through to their return and resettlement in their home communities.

Flight

The United Nations High Commissioner for Refugees (UNHCR) estimated the total number of people displaced by armed conflict in 2004 at 34 million: 9.3 million were refugees in neighbouring states, and another 25 million were internally displaced in their home countries.[44] According to the United Nations Secretary-General, "The differential impact of armed conflict and the specific vulnerabilities of women can be seen in all phases of displacement."[45]

During flight, women and girls remain at high risk for sexual violence — committed by bandits, insurgency groups, military and border guards. Many women must flee without the added safeguard of male relatives or community members, further increasing their vulnerability. In the case of 17-year-old "Tatiana" from the DRC, the results were devastating:

Tatiana was eight-and-a-half-months pregnant when her husband and her two-year-old son were hacked to death by irregular militia in May 2003. When she, her mother and two younger sisters heard that the same militia intended to raid the district of Bunia, where they lived, they fled. Six days later, they reached a militia checkpoint, but her mother could not pay the $100 demanded. The militia cut her throat, killing her. When Tatiana's 14-year-old sister began to cry, she was shot in the head. Her other sister, age 12, was taken to a nearby clearing and gang-raped. Tatiana was told to leave at once or suffer the same fate. After six days walking, she went into labour and gave birth to a girl. Although she had lost a lot of blood, she had to take to the road again the following day. The baby later died.[46]

Without money or other resources, displaced women and girls may be compelled to submit to sex in return for safe passage, food, shelter or other resources.[47] Some may head towards urban settings, possibly in search of the relative security of a densely populated area or in the hope of obtaining employment. Whatever the motivation, both internally displaced and refugee women and girls in urban settings are at risk of exploitation by local residents, especially because they are less likely than encamped populations to be targeted for assistance and protection by governments or by humanitarian agencies.

Afghan refugee women living in the city of Peshawar, Pakistan, for example, described being forced to exchange sex for rent-free housing.[48] In Colombia, the Ministry for Social Protection reported in 2003 that 36 percent of internally displaced women in the country had been forced by men into having sexual relations. This statement was later confirmed in a study undertaken in the same year, which found that displaced women living in *barrios* in or near the city of Cartagena had suffered higher levels of physical and sexual violence after their displacement.[49] Unaccompanied girls are likely to be among the most vulnerable to sexual exploitation. A 1999 government survey of over 2,000 prostitutes in Sierra Leone found that 37 percent of the young women were under the age of 15, and that the majority of them had been displaced by conflict and were unaccompanied by family.[50]

Still others attempting to escape from war may be the target of traffickers. The absence of border controls and normal policing make conflict-affected countries prime routes for traffickers. In Colombia, the ongoing internal conflict has given rise to one of the western hemisphere's most active trafficking networks. Colombia's Department of Security estimated that 35,000 to 50,000 women and girls were trafficked in 2000, the majority to countries in Asia and Western Europe, as well as to the United States.[51] Myanmar, also wracked by long-standing civil conflict, is thought to supply some 40,000 trafficked women and girls annually for work in brothels, factories and as domestic labourers in Thailand.[52]

Displacement to camp settings

Camps for internally displaced persons (IDPs) or refugees may offer only limited protection from sexual violence. Humanitarian aid workers have consistently identified the danger to women who must venture far

outside the confines of camps to search for firewood or other staples unavailable in the camp. Research undertaken almost 10 years ago among refugees living in camps in Dadaab, Kenya, found that more than 90 percent of reported rapes occurred under these circumstances.[53] Despite the long-standing evidence, however, not enough has been done to anticipate and avert this predictable risk in more recently established camps.

One 27-year-old Liberian woman who had been raped twice before seeking safety in an IDP camp described the circumstances of her third rape, in 2003, when she left the camp to look for firewood:

"There were three government soldiers with guns. One of them saw me and asked, 'Where are you going?' I said I was looking for wood. Then

A 1999 government survey of over 2,000 prostitutes in Sierra Leone found that 37 percent of the young women were under the age of 15, and that the majority of them had been displaced by conflict and were unaccompanied by family.

he told me, 'You are assigned to me for the day.' I was very afraid. He forced me to go far into the bush, and he undressed me. Then he raped me. When I got dressed afterwards, he took 50 Liberian dollars from me. … My stomach is very painful, but I don't have any money to go for treatment."[54]

The trend continues for encamped women displaced by the conflict in Darfur, Sudan, but in this instance, repeated reports by a number of international human rights organizations resulted in recent efforts to improve policing and security related to firewood collection.[55] For many women, however, these security measures have come too late.

Women are also at risk of rape in or near camps, particularly when the camps are poorly planned and/or administered. In a 1996 survey of Burundian refugee women displaced to a camp in Tanzania, more than one in four reported being raped during the prior three years of conflict, with two-thirds of the rapes occurring since displacement, either inside or close to the camp. The majority of perpetrators were other refugees (59 percent), followed by local Burundian residents (24 percent), and then local Tanzanians, soldiers and police.[56] As with firewood collection, advocates and humanitarians have for several years spoken out about the relationship between ill-considered camp design and violence against women, and have put forth recommendations for reducing women's vulnerability.

A Sudanese refugee who was shot in the shoulder and leg as he defended his daughters against the *Janjawid* militiamen who were trying to rape them. The militiamen later tortured him by tying a cord around his testicles and pulling on it. The ubiquity of rape as a weapon of war places enormous strain on male family members, who often are helpless to prevent such assaults.
Photographed in Goungour, Chad, in 2004.

Image: Francesco Zizola/Magnum

Former abductees — some of whom spent years as forced labourers and "wives" for the Lord's Resistance Army in northern Uganda — relax in the Gusco Rehabilitation Centre. One girl holds a baby while another reads a newspaper with the headline, "Love: Don't force it. Don't rush it. Don't hurt it."

Nevertheless, the problem persists in many settings. A risk assessment carried out in 2004 in seven IDP camps in Montserrado County in Liberia concluded that overcrowded conditions, insufficient lighting at night, the close proximity of male and female latrines and bathhouses, and poor or unequal access to resources all conspired to increase the likelihood of sexual violence against women and girls.[57]

In a study undertaken in Northern Uganda, also in 2004, a woman living in one of many IDP camps in the region told investigators, "Rape is rampant here ... a woman was recently harassed by two men who held her legs wide open and used a flashlight to observe her private parts and allowed another man to rape her while they observed.[58]

Lack of institutional protection

Not unlike rape in war, these acts of violence flourish in the environments of impunity that too often circumscribe the lives of displaced populations. The problem can be especially dire for IDPs. Despite the fact that in 1998 the United Nations produced guiding principles on the protection of displaced populations, there is still no United Nations agency specifically mandated with their care and protection. UNHCR is increasingly stepping in to fill the void, but in 2004 the refugee agency assisted only 5.6 million of the estimated 25 million internally displaced persons around the world.[59] More often, the responsibility for IDPs falls primarily to national governments, whose resources are likely to be drained or diverted by the conflict. A global evaluation of the reproductive health of refugees and IDPs by an interagency working group found that reproductive health services are most lacking among IDP populations, of which services addressing gender-based violence are the least developed.[60]

The scenario may be only marginally improved for refugees. In too many instances there are not enough UNHCR staff on the ground who are designated to address the issue of gender-based violence. Even where staffing is sufficient, UNHCR's ability to provide sustained protection against sexual violence is all too often only as good as a host country's commitment to addressing the issue. Wherever a host government or local community is hostile, the risk of all forms of violence against refugees — including sexual violence — is higher.

Following a statement issued in 2000 by the president of Guinea, for example, in which Liberian and Sierra Leonean refugees were blamed for sheltering armed rebels responsible for attacks on Guinea, women and girl refugees reportedly were raped in mob reprisals launched by Guinean

police, soldiers and civilians.[61] Some 50 Burundian refugee women in Tanzania allegedly were attacked in May 1999 by a group of over 100 Tanzanian men who were apparently avenging the death of a local schoolteacher.[62] Thousands of Afghans in Pakistan and Burmese in Thailand have never been granted official refugee status by their host

> What is perhaps more surprising is the extent to which humanitarian actors — those whose commitment is to provide assistance — have been implicated in sexual crimes against refugees and internally displaced persons.

governments. The fear of forced return means that they are unlikely ever to report a case of sexual violence committed against them to local authorities. Not surprisingly, in both Pakistan and Thailand multiple incidents have been recounted by refugee women and girls of local police or security colluding in or even perpetrating sexual violence against them.[63]

What is perhaps more surprising is the extent to which humanitarian actors — those whose commitment is to provide assistance — have been implicated in sexual crimes against refugees and IDPs. A 2002 report jointly published by Save the Children (UK) and UNHCR documented allegations against 67 individuals working in 40 aid agencies serving refugees in three countries in West Africa. One young refugee mother told researchers, "I have to sleep with so many men to make 1,500 GNF (37 cents) so that I can feed myself and my child. [The locals] pay me 300 (7 cents) each time, but if I am lucky and I get [an aid] worker, he can pay me 1,500." Another refugee suggested, "In this community, no one can access CSB [a soy nutrient] without having sex first."[64] Although a United Nations-sponsored investigative team following up on the allegations questioned the verity of the report, multiple subsequent incidents of sexual exploitation by aid workers in camps in Kenya, Zimbabwe and Nepal, among others, have continued to draw attention to the seriousness of the problem.[65]

Reconstruction or exploitation?

Evidence suggests that sexual violence does not necessarily end with the cessation of armed conflict. Incidents of rape are reported to have increased sharply in the context of ongoing insecurity in post-war Iraq, for example. One of the victims, "Dalal", was abducted, held overnight and allegedly raped in 2003 by four Iraqi men who she believes "wanted to kidnap anyone ... to take what they wanted."[66] In other post-conflict settings, incidents of rape may decrease, but risk of exposure to forced or coerced prostitution, as well as trafficking, may increase. Events in the Balkans — where prostitution and trafficking burgeoned in the aftermath of wars in the former Yugoslavia — illustrate how criminal elements may replace fighting factions in the continued sexual victimisation of women and girls. The added presence of peacekeeping forces, who have been implicated as users of commercial sex workers in places such as Bosnia-Herzegovina, Sierra Leone, Kosovo, Timor Leste and the DRC, may supply a notable portion of local demand.

In many instances, the risk to women and girls of falling prey to sexual exploiters is exacerbated by reconstruction programmes that fail to specifically target their needs, or to address long-standing patriarchal traditions that discriminate against women. After the genocide in Rwanda, for example, inheritance laws barred surviving women and girls from accessing the property of their dead male family members unless they had been explicitly named as beneficiaries. As a result, thousands were left with no legal claim to their homes and land.[67] Such impoverished women, returning to their communities without family or resources, are more likely to be caught up in the sex trade.

Ironically, and sadly, women and girls who experienced sexual violence during conflict are probably the most vulnerable of all to further exploitation in post-conflict settings. Some rape victims may be rejected

"Armed conflicts ... increasingly serve as vectors for the HIV/AIDS pandemic, which follows closely on the heels of armed troops and in the corridors of conflict."

by their families and communities for having "lost their value."[68] In Burundi, women who had been raped told researchers in 2003 that "they had been mocked, humiliated and rejected by women relatives, classmates, friends and neighbours because of the abuse they had suffered."[69] Raped women may be abandoned by husbands who fear contracting HIV, or who simply cannot tolerate the shadow of "dishonour" they believe their raped wives have cast across them. Without prospects for the future, prostitution may seem the only viable option to these women.

For other women and girls, their histories of victimisation may dull them to the dangers of entering the sex trade. One young girl in Sierra Leone who previously had been abducted by rebels voluntarily became a prostitute after she was released by her captors. She reportedly "considered herself fortunate that she was now being paid."[70] In

Rwanda, an HIV-positive woman in Kigali spoke of her sister's resignation: "After the war, we saw our family decimated ... my little sister for whom I care is a pseudo-prostitute because she has no money. She says that she will continue this lifestyle even if she becomes HIV-positive. She says she looks at my health degrading and insists that she wants to taste life before she dies."[71] Disregard for one's own wellbeing is only one of the many potential devastating effects of sexual violence on its survivors.

The impact on the survivor

Sexual violence against women in war and its aftermath can have almost inestimable short and long-term negative health consequences. As a result of the systematic and exceptionally violent gang rape of thousands of Congolese women and girls, doctors in the DRC are now classifying vaginal destruction as a crime of combat. Many of the victims suffer from traumatic fistula — tissue tears in the vagina, bladder and rectum.[72] Additional long-term medical complications for survivors may include uterine prolapse (the descent of the uterus into the vagina or beyond) and other serious injuries to the reproductive system, such as infertility, or complications associated with miscarriages and self-induced abortions.[73] Rape victims are also at high risk for sexually transmitted infections (STIs). Health clinics in Monrovia, Liberia, reported in 2003 that all female patients — most of whom said they had been raped by former government soldiers or armed opposition — tested positive for at least one sexually transmitted infection.[74] Untreated STIs can cause infertility — a dire consequence for women and girls in cultures where their value is linked to reproduction. STIs also increase the risk of HIV transmission.

HIV/AIDS is among the most devastating physical health consequences for survivors of sexual violence — as evidenced by the continued suffering of women in Rwanda. In a study of over 1,000 genocide widows undertaken in the year 2000, 67 percent of rape survivors were HIV-positive. In the same year, the United Nations Secretary-General concluded, "Armed conflicts ... increasingly serve as vectors for the HIV/AIDS pandemic, which follows closely on the heels of armed troops and in the corridors of conflict."[75] Despite the level of recognition of the urgency of the problem of HIV/AIDS in war, insufficient resources have been dedicated to addressing the issue. In Rwanda, as elsewhere, treatment for rape victims infected with HIV has been characterised as "too little, too late."[76] The story of one HIV-

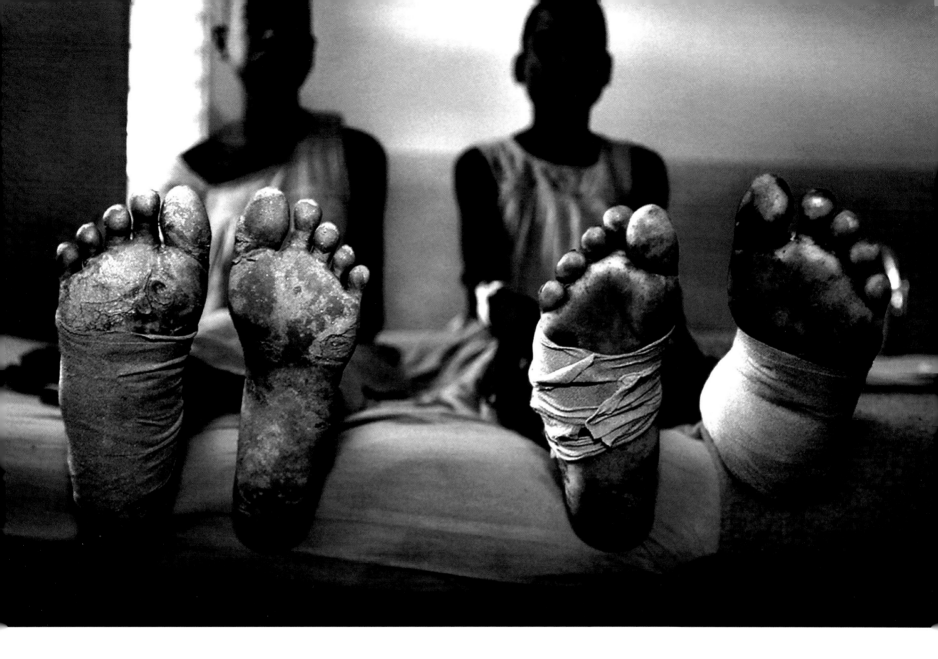

Recently liberated girls, who were forced to work as porters and domestic "slaves" for the Lord's Resistance Army in northern Uganda, await treatment for their injured feet in Kitgum at St Joseph's Hospital. They are among the tens of thousands of children who have been — and continue to be — abducted and made to serve the rebels. During the two-decade-long conflict, young girls and women have been vulnerable to physical and sexual abuse, not only from the rebels but also from government soldiers.

Image: Sven Torfinn/OCHA

In 2002, this woman fell victim to the Revolutionary United Front (RUF) rebel forces. In both Sierra Leone and neighbouring Liberia, the RUF amputated civilians' arms and hands to intimidate communities and spread terror. Despite the peace in the region today, thousands of men, women and children live with the irreparable reminders of these brutal tactics.

Image: Brent Stirton

positive victim of the genocide illustrates the tragic consequences:

"Since I learned I was infected [in 1999], my husband said he couldn't live with me. He divorced me and left me with three children, so now I don't know how to pay for food, rent, school and so on. I have no family left. My six-year-old has many health problems, and she must have HIV.

"I regret that I'm alive because I've lost my lust for life. We survivors are broken-hearted. We live in a situation which overwhelms us. Our wounds become deeper every day. We are constantly in mourning."

She should be on antiretrovirals, but there isn't the money. Since I was married after the war, it is difficult for me to access help from the Genocide Survivor's Fund. My greatest worry is what will happen to my children if I die. I want to get sponsors for them, so at least I can die in peace."[77]

The challenges of meeting the myriad health needs of survivors of war-related sexual assault are complicated by the absence of adequate facilities and trained staff in many war-torn settings. In research conducted in post-conflict Timor Leste and Kosovo, and among internally displaced women in Colombia, over two-thirds of women interviewed reported that reproductive-health services were difficult to access.[78] Even where services do exist, they may not be free — as is the case in many countries in Africa, where state-run health centres operate on a cost-recovery basis. Moreover, many health clinics are constructed with open waiting areas where women and girls may be expected to disclose their reasons for seeking care; in the absence of confidentiality, they are likely to conceal their victimisation. Health workers' beliefs that it is their responsibility to "prove or disprove" rape is also a limiting factor in quality of care. In some settings, a woman seeking medical treatment may be required first to report her case to the police in order to get a medical referral. This prerequisite, in turn, may expose women to further violence.

Rape victims in Darfur, for example, have been arrested for "illegal" pregnancies (occurring outside the context of marriage). One 16-year-old Sudanese girl, who had already suffered the rejection of her family and fiancé, endured additional abuse at the hands of police:

"When I was eight months pregnant from the rape, the police came to my hut and forced me with their guns to go to the police station. They asked me questions, so I told them that I had been raped. They told me that as I was not married, I will deliver this baby illegally. They beat me with a whip on the chest and back and put me in jail. There were other women in jail who had the same story. During the day, we had to walk to the well four times a day to get the policemen water, clean and cook for them. At night, I was in a small cell with 23 other women. I had no other food than what I could find during my work during the day. And the only water was what I drank at the well. I stayed 10 days in jail and now I have to pay the fine — 20,000 Sudanese dinar [$65] they asked me. My child is now two months old."[79]

For those who are subject to discrimination by family and community, and who also do not receive basic psychological support, the emotional effects of their violation may be as debilitating as any physical injuries. Many rape survivors in Rwanda reportedly "still live under a constant shadow of pain or discomfort which reduces their capacity to work, look after and provide for their families."[80] One such survivor, who was gang raped and beaten unconscious during the genocide, woke up only to witness the killing of people all around her. Ten years later, she says:

"I regret that I didn't die that day. Those men and women who died are now at peace whereas I am still here to suffer even more. I'm handicapped in the true sense of the word. I don't know how to explain it. I regret that I'm alive because I've lost my lust for life. We survivors are broken-hearted. We live in a situation which overwhelms us. Our wounds become deeper every day. We are constantly in mourning."[81]

The implications of such testimony make clear the fact that programming to assist survivors is imperative to any lasting efforts at reconstructing the lives and livelihoods of individuals, families and communities in the wake of armed conflict. In most conflict-affected settings, however, human rights and humanitarian activists are still fighting to ensure that the most basic services are accessible. The ultimate goal — putting an end to the epidemic of sexual violence against women and girls during war — seems an even more distant aspiration than developing adequate response services.

Assisting and protecting survivors

International humanitarian initiatives aimed at addressing violence against women in refugee, internally displaced and post-conflict settings are relatively new. Most have been introduced only in the last 10 years. Particularly during the late 1990s, a number of relatively small-scale but nonetheless vital projects were implemented in various sites around the world. The lessons learned from these efforts gave rise to a theoretical model, currently promoted by UNHCR and others, that recognises the importance of integrating prevention and response programming within and across service-delivery sectors, specifically in the areas of health, social welfare, security and justice.[82] In other words, survivors must have access to medical care as well as psychosocial assistance; they should be able to rely on the protection of the police, peacekeepers and local military; and they are entitled to legal assistance should they choose to prosecute those who perpetrate violence against them. Addressing sexual violence also requires national education and sensitisation — at the family and community level and at the level of service provision — so that doctors, lawyers, judges and police are able to respond to survivors efficiently, effectively and supportively. It further requires advocating for improved legislation to protect women and girls, as well as policies that support gender equity and equality.

While the broad outline of roles and responsibilities within this "multisectoral model" provides a general framework for addressing violence against women, an assessment undertaken in 2001 concluded that the implementation of the model was weak in virtually every conflict-affected setting around the world.[83] Foremost among the

...the last decade has produced significant advances in international standards and mechanisms of accountability for those who commit sexual violence.

limitations to establishing multisectoral programming was the failure — at both the international and national levels — to prioritise violence against women as a major health and human rights concern. The result was a lack of financial, technical and logistical resources necessary to tackle the issue. Many survivors, the 2001 assessment observed, were not receiving the assistance they needed and deserved, nor was sufficient attention being given to the prevention of violence. The outcomes of an independent experts' investigation spearheaded by the United Nations Development Fund for Women the following year echoed these findings in their conclusion "that the standards of protection for women affected by conflict are glaring in their inadequacy, as is the international response."[84]

These inadequacies persist even today. However, the number of field-based initiatives addressing the issue of sexual violence against women and girls continues to grow, even against a wearisome backdrop of

limited funding. Methodologies are being refined by many humanitarian organizations to try to extend and improve services for survivors, as well as to build the capacity of local agencies to take on the issue. Standardised procedures for medical management of rape are being adopted in an increasing number of settings. Training modules have been developed to build local capacity to meet the psychosocial needs of survivors. Efforts are being made, most evidently in post-conflict settings but also in some refugee settings, to support legal reforms that would provide greater protection against multiple types of gender-based violence against women and girls.

Widespread community-based education aimed at changing attitudes and behaviours that promote sexual and other forms of violence against women has been carried out in a number of settings. Research on the nature and scope of the problem has also multiplied in recent years, and is bringing pressure to bear on international actors as well as on states to take more aggressive measures to address violence against women in conflict and its aftermath.

In addition, several high-level international initiatives are currently underway to promote more coordinated and comprehensive action by humanitarian aid organizations. New guidelines issued by a task force of the United Nations Inter Agency Standing Committee (IASC) provide detailed recommendations for the minimum response required to address sexual violence in emergencies and hold all humanitarian actors responsible for tackling the issue in their respective areas of operation. The IASC released a statement in January 2005 reconfirming their commitment to "urgent and concerted action aimed at preventing gender-based violence, including in particular sexual violence, ensuring appropriate care and follow-up for victims/survivors, and working towards holding perpetrators accountable."[85]

To this end, a global initiative to "stop rape in war" is being developed collaboratively by United Nations entities and nongovernmental organizations. The two major pillars of the initiative include conducting advocacy at the international, regional, and local levels, and strengthening programming efforts among those currently engaged in addressing the issue of sexual violence in conflict. One of the notable outcomes of the proposed initiative is to reduce the prevalence of rape in target countries by at least 50 percent by 2007. Such ambitions will require a "quantum shift" in approaches to sexual violence in war, most especially in terms of prioritising all efforts to end the levels of impunity

Girls chat together in the dormitory of the Gusco Rehabilitation Centre in northern Uganda. Most of the former abductees at the facility were virtual slaves to the rebel Lord's Resistance Army (LRA) and forced into sexual relationships with its soldiers. "Cecilia" (not pictured here), aged 20, was abducted from a secondary school in Pader when she was 15 and spent five years in captivity. She is now at a rehabilitation centre in Kitgum.

"I was given to John Okech, one of [LRA leader Joseph] Kony's senior commanders. I was his fourth wife. He soon brought in four other young girls. They were to become his wives when they were slightly older. In the meantime, they were told to baby-sit for his other wives. When you are given a commander as your husband, you're expected to produce food. You're also given a gun and expected to fight. I was often picked to go out on patrols.

"I became pregnant in early 2002, when Kony predicted an attack from the UPDF [United People's Defence Forces] on our bases in Sudan. By June, our whole group sneaked back into Uganda and hid in the Imatong mountains. This was the most difficult time for captives. My husband was part of the attack on Anaka [a village in Gulu district]. He was shot in the chest by the UPDF. He died a few days later. I gave birth to a baby boy, but he died after a month.

"I was released after my husband died. I only returned from the bush a few days ago. I'm still haunted by frightful dreams. I dream only that I'm still in the bush. I hear children crying. I dream that we are being attacked, or fighting, walking for days in the hot desert without food or water. I'm happy to be back, but I have no hope of returning to school. I heard that my entire family was displaced. They are scattered in camps in the district."

[Excerpted from *"When the sun sets, we start to worry …" An account of life in northern Uganda* published by the United Nations Office for the Coordination of Humanitarian Affairs (OCHA)/Integrated Regional Information Networks (IRIN) in 2003.]
Image: Sven Torfinn/OCHA

Due to the unending insecurity in northern Uganda, over 1.6 million people currently are living in over 200 camps for internally displaced persons (IDPs). Residents at the camps report that IDP life has had a disastrous effect on their society. Signs of the social breakdown include high levels of promiscuity, substance abuse, unprotected sex and increased numbers of child mothers. As people stay longer and longer in the camps, what is left of their dignity is gradually eroded. Disrespected by the traumatised youth, forced to look on, powerless, as their society is turned inside out by violence and fear, some of the older adults become mentally ill, according to camp leaders.

For households headed by women, the difficulties are heightened. One woman, "Risper", said that residents who sleep in their huts in the camp at Kitgum face great danger. Risper, whose husband died in 2003 of an AIDS-related illness, is raising her three children on her own. The youngest is two years old and seriously ill. Risper could not find anyone to help her build her hut. "Everybody wants money," she said. While it normally would have taken one day to finish, Risper has been working for days. "I am not strong enough to finish the work quickly," she said. "I also have other responsibilities." After working on the house, she had to cook the children their sole meal of the day. The only ingredients she had at hand were a cup of sorghum flour and some green vegetables. "We will eat and then find a place to sleep," she said. "We don't sleep in our huts."

that have given rise to the "shocking scale and stubborn persistence" of the violence.[86]

The final frontier: ending impunity

Along with an increase in field-based programming, the last decade has produced significant advances in international standards and mechanisms of accountability for those who commit sexual violence. International criminal tribunals for Rwanda and the former Yugoslavia have prosecuted sexual violence as crimes of genocide, torture, crimes against humanity and as war crimes. The Rome Statute of the recently established International Criminal Court (ICC) has enumerated rape, sexual slavery and trafficking, enforced prostitution, forced pregnancy, enforced sterilisation and other forms of sexual violence and persecution as crimes against humanity and as war crimes. The ICC is initiating investigation into cases from several conflict-affected countries.

Another groundbreaking advance was the United Nations Security Council's adoption of Resolution 1325 in 2000, which specifically "calls upon all parties to armed conflict to take special measures to protect women and girls from gender-based violence, particularly rape and other forms of sexual abuse, and all other forms of violence in situations of armed conflict."[87] Since that time, the United Nations Secretary-General has submitted two reports to the United Nations Security Council on the implementation of Resolution 1325. While these reports concede that much remains to be done, especially in terms of holding states accountable for the actions of fighting forces and in increasing the level of participation of women in all stages of peace-building, they also note that major advances have been made in introducing codes of conduct that establish "zero tolerance" for all United Nations personnel, including peacekeepers, who might sexually exploit those they are meant to serve. Since these codes of conduct were implemented, action has been taken against offenders in a number of countries, such as the DRC, where an inquiry into allegations of sexual exploitation committed by over 100 peacekeepers is underway.

However, grave problems with impunity persist in virtually every conflict-affected setting around the globe. International tribunals can only prosecute a fraction of cases, and many national governments do not have the resources or the commitment to pursue the perpetrators of sexual crimes against women. In some cases national jurisdiction does not extend to foreign fighting forces who commit abuses within their territory. In others, governments do little to support victims in coming forward. Evidentiary requirements often mean that the burden of proof lies with the victim. Some must pay for legal assistance. Where forensic evidence is required, healthcare providers must be able to collect it in a timely manner and be prepared to present that evidence at a trial. Police or relevant security forces must be trained to investigate and appropriately document their findings. The frustrating reality for many survivors of sexual crimes in conflict-affected settings around the world is that there are no systems to ensure basic protection to survivors, let alone access to justice.

Such impunity both reflects and reinforces the widespread cultural norms that acquiesce to the inevitability of violence against women and girls whether in times of peace or of war. And it is these norms that must be targeted aggressively in order to ensure reductions in levels of abuse: "In a world where sex crimes are too often regarded as misdemeanours during times of law and order, surely rape will not be perceived as a high crime during war, when all the rules of human interaction are turned on

...grave problems with impunity persist in virtually every conflict-affected setting around the globe. International tribunals can only prosecute a fraction of cases, and many national governments do not have the resources or the commitment to pursue sexual crimes against women.

their heads, and heinous acts regularly earn their perpetrators commendation. ... What matters most is that we combine the new acknowledgement of rape's role in war with a further recognition: humankind's level of tolerance for sexual violence is not established by international tribunals after war. That baseline is established by societies, in times of peace. The rules of war can never really change as long as violent aggression against women is tolerated in everyday life."[88]

In a world where thousands of women and girls suffer sexual violence committed with impunity in the context of conflict, the message needs to be made clear: A single rape constitutes a war crime. n

"Helena" is 25 years old and the victim of rape by a soldier in Sake, Democratic Republic of Congo. Her daughter "Fara", the child of the rape, is two-and-a-half years old.

"I was sent to buy salt one night and was grabbed by a group of soldiers hanging around by the market. They dragged me to a disused house nearby, where they regularly raped people they had taken from the market. There were 10 men, one of whom raped me. He pushed me to the floor and beat me, helped by the others. I told the man that I was a child and didn't want to do such things, but he just carried on. I felt so much pain in my stomach. I was taken by force to Kimbumba, 30 kilometres from Goma, where he kept me for a week until he was sent to war. I was left there, pregnant with his child. My parents had thought I'd disappeared so they welcomed me back into the home when I returned. But I have many problems: I rely on my mother for food, but sometimes we don't eat at all. I feel rejected by society because of what happened."

Images: Georgina Cranston/IRIN

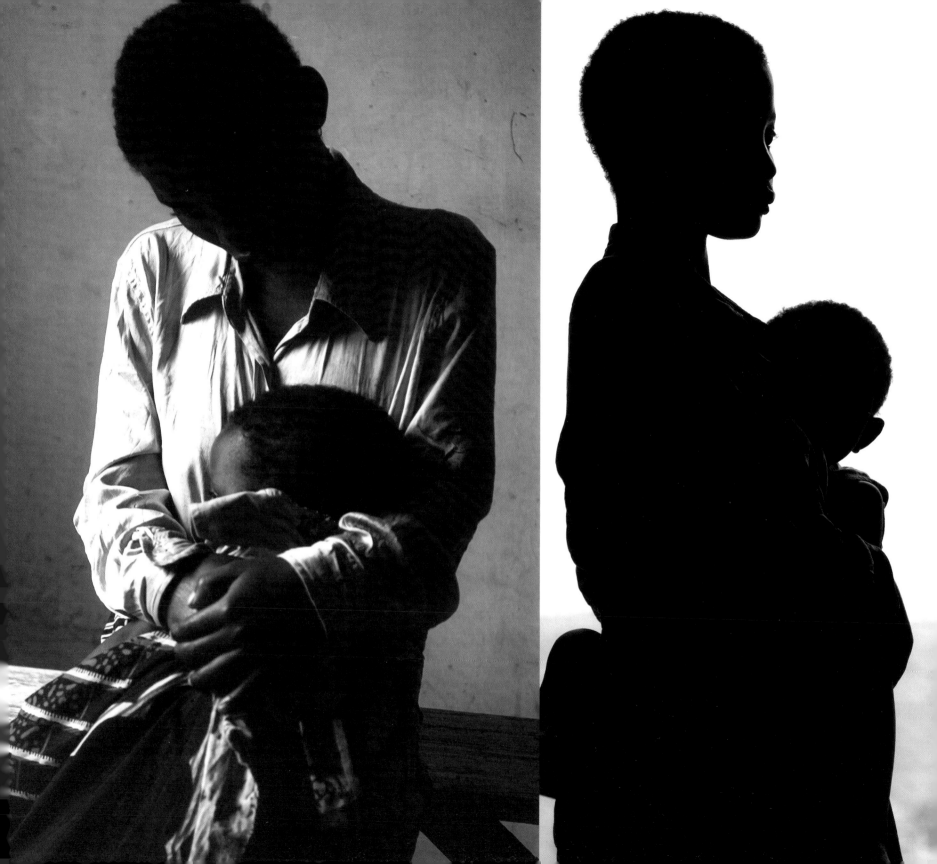

"Elizabeth" and her four-year-old daughter were brutally raped and beaten by six militiamen near their home in Masisi, Democratic Republic of Congo. Her daughter was carried away by their attackers, and the baby son that Elizabeth was carrying on her back throughout the assault subsequently died. Through counselling provided by Doctors On Call Services (DOCS), Elizabeth has been able to begin the healing process.

"I am now ready to talk about my story. Before I was raped, both my parents were killed in the war, as were many of my relatives. In fact, my three sisters are widows because their husbands were all killed.

"One morning in November 2004 I went to look for food in the field with two of my children. My four-year-old daughter and I were carrying baskets, but my son was just a baby so I had him on my back. We were going to our *shamba* [fruit and vegetable garden] 15 kilometres away to look for bananas, plaintain and pineapple, when the militiamen appeared in front of and behind us. The six men pushed us from the path to the nearest field and tied my daughter's and my arms behind our backs. They started to beat us with their guns, and also beat and kicked my baby. I still suffer from intense pain now, even if I carry the smallest bucket.

"As they were beating me, I fell to the ground with my baby still on my back. It was then that they took off my skirt and began raping me, with my baby on my back throughout. It was impossible to resist — we couldn't even make any noise. I was raped by three men and my daughter was raped by the other three at the same time, lying next to me on the ground. While one raped each of us, the other two would point their guns and hold us down with their feet. When one finished, the next would start. I felt totally useless — there was no way to shout as they would have killed us. When it was over, they took my daughter away with them. I have not seen her since.

"I had such terrible pains in my stomach, vagina and back that they had left thinking I was dead. I could only crawl, and crawled through the bush for three days. They had taken everything I had, so I was completely naked. I put leaves on my body, and carried my baby, who was very sick. He had been beaten badly and when I fell to the ground I had landed on him. He died a week after the attack.

"Some people passed me in the bush and I sent them to fetch my sister. She took me back to Masisi, where I found that my house had been looted the same day that I was raped. Everything had been taken. My husband, who had married again and was living in Mweso with his new wife, and I had been friends, but after the rape he rejected me entirely.

"Through my sister I met the counsellors [connected to DOCS] who helped me. I was taken to hospital a week after the attack, where they told me that my stomach was damaged. I was unable to walk, so I was sent home, and I am now waiting until I am strong enough to travel to DOCS. They wouldn't let me travel before, as my condition was so bad that they thought I might die on the way. I am getting stronger but my back is still very bad.

"I used to go to our *shamba* every day, but my back was so damaged by the beating and the rape that I can't anymore — I just don't have the strength. I am also too scared to go. Sometimes I have nightmares and can't sleep. At other times I wake up and lose all hope, as I have been dreaming of dying. Support from my community has helped me, as has my faith in God. DOCS came to counsel us — they gave us hope and encouraged us to continue living.

"DOCS has also given me a goat, beans and a hoe. I am so happy — it proves to me that I am loved. I live with my six children and had to beg for food as before today I didn't have the materials for working. We are so poor, my children can't go to school. But I am going to rear the goat and grow the beans for food."

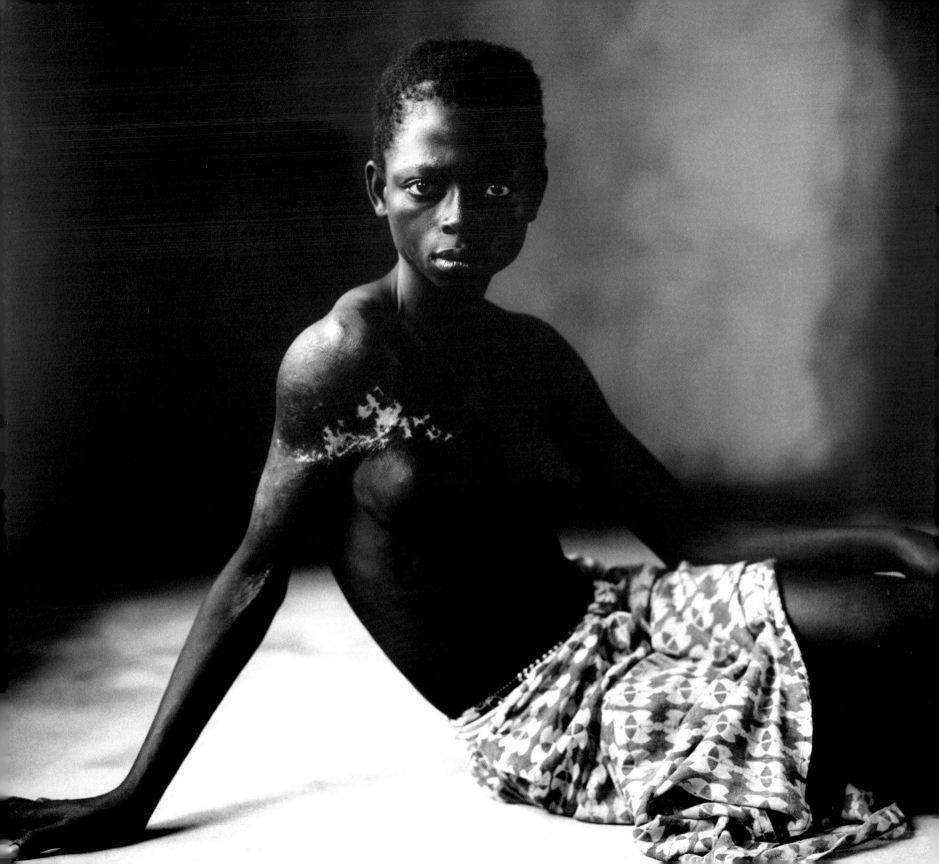

A young former "bush wife" in Sierra Leone, who was abducted from her family at age 10 by rebels from the Revolutionary United Front. After a killing spree that decimated most of her village, the rebels took her away with them to work as a cook, porter and sex slave. When she tried to escape, the rebels poured acid over her arm and breast as a warning to other abductees. After two years in captivity, she was able to escape. She recently joined a small self-help group of female torture victims. Sierra Leone has only one psychologist, and there are thousands of female victims of sexual abuse and torture — who have no choice but to help themselves.

Image: Brent Stirton

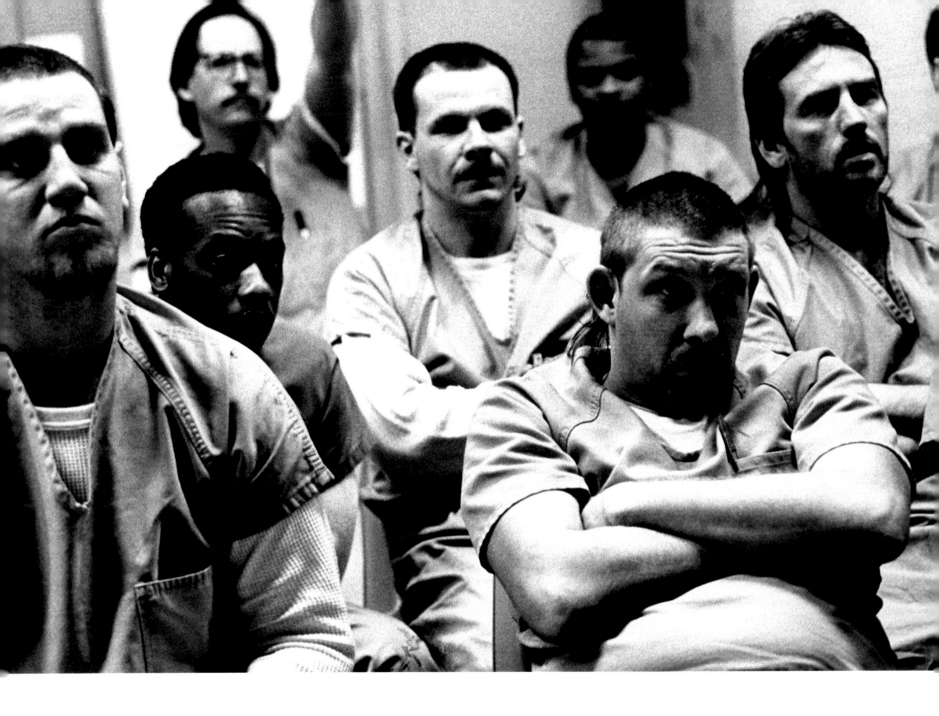

Men who have been convicted of domestic violence and stalking attend "diversion" sessions at a prison in the United States as part of efforts to help them change their behaviour. Many perpetrators of domestic violence never serve time in jail or have their crimes exposed or reported.

Image: Donna Ferrato/Network Photographers

perpetrators

"The ratio of male to female offenders for all types of crime has been narrowing steadily during the last few decades. But the fact remains that, today, about 80 percent of crimes against property are committed by men, as are 95 percent of crimes involving violence."[1] By contrast, any reflection upon the level and nature of female crime is a salutary experience for men, who would be forced to conclude that if men behaved like women the courts and prisons would be virtually empty.

The prevalence of male perpetration

The overwhelming majority of violence against women and girls is committed every day and in every nation by men. Where sexual violence and exploitation takes place against men and/or boys, the perpetrators are, again, overwhelmingly male. In categories where violence is embedded in tradition, such as child marriage, female genital mutilation and "honour" crimes, women may also play an active role.

Despite the progress that has been made to introduce legal and social reforms to address gender inequality, violence against women and girls continues. Evidence suggests, in fact, that violations such as trafficking, rape, child abuse, child prostitution and pornography are on the rise.[2] The majority of studies of gender-based violence echo the findings of two psychologists whose research led them to conclude, "Most sexual offenders are men. Men commit most of the aberrant and deviant sexual behaviours such as rape, child molestation and exhibitionism. ... " Furthermore, and more relevantly, when females are involved in aberrant or illegal sexual behaviour, coercion and violence is less commonly employed.[3]

Even though most acts of violence are committed by men — and studies confirm that men have a higher propensity for violent behaviour than women   not all men behave violently. Are men genetically motivated, or hard-wired, in a significantly different way than women? Or does society teach the sexes to act the way they do?

The nature / nurture polarity

Most researchers reject the notion that biology can be blamed for violent behaviour. Male violence, they say, is not genetically based but is instead perpetuated by a model of masculinity that permits and even encourages men to be aggressive. "Men's monopoly of violence stems from lifelong training in sexist models of masculinity."[4] Anthropological research shows that domestic violence is virtually nonexistent in some societies, and therefore not an inevitable human condition.[5]

Generally, the "nurture" position rejects the idea that men have a natural propensity to violence or that men have "uncontrollable" violent and sexual urges. In the case of intimate-partner abuse, for example, observers point out that men are able to control themselves in settings where the social or professional cost of their behaviour would be too high, but are unwilling to exercise the same restraint when they are behind closed doors.

Those advancing this perspective challenge apologists for male violence, who use biological arguments or the "psychopathological model" for male sexual violence to explain men's behaviour. Instead, they insist that these men are not "sick" or pathological and are responsible for their actions, behaving reprehensibly, with free, conscious choice.[6]

The counterargument to this opinion — which is regularly reinforced and perpetuated via popular culture and religious dogma — claims that men are captive to their libidos. This view maintains that the historic and global evidence of male's natural aggression and the biological

Violence is also a learned behaviour that may be passed down the generations. "The highest risk marker for a man to use violence against his wife and child is early exposure to violence in his childhood home."

imperative cannot be ignored. While socialisation may play an important role in how people behave in different societies and at different points in history, the "nature" position argues that sexual violence is too widespread and too overwhelmingly perpetrated by males to suggest that men and women are not motivated and driven by different forces. These arguments appear to echo 19th-century pseudo-medical claims promoted by some scientists that men were a breed apart and slaves to uncontrollable testosterone, where male promiscuity is seen as a critical vestige of evolutionary forces conferring "selective advantage" on men who impregnate multiple partners.

Other theorists, however, are situated between the two poles of "nature" and "nurture". They acknowledge a degree of "natural male inclination", which in combination with repeated negative socialisation reinforces violent characteristics.[7] In patriarchal societies, a significant manifestation of male aggression is man's perpetration of sexual coercion and violence against women.

Popular perceptions

Irrespective of this debate, there is a virtually universal *de facto* acceptance amongst people and communities worldwide that men and women have different natures and different roles to play. Whatever the origin of male violence, most people are caught up in their societies and the times they live, and are products of cultural influences. Women may internalise stereotypical models of male and female behaviour as much as men and, as a result, may play a strong part in the maintenance of these stereotypes.

In many countries, gender roles are deeply entrenched and reinforced by cultural norms, to such an extent that questioning the status quo involves risk.[8] Even in countries that are seemingly less bound by tradition, where equal rights are codified in law and widely accepted, these stereotypes still dominate the popular mindset.

The United States and Australia are examples of industrialised countries where sexual stereotyping and violence-supporting attitudes remain entrenched among the majority. High incidents of rape, domestic abuse and child abuse in these countries are thought to be linked to a general acceptance of these stereotypes. One study recently estimated that during a 12-month period in the United States, more than 302,000 women and almost 93,000 men experienced a completed or attempted rape.[9] In a 1995 study in Australia, 37 percent of the male participants disagreed with the statement that "Women rarely make false claims of rape." One in six respondents to the survey agreed that "Women who are raped often ask for it."[10] Rape is, of course, only an indirect indicator of such beliefs or stereotypes.

Psychological research demonstrates strong evidence that violence is a learned behaviour that may be passed down the generations. "The highest risk marker for a man to use violence against his wife and child is early exposure to violence in his childhood home."[11] A negative finding when one considers the current number of boys witnessing their fathers' violent behaviour, but also one that offers hope, perhaps, that nonviolence can be similarly learned.

Belgian child killer and rapist Marc Dutroux throws himself to the ground while pretending to have a heart attack on the way to his first court appearance in October 2002. A doctor who was called to the scene proclaimed him fit for trial. Dutroux was arrested in August 1996 for the kidnapping and rape of six young girls and the murder of two of them. His highly publicised case and disturbing trial shook the Belgian establishment. Dutroux was given a life sentence.

Image: Jorgen Hildebrandt/Panos

Two brothers, aged 12 and 13, wash the ink off their hands after being fingerprinted by police in Cape Town, South Africa. The brothers and their 11-year-old friend were taken in by the Police Child Protection Unit after being identified as the sexual assailants of a three-year-old boy who lived near them. The boys allegedly forced the younger child to perform oral sex on them and then did the same to him.

Image: Mariella Furrer

A man is led away after being found guilty of stabbing his wife to death in a savage example of domestic violence in the United States. He stabbed her 17 times in front of their two children and other adult witnesses.

Image: Donna Ferrato/Network Photographers

Making man myths

Cross-cultural studies reveal that in most communities simple anatomical maleness is not enough to be a man. Real manhood lies elsewhere and is often a "precarious or artificial state that boys must win against powerful odds."[12] Does this "masculine mystique" encourage toughness, dominance and extreme competitiveness at the expense of honest emotion, empathy and communication?[13]

Violence against women is more predominant in cultures where the idea of manhood is linked to entitlement to power or male honour.[14] Historically, wars have been intensely masculine endeavours and the majority of all warriors, soldiers, generals, admirals, police, militias and prison wardens are and have been men. In addition, bureaucrats, politicians and those who monopolise the systems of collective or institutional violence throughout the world are men.

As boys become men within these societies, attributes of action, decisiveness, aggression and supremacy are prized and closely associated with "manhood". These qualities, however fallacious, are perpetuated and considered the "natural" order and the preserve of masculinity. The expression of these characteristics in different societies can range from subtle to overt. Socialisation of this kind negatively impacts both women and men. A recent publication from Brazil called *Dying to Be Men* — based on studies of violent male behaviour in the United States, the Caribbean, Brazil and Nigeria — suggests that because young men are losing their lives in their attempts to embody certain models of masculinity, they are literally "dying to be men".

In many non-Western societies, strict social rules that perpetuate the notion of the dominant male also deny women access to public life, private property, or even joint custody of their children. A woman is the protected possession of a man — his housekeeper, cook, monogamous sex partner and mother of his children. Even in countries that are considered more advanced in terms of democracy and representation — those with gender-sensitive legislation and significant structural equality between the sexes — violence against women continues. Many observers blame the influence of modern media, in particular television, films and advertising, for both subtly and explicitly perpetuating patriarchal role models for men and women.[15]

Myriam Miedzian's *Boys Will Be Boys: Breaking the Link Between Masculinity and Violence* examines how and why males are increasingly resorting to violence and what society can do about it. "As long as male behaviour is taken to be the norm," she writes, "there can be no serious questioning of male traits and behaviour. A norm is by definition a standard of judging; it is not itself subject to judgement."[16]

Violence and sexual abuse in marriage

In South Africa, researchers for the Medical Research Council estimated in 2004 that male partners kill their girlfriends or spouses at the rate of one every six hours — the highest mortality rate for domestic violence ever recorded, they claim. According to a United Nations report that same year, domestic violence accounted for more than 60 percent of murder cases in court in Harare, Zimbabwe. In Zambia, a recent study found that nearly half the women surveyed had been beaten by a male partner.[17]

Outside Africa and throughout the world, similar statistics for domestic abuse are staggering, with only a small minority of communities apparently free of this violence. "For God's sake!" exploded one Nigerian when questioned about his wife-beating. "You are head of the home as the man — you must have a home submissive to you."[18]

A high number of women who report domestic violence also report rape within their relationship. "My sex life in marriage has been dominated by

> **"As long as male behaviour is taken to be the norm, there can be no serious questioning of male traits and behaviour. A norm is by definition a standard of judging; it is not itself subject to judgement."**

rape, rape, rape — and nothing to do with love," concluded one woman from Latin America, echoing similar claims by women interviewed in different contexts around the world.[19]

All too often sex in marriage is not a mutually pleasurable event but a brutal service exacted by force, threat or social convention.

According to one expert on domestic violence, "At an individual level, some men are more likely to sexually assault women: men who have hostile and negative sexual attitudes towards women, who identify with traditional images of masculinity and male gender role privilege, who believe in rape stereotypes, and who see violence as manly and desirable. … Men with more traditional, rigid and misogynistic gender-role attitudes are more likely to practise marital violence."[20]

The perpetrators of rape within marriage are not readily characterised as any particular group. Using force in marriage to gain sexual access is a cross-cultural and cross-societal phenomenon that is not the monopoly of any economic or social class. In many cases those who are accused or — in isolated instances — convicted of rape in marriage may not conform to popular notions of what a rapist is. Perpetrators of rape in cultures that expect and condone the brutal deflowering of a young bride (sometimes with knives) may be committing a severe assault and rights abuse, but they would be surprised to be labelled a rapist, which illustrates the complexity of dealing with these issues on a global basis.

There are common myths about perpetrators of domestic violence. These include the notion that domestic violence is rare or that perpetrators are somehow "abnormal" men who cannot control their anger. In reality, most men who beat their wives do not exhibit violent or antisocial traits outside the home. The idea that perpetrators are driven to violence by the behaviour of their partners is also a myth, as perpetrators are often unaffected by their partners' efforts to change or avoid so-called "provocative" behaviour. The notion that poverty causes violence is a myth as well: Poverty can be a contributing factor to domestic abuse, but intimate-partner violence exists at every socioeconomic level.[21]

Whatever the myths may be, it is indisputable that domestic violence has especially frightening and tragic implications for victims, who are locked socially, economically and often emotionally into the abusing relationship and share a home with their abuser. In many countries, the

In many countries, the environment outside the home is fiercely unwelcoming to women who leave or divorce violent husbands, seek refuge or protective custody away from their partners, or seek legal redress.

environment outside the home is fiercely unwelcoming to women who leave or divorce violent husbands, seek refuge or protective custody away from their partners, or seek legal redress. In Nigeria, where there are over 130 million people and wife battering is widespread, there are only two shelters for battered women.[22]

Law enforcement in many countries will not intervene in what is still regarded as a domestic quarrel, despite evidence indicating that without intervention (legal or social) abusers are unlikely to seek rehabilitation or stop their battering behaviour. In most cases law enforcement and the judiciary are run entirely by men, who are part of the patriarchal society

that tacitly or overtly perpetuates attitudes that tolerate beating women. Numerous reports from Latin America, the Middle East and Central and South Asia cite examples where law enforcement officials have delivered wives who had been beaten back to the very families and perpetrators from whom they sought refuge.

Training programmes and special units of law enforcement to assist victims of domestic violence have been developed only recently in a select number of countries. It was originally believed that if a victim of domestic violence could leave the abusive relationship the violence would stop, but now it is widely accepted that leaving does not guarantee an end to the abuse. In fact, separation is often the riskiest time for women, as many abusive men continue to harass, stalk and harm their victims long after the separation, sometimes resulting in murder. In one United States study, 70 percent of the reported injuries from domestic violence occurred after a couple separated.[23]

Many working in the field maintain that the most effective way to stop perpetrators abusing their partners is arrest and incarceration. Legally and socially, however, societies still struggle with the complexities of domestic violence, the gravity of the crime and their overall commitment to tackling it.

Great strides have been made in terms of highlighting the scale and scope of intimate-partner violence over the last two decades. While the problem remains great, there is some evidence of progress, particularly in settings where women's rights and choices have increased and they have gained more economic independence. But in more traditional societies, where a woman is secondary to the male head of the house and where male domination or patriarchy is more overt, the overwhelming majority of violence against women goes unreported, forcing women to suffer in silence. Documenting the prevalence of male violence against women in the home in more traditional cultures warrants further research.

In recent years, much has been made of certain studies indicating that men are also victims of domestic abuse where the perpetrators are women. Some suggest that there is a degree of "gender symmetry" in domestic violence — that women abuse at their partners at similar rates as men — but a closer look at the methodology used in these studies casts doubts over the veracity of these claims. Opposing studies show that only 5 percent of domestic violence cases involve female

A Roman Catholic priest in Cape Town, South Africa, hangs his head as police search his home. He was arrested in July 2005 after police received reports from several men alleging that he had abused them when they were boys. In 2002, a child-abuse scandal implicating Catholic priests affected nearly every diocese in the United States, and more than 200 priests were removed from their ministries. According to surveys, some of the abusive priests defended themselves by asserting that mutual masturbation, fellatio or touching children's bodies, while sinful, did not violate their vow of celibacy.

Image: Mariella Furrer

Bosnian Serb rapist Dragoljub Kunarac shocked the United Nations International War Crimes Tribunal for the former Yugoslavia (ICTY) in his initial court appearance by pleading guilty in 1998 to raping Muslim women. During the Balkans conflict, there was widespread and systematic use of rape by all belligerents — in particular the Serbian forces. During the ICTY trials, rape, which was closely associated with ethnic cleansing was officially recognised for the first time as a war crime.

Image: Jerry Lampen/AFP

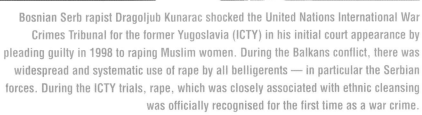

One of the accused cries as she is led from the courthouse in Angers, France, in July 2005 after hearing the verdict in the biggest ever paedophilia trial in French legal history. In total, 65 men and women were accused of the rape and sexual abuse of numerous children — some of them their own — over a period of years. Some of the children were only a few months old. The six principle defendants were accused of organizing the child-abuse network in a poor district of Angers.

Image: Alain Jocard/AFP

perpetrators.[24] An examination of the reality of power relations, access to economic resources and possibilities for separation or divorce indicates that by any standards the violence and vulnerability of men who are abused by female partners is of a different calibre than the pandemic of abuse of women by male partners throughout the world.[25]

A dangerous catalyst

Studies of the link between intimate-partner violence and rape and substance abuse indicate that "a large proportion of incidences of physical and sexual violence involve alcohol or drug use by perpetrator, victim or both."[26] Research has shown that sexually aggressive dates are more likely to drink heavily or use drugs. Other studies mention that while the consumption of alcohol may lower inhibition for some men who are predisposed to sexual aggression, the pharmacological effect of alcohol on physical arousal may actually impede a man's ability to complete a rape.

Numerous testimonies from battered and sexually abused women confirm that alcohol — while not a cause of violence — can be a common catalyst to abuse. Research indicates an association between heavy alcohol consumption and sexual and physical violence against women, but it is unclear, however, how alcohol increases the risk of violence.[27] Drunkenness can provide an excuse for antisocial behaviour, such that men feel they will not be held accountable for their actions. There is evidence that men with alcohol problems tend to be violent more frequently and inflict more serious injuries on their partners.[28]

Dishonouring women and girls

"Pakistani police have arrested five men on charges of kidnapping and gang-raping a woman in the latest of a string of so-called honour crimes. The married woman was attacked because one of her male cousins had an affair with a woman whose father disapproved of the relationship, police said. ... "[29]

Despite popular perceptions, the concept of "honour" as a pivotal force around which family and society are formed is by no means the monopoly of Muslim culture. Research in Latin America, Mediterranean countries, the Middle East, Asia and the Far East, as well northern and sub-Saharan Africa, shows that patriarchal models of honour dominate cultural and social arrangements. The threat to women's basic human rights and personal safety is severe in these environments, where perpetrators of honour-restoring violence neither see themselves as wrongdoers, nor are seen as wrongdoers by their society. In the preceding example from July 2005, the perpetrators were required to carry out the judgement on orders from a village council in a rural area in Pakistan where tribal customs still hold sway.

Honour crimes have been described as a "retrogressive patriarchal tradition".[30] They are based on the idea that a man's honour is predicated largely on his ability to control the behaviour, especially sexual, of his womenfolk. Institutions that foster male domination and sexual segregation have accordingly become fundamental to the social order in such societies.

In a context that would be considered extraordinary outside of these communities, a father, brother or uncle may be the perpetrator of femicide and not consider it a crime or anything other than the right thing to do. "This is my daughter's wedding night and those people are pretending that my daughter is not a virgin," an Algerian father shouts

> "This is my daughter's wedding night and those people are pretending that my daughter is not a virgin. I want you to examine her and clear my honour. I swear if she is not a virgin I will kill her right now."

to doctors at 3 a.m. in a hospital emergency room. "I want you to examine her and clear my honour. I swear if she is not a virgin I will kill her right now."[31] Loss of virginity, or perceived loss of virginity, brings permanent dishonour to an unmarried woman and her family. The only way to cleanse the family honour is to kill the woman.

In these cultures, the police and judiciary display gender bias in favour of men who have killed women or girls for alleged breaches of honour. Where there is legislation, it is often ineffective in prosecutions and frequently regarded as Western or modern/urban by communities that predominantly live according to centuries-old customary law and informal tribal jurisdiction.

Documented cases from Brazil, Palestine, Pakistan, Turkey, Saudi Arabia, Jordan, Morocco, Syria and Lebanon (amongst many other countries) illustrate present-day examples of lenient judgements for wife murdering. This exists on a universal scale and therefore does "not result from religious or cultural factors but from a shared attitude to do with a woman's worth and their proper role in society."[32] In such cases the perpetrator may even be exonerated.

In these contexts what can we say of the perpetrators? Are they individuals guilty of gross human rights abuses and murder or are they part of a culture, a system that is collectively perpetrating these abuses?

The hegemony of patriarchy

While significant progress has been made in the last 20 to 30 years in challenging patriarchal systems in many parts of the world, structures of male dominance are so pervasive in most cultures that many women and men accept them and live out their days without questioning the "norms" under which they live. The inevitable involvement of women in particular forms of gender-based violence is therefore significant and, in some cases, instrumental. This is perhaps most evident where traditional gender roles remain entrenched.

Practices such as sex-selective abortion, female infanticide, child marriage and female genital cutting survive and persist with the direct endorsement and participation of women. Mothers, grandmothers, aunts and sisters all live under the hegemony of a cultural system of codes and practices that stem from male-dominated attitudes towards a woman's worth, her commoditisation, her subjugation and the importance, at any cost, of ensuring a woman's fidelity through the control of her sexuality.

As a result, these practices are often perpetrated and facilitated by women, who, like their male counterparts, do not seek to change their customs. The same is true in societies where crimes related to "honour" continue. It would be erroneous to suggest that women are united against the men of their societies over issues of honour. The extent to which women are implicated and involved as perpetrators of practices which harm their own sex illustrates how slow and complicated any future change will be.

Rape and sexual abuse

Rape is a pandemic of huge proportions that affects millions of people across the globe. The perpetrators are almost exclusively male and the victims predominantly women and girls. Their victims may be infants, adolescents, women in their reproductive years and older women. Men

and boys are also raped in high numbers, usually by heterosexual males. Rape may happen in the context of "dating", in marriage, or as part of gang initiation. Rape is widespread in areas of civil unrest and where the rule of law is weak. Rape and sexual abuse are also rife in protected and "captive" environments such as prisons, refugee and displaced person's camps, the armed services and schools.

Countries of recent notoriety for high numbers of reported rapes are South Africa and the Democratic Republic of Congo, but the rates of rape in India, the United States and many other countries are equally high. Research shows that amongst developed countries the United States has unusually high levels of rape. In 1980 the rate of reported rape in the United States was 18 times higher than the corresponding rate for England and Wales.[33] More recent data from the State Department of the United States in 2000 indicated that a woman is raped in that country every 90 seconds. According to a 2002 study in Ireland, 6.4 percent of the female population reported having been raped.[34]

Cultural definitions of manhood that stress the importance of sexual conquest and potency place women at increased risk of sexual assault. Many rapists do not consider their aggressive or coercive tactics to be

> Traditional practices such as sex-selective abortion, female infanticide, child marriage and female genital cutting survive and persist with the direct endorsement and participation of women.

criminal and often feel justified in forcing a women into having sex. Studies have shown that men do not place as great a value on sexual consent as women.[35]

The act of sexual violence may be motivated by different impulses depending on the rapist and the social or political context in which the violation is performed. Many researchers have concluded, however, that rape is essentially an expression of power rather than an act committed for sexual gratification. They argue that while sexual arousal and even sexual gratification may be a by-product of rape, sex serves as the medium through which perpetrators of rape both demonstrate and exercise control over their victims.

Even when acting according to the same basic impulse, rapists are as varied as those who are raped, and efforts to pin down specific characteristics of rapists are inconclusive. Despite the popular representation of rapists as "sick" or depraved monsters, studies have

Police surround the body of convicted rapist Carlos Pardilla outside a Manila court in the Philippines in June 1999. Pardilla leapt to his death from the fifth floor of the courthouse after being sentenced to death by legal injection for raping his daughter.

Image: Mike Alquinto/AFP

David Potse, age 23, after being convicted in a South African court of raping a nine-month-old baby. Potse's DNA matched samples taken from the victim, and his girlfriend, who witnessed the rape, testified against him. He was given a life sentence for the rape, with an additional 18-year sentence for indecent assault.

Image: Emile Hendricks/AFP

Doctors check for any remaining signs of life in the bodies of two Saudi men and one Kuwaiti man, which hang from the gallows in front of the interior ministry in Kuwait City in 2004. The men were convicted of the rape and murder of a six-year-old girl they had kidnapped in 2002. After taking the child from her home, they drove to a remote desert area, where they raped her and then stabbed her five times in the chest before slitting her throat.

Image: Yasser al-Zayyat/AFP

shown that fewer than 5 percent of men were "psychotic" when they raped.[36] The central assumption in the psychopathological model is that violent male sexual aggression is strange or abnormal, but the prevalence of rape and the range of perpetrators links sexual aggression, instead, to social and environmental variables.

A study of 114 convicted and incarcerated rapists in the United States revealed a range of motivations from the perpetrators' perspective. A number of rapists used sexual violence in revenge against another male and/or as punishment — by abusing another man's woman they punish the man — while others used it as a means of gaining sexual access to unwilling or unavailable women. In one example, a man had an argument with victim's husband. "I grabbed her and started beating the hell out of her. Then I committed the act. I knew what I was doing. I was mad. I could have stopped but I didn't. I did it to get even with her and her husband."[37]

In some cases perpetrators said that rape was just a "bonus" added to burglary or robbery. The rapists found themselves in a position of power and the opportunity presented itself. One man interviewed said, "Rape was a feeling of total dominance. Before the rapes, I would always get a feeling of power and anger. I would degrade women so I could feel there was a person of less worth than me."[38]

Rape also was considered by some to be a recreational activity. The act was described as an adventure and an exciting form of impersonal sex which gave the rapists power over their victims. A common thread in

Organized rape can be used as a tactical device ... to intimidate, to punish individual women and social groups, to destabilise and demoralise communities or to drive unwanted people from their land.

these interviews was the objective of dominance. The analysts of this study concluded, "The pleasure these men derived from raping reveals the extreme to which they objectified women. Women were seen as sexual commodities to be used and conquered rather than as human beings with rights and feelings."[39] Researchers came to the final conclusion that perhaps they were asking the wrong question. "Instead of asking men who rape 'why?' perhaps we should be asking men who don't 'why not?'"[40]

Organized rape can be used as a tactical device to accomplish particular political and social ends. It may be used to intimidate, to punish individual women and social groups, to destabilise and demoralise communities or to drive unwanted people from their land.[41] Conflicts in the last decade in the Balkans and the present atrocities in Darfur, western Sudan, as well as the mass rape of women and girls during the 1994 genocide in Rwanda are examples of rape being used to achieve these kinds of ends. Men may be forced at gunpoint to rape female family members or other men, as part of the use of rape to terrorise and humiliate people.

The perpetrators in these cases are a wide range of men, uniformed and civilian, who act with the tacit or explicit approval of their political or military leaders. While many rapists in these contexts may claim, after the event, that they were coerced into committing rape, there is a long history of rape being seen and enjoyed as the spoils of war.

The role of vice and greed

There are categories of gender-based violence — such as trafficking of women and children, the sale and use of child pornography, and forced prostitution (adult and child) — where the perpetrators are engaged in illegal activities for financial gain. The activities may be neither culturally acceptable nor allowed by national or international law, but unlike other forms of violence against women and girls, the perpetrator's primary interest in his victim is as a lucrative commodity.

The intended end of a perpetrator's activities in these instances is to earn income, and the means involve coercion and infringement of other people's rights. While the violent gangs that often control trafficking and prostitution may directly sexually abuse the women and children they control, vice and greed are the primary motivation for their activities.

Patriarchal societies which already victimise women and girls create the preconditions for trafficking and forced prostitution to exist. The exploitation of women and girls occurs within contexts that deny them their most basic human rights.

Perpetrators who organize, plan, invest in and dominate aspects of the illegal sex industry are predominantly male, but women are also complicit at different levels. Female agents are directly involved in running brothels, disciplining and maintaining prostitutes and recruiting girls for trafficking.

The users of Internet pornography involving minors, the global patrons of women who are forced into prostitution, and those who keep trafficked women in virtual slavery (as domestic or sexual slaves) are no less perpetrators of sexual crimes.

The sex "industry" operates within market dictates of supply and demand, and both sides have to take responsibility. Perpetrators on the supply side of the illegal sex industry are normally criminals and organized in what is a highly competitive and lucrative multimillion-dollar economy. On the demand side, users of prostitutes and Internet pornography throughout the world are demographically diverse, and include men of all ages and characters. Women also use these sex services, although it is less common. Sometimes these users may be ignorant — or choose to be ignorant — of the gender-based violence they involve themselves in.

National laws in various Western countries are beginning to reflect this sense that the users of these "services" are complicit in the illegal activity irrespective of where the crime occurs. In recent years, cases of British sex tourists being prosecuted for activities committed in Cambodia or the Philippines, or Australians when visiting Thailand are sobering reminders to perpetrators that international boundaries no longer provide them with the immunity that they previously enjoyed. There also have been initiatives in some countries to criminalise domestic prostitution by policing and punishing the clients rather than the sex workers themselves.

Perpetrators of child abuse

"There are many perpetrators who have committed sexual crimes against children, some of their own children, in a very deliberate, systematic, premeditated, thoughtful, manipulative and conniving sort of way. These are not sick, demented abnormal people. These are thoughtful, intelligent planned initiatives undertaken by perpetrators to get what they want."[42] This psychotherapist from Canada echoed the conclusions of numerous studies that focus on the characteristics of perpetrators of child sex abuse.

Sexual abuse of children and adolescents is one of the most invisible forms of sexual violence because of the considerable taboo surrounding the notion of incest and child abuse in most cultures. Research shows that the majority of perpetrators are men; only a small percentage of the abuse — between 3 percent and 10 percent — is conducted by women.[43] The male perpetrator is normally a father, brother, uncle, step-father or grandfather. One study suggested that while 13 percent of all perpetrators of female incest were the biological fathers and 12 percent

> "There are many perpetrators who have committed sexual crimes against children, some of their own children, in a very deliberate, systematic, premeditated, thoughtful, manipulative and conniving sort of way."

were brothers, only 0.5 percent were mothers.[44] In many cases the victim's fear of testifying against the known perpetrator, combined with the considerable social disapprobation for the perpetrator if exposed, means that countless cases of child abuse are hidden by families or communities. Victims of child abuse within the family suffer a special sense of harm: The violations break spoken and unspoken rules of kinship that traditionally codify the identity of the child.[45]

As with other gender-based crimes, people who prey on children are not a homogenous group. They range from those clinically defined as "preferential paedophiles", to situational abusers, to those who are indifferent to the age of their sexual partners and finally to those who perpetrate infant rape. Situational abusers may not be exclusively attracted to children but in a single case or series of cases may take advantage of a situation where they engage in sex with a minor. "Indifferent" abusers are unlikely to seek out young children but are nevertheless willing to pay for casual sex with underage girls, particularly when abroad. The motivations for perpetrators of infant abuse and rape may be the most unclear, although in some cultures those who believe in the myth of the "virgin cure" may rape infants in hopes of being protected against and/or cured of HIV/AIDS and other sexually transmitted infections.[46]

It is likely that all child abuse is underreported, but this may be even more the case when the victims are boys. Evidence suggests a causal relationship for boys between being abused as a child and becoming a perpetrator of abuse as an adult.[47] Studies of female victims, on the other hand, indicate they rarely become perpetrators of child abuse. Instead, girls are more likely to have other problems such as early pregnancy, substance abuse and abusive relationships.

Witnessing domestic/marital violence as a child appears to increase the

In civil wars, when the rule of the gun replaces the rule of law, women and girls are at great risk of all forms of violence.

Image: Georgina Cranston/IRIN

In efforts to combat the increasingly publicised tide of violence and sexual abuse in South Africa this billboard in Johannesburg asks, "What kind of man are you? … Violence against women hurts us all."

Image: Mariella Furrer

likelihood of a male abusing a partner later in life.[48] Notably, being directly abused appears to be less of a risk marker for committing future abuse than is witnessing violence, but it is nevertheless significant. In other words, violence in adult relationships is in part a learned response of young boys who grow up in violent homes. However, exposure to family violence is not a prerequisite for future abuse. For example, one study found that 38 percent of wife abusers had neither witnessed nor experienced physical aggression as a child.

Addressing the prevalence of perpetration

Whether the by-product of cultural tradition or predatory and impulsive masculinity, gender-based violence throughout the world is perpetrated in the main by men. In every category of sexual violence and gender-based discrimination, the victims are predominantly women. Violence against women and girls is a global epidemic that permeates, in some form, all cultures and communities.

This chapter seeks to explore the motivation that drives perpetrators of some aspects of gender-based violence against women. Many writers and commentators describe the behaviour of perpetrators in different ways, using sociological, cultural or psychological constructs, but some of the individual testimonies researched for this book were so gratuitously brutal, so monstrous in intent and so utterly careless of the suffering of the victim that the term "evil" seems to be the only suitable description. This writer was at a loss to understand or explain the motives of some perpetrators — whose actions were violent in the extreme and directly targeted against women — in any other way.

Most men, however, are not violent towards women and treat the women and girls in their lives with care and respect. There are a growing number of groups and networks of men around the globe who are now taking action, often in alliance with women, to help stop gender-based violence. Amongst various initiatives, perhaps the best known example of men's antiviolence activism is the White Ribbon Campaign. Started in 1991 in Canada, it has now spread to the United States, Europe, Africa, Latin America and Australia.[49]

Responding to perpetrators of different forms of gender-based violence is a major challenge due to the scope and extent of the violations themselves and the involvement of such a wide spectrum of men. The problem is compounded and facilitated by the fact that most societies are patriarchal, with structures and systems that directly or indirectly defend and reproduce perpetrators of physical violence and sexual assault and abuse.

Research shows that these forms of violence, and in particular child abuse, are most often transmitted intergenerationally through those who have been subject to, or witness to, abuse.[50] In such an environment, it is difficult to see how real changes will take place to break the cycle of violence unless men themselves, as chief perpetrators, take a leading role in creating societies that structurally and socially reject gender-based violence in all its forms. n

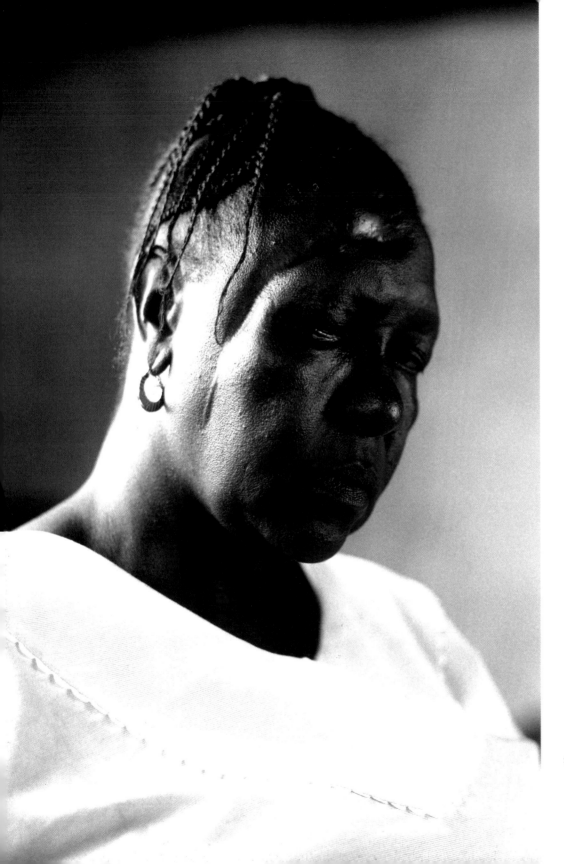

Recent conflicts in West Africa, Democratic Republic of Congo, Uganda and Sudan are examples of wars in which government soldiers, militias, rebels and criminals have perpetrated many thousands of brutal rapes. This woman, a nurse by profession, was abducted by rebels in Sierra Leone to live as a "bush wife". The scar on her forehead is from a bullet wound she sustained when the soldiers, after gang-raping her, tortured her by seeing how close they could come to killing her with an AK-47.

Image: Brent Stirton

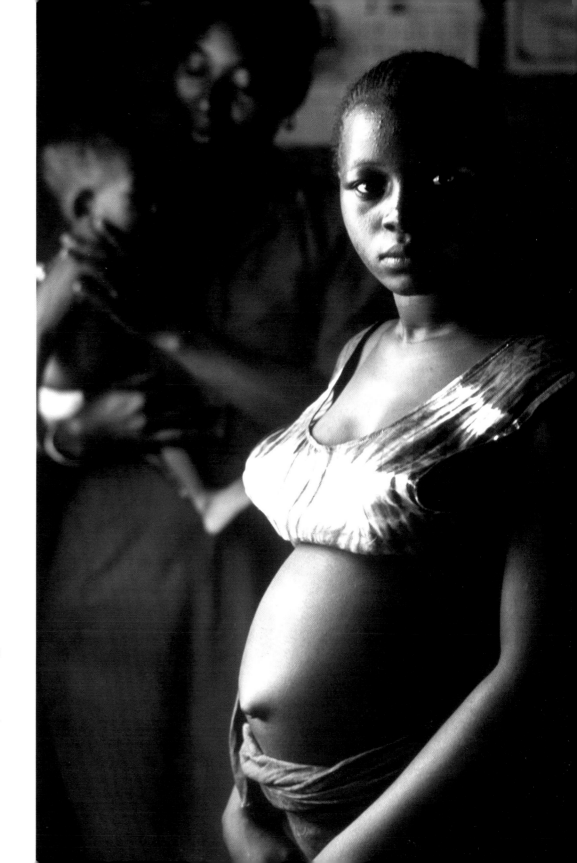

A 13-year-old girl and former "bush wife" who became pregnant through rape in Sierra Leone. She was fortunate enough to return to her family after peace accords were signed, but shortly afterwards her father threw her out of the household for bringing "dishonour" to the family. In the countless stories of this nature, the perpetrators are never brought to account for acts that shatter women's and girls' lives. In many cases victims suffer the secondary impact of rejection by their families and communities. Frequently, girls in this predicament find that prostitution is their only means of survival.

Image: Brent Stirton

The international movement challenging discrimination and violence against women is driven by hundreds of formal and informal groups around the world that have mobilised for change.

Image: Zana Briski

turning the tide

"There must be no impunity for gender-based violence. Let me be clear. What we are talking about is not a side issue. It is not a special interest group, of concern to only a few. What we are talking about are not only women's rights but also the human rights of over one half of this globe's population. ... Violence against women concerns not only women but above all the rest of us."[1]
— *the late Sergio Vieira de Mello, former United Nations High Commissioner for Human Rights*

The fight to end violence against women is both historic and universal. Historic, because gender inequality, which lies at the root of this violence, has been embedded in human history for centuries and the movement to end it challenges history, custom and, most critically, the *status quo*. Universal, because no society is an exception to the fact that violence against women is perpetuated through social and cultural norms that reinforce male-dominated power structures. The struggle is nothing less than a demand for full human rights to be unconditionally extended to all people everywhere.

Those engaged in this struggle recognise that despite important advances that have laid the foundation for universal human rights, the work has only just begun. In October 2004, on the 25th anniversary of the landmark Convention on the Elimination of All Forms of Discrimination against Women, the committee monitoring international implementation stated, "In no country in the world has women's full *de jure* and *de facto* equality been achieved."[2]

In most countries, in fact, the reality remains bleak. Discriminatory social norms and practices continue to impede women's full enjoyment of their human rights. Insufficient political will, the extensive underrepresentation of women in decision-making positions and a lack of resources to address the issue are further impediments to progress.[3]

Asserting human rights

The Universal Declaration of Human Rights, adopted without dissent by the United Nations in 1948, recognises the "equal and inalienable rights" of all people, "without distinction of any kind."[4] Violence against women contravenes a number of the fundamental human rights laid out in this

Declaration, such as the right to security of person; the right not to be held in slavery or subjected to inhuman treatment; the right to equal protection before the law; and the right to equality in marriage.[5] Nevertheless, states sometimes deploy the argument of cultural relativism to defend practices that abuse women. According to the first United Nations Special Rapporteur on Violence against Women, "The universal standards of human rights are often denied full operation when it comes to the rights of women."[6]

This book highlights through written description and visual representation many of the persistent expressions of gender-based violence. The testimonies of women and girls emphasise that there is no room for complacency or a false sense of rapid progress in the fight against inequality. To the countless women still suffering today, any positive changes that have been achieved must bear little relevance to their immediate reality. Nevertheless, remarkable developments have taken place in recent years, due in large part to the commitment of a few to change the behaviour of many. In the face of formidable forces maintaining the patriarchal systems that give rise to both discrimination and violence against women, there is evidence that the tide may be turning.

The emergence of an international movement

The protection of women from systemic violence and discrimination has its roots in the movement of female emancipation at the turn of the 18th century. However, it was only in the latter half of the 20th century, after the founding of the United Nations, that women's activists began applying international standards of human rights to expose the links between sex-based discrimination and violence against women, and to argue for state accountablity. By the 1970s, their efforts were taking root. The first World Conference on Women was held in Mexico in December 1975 and heralded the United Nations Decade for Women: Equality, Development and Peace, spanning the years 1976 to 1985.

Once the preserve of women's rights activists, the struggle to end violence against women is now becoming mainstreamed in government policies and development programming and increasingly recognised as an international priority.[7] Academic scrutiny and public awareness of the issue also have accelerated in the last two decades. Key actors in the campaign are the United Nations — in particular the the Development

Fund for Women (UNIFEM), the World Health Organization (WHO), the United Nations Fund for Population and Development (UNFPA) and the Division for the Advancement of Women (UNDAW), as well as

At the international level, there is no shortage of detailed declarations that address all aspects of violence and discrimination against women — a major achievement, but one that requires political will at the national and local levels in order to become a reality on the ground.

a wide range of intergovernmental and nongovernmental organizations and local community-based groups.

An evolving body of international agreements and declarations is providing all these actors with a powerful normative framework for promoting and protecting women's right to be free from violence. In 1979, the General Assembly of the United Nations adopted the comprehensive and detailed Convention on the Elimination of All Forms of Discrimination Against Women, which is often referred to as the "bill of rights for women". As of 2003, the Convention had been ratified by 174 states. It does not, however, specifically detail the issue of violence against women. Instead, this subject was taken up in 1993, with the adoption of the United Nations Declaration on the Elimination of Violence Against Women. The Declaration calls upon states to condemn violence against women and to avoid invoking custom, tradition and religion to obstruct their obligation towards its total elimination.

The Fourth World Conference on Women in Beijing in 1995 and its follow-up conference in 2000, known as Beijing +5, have been important reference points for much of the activism and campaigning in recent years. Both conferences called for a re-engagement and intensification of focus by world governments and civil society on issues of violence and discrimination against women and girls. International commitments to the elimination of gender-based violence were strengthened with the appointment of a United Nations Special Rapporteur on Violence Against Women in 1993, the adoption of the Beijing Platform for Action in 1995 and the establishment of the United Nations Trust Fund to Eliminate Violence against Women in 1996.

At the international level, there is no shortage of detailed declarations that address all aspects of violence and discrimination against women — a major achievement, but one that requires political will at the national and local levels in order to become a reality on the ground.

A group of sex workers in Freetown, Sierra Leone. Many of these girls, who were displaced from their villages by civil conflict, fled to the capital and, without a means to support themselves, were forced to work as prostitutes.

Image: Brent Stirton

Women who have suffered violence need economic opportunities in addition to medical and psychological support.
Thousands of women in conflict-affected settings are rebuilding their lives support through training and microcredit initiatives.

Bringing the fight home

Today, agencies working to end violence against women — as well as leading researchers, writers and activists — agree that there are specific activities that need to take place at the national and local levels if the fight against gender-based violence is to have a long-term impact. These involve creating increased protection for women through partnerships with institutions and governments to ensure legislative reform and implementation. They also involve measures to guarantee that survivors have access to support services, which can mitigate the impact of violence and reduce the likelihood of its recurrence. They further involve raising awareness and developing public and institutional support through research and advocacy efforts. Lastly, they involve the empowerment of women through education, greater employment opportunities and equal participation in decision-making.[8]

Changes in national legislation

Significant advances have been made in criminalising forms of gender-based violence at the national level. For example, by 2003, legislation explicitly banning intimate-partner violence was in place in 45 countries; a further 21 were drafting such legislation. In an additional 45 countries, this type of violence was covered implicitly by other laws. Legislative reforms in some countries have facilitated prosecution for sexual assault, notably by broadening the definition of rape, revising the conditions regarding evidence and removing demands that victims' accounts be corroborated.[9] Twenty-five countries have enacted legislation explicitly or implicitly criminalising female genital mutilation (FGM).[10]

Notwithstanding these gains, overall progress has been limited — the Special Rapporteur on Violence Against Women declared in recent years that "states are failing in their international obligations to effectively prevent, investigate and prosecute violence against women."[11] In only three countries is violence against women in itself legally considered to be a criminal activity.[12] While there are 130 countries with legislation in place that can be applied to sexual assault, only 16 countries have specific laws against it, and although marital rape is considered a crime in 50 countries, only five countries have specific legislation against it. Seventy-nine countries have no legislation whatsoever covering intimate-partner violence, despite its prevalence, and very few nations have any mechanism to address the issue of gender-based violence in times of war.[13]

In some countries, laws may even exacerbate women's risk of violence. Legislation may favour family preservation in the event of domestic violence, suspend rape sentences if the perpetrator marries the victim or permit "honour" to be used as a mitigating factor in criminal penalties.[14]

… by 2003, legislation explicitly banning intimate-partner violence was in place in 45 countries; a further 21 were drafting such legislation.

Women may be unable to own or inherit property and secure their financial independence.[15] Marital laws may enshrine unequal divorce rights, making it impossible for women to instigate separation.

Even where legislation prohibiting violence against women exists, there is no guarantee that it will be applied effectively. Enforcement requires the existence of a rule of law and an interested and impartial criminal justice system, which many countries lack.[16] Regional assessments on violence against women commissioned by UNIFEM in recent years documented that "nearly every area reported failure to implement antiviolence legislation as an egregious problem."[17] Gender bias is strongly evident in the male-dominated law enforcement and judiciary sectors in many countries, where domestic violence, for example, may be dismissed as a "family" issue, and information regarding a rape victim's sexual history can be used in court to discredit her testimony. Despite the enactment of national legislation against female genital mutilation, the persistence of the practice in some countries continues unabated, while evidence of prosecution of those practising FGM has occurred in only six countries.[18]

Assisting victims of violence

Over the last 20 years, particularly in industrialised settings, services for survivors have significantly improved in scope and quality. Due in large part to the efforts of women's organizations, coordinated responses to intimate-partner violence and sexual assault have become standardised and are increasingly addressing a variety of needs, from the provision of medical treatment, counselling, legal aid, protection and shelter, to assistance with reintegration of victims into society.

Innovative initiatives include women's police stations and "one-stop" crisis centres that provide survivors support through the criminal-justice process. Some countries have networks of "safe houses" to which women can go for temporary shelter from abusive partners. "Rape suites", staffed by social workers as well as doctors, ensure that survivors receive supportive care during forensic examinations.[19] Specialised treatment programmes also have been established for child victims of abuse, as well as for the elderly.[20] Many countries have initiatives to sensitise those working in the health, security and legal sectors to the issues surrounding violence against women. Such measures seek to challenge the gender biases that discourage women from reporting incidents of violence and in turn increase impunity levels.

The standards established in certain countries are by no means global. In many parts of the world, specialised services for survivors continue to be minimal or nonexistent. Barriers include a lack of resources and technical competence, as well as institutional constraints such as limited coordination between service providers and perceptions that violence against women is unimportant.[21] The failure by the healthcare and legal sectors to offer free, confidential and safe advice and care, the absence of standards for the sensitive and accurate collection of forensic evidence, and prevailing victim-blaming attitudes discourage victims from seeking assistance.[22] Poor infrastructure and lack of affordable transport also mitigate against women receiving support. Overall the issue of adequate and appropriate service provision continues to be a huge challenge — particularly in areas where it is most needed.

The power of data

Data on the scope, causes and implications of gender-based violence are vital to designing and monitoring both prevention and response strategies, informing advocacy and awareness campaigns, and advancing legislative reform. Especially in the last 10 years, research efforts have improved considerably, and in some countries population-based studies and standardised collection of service-delivery data are now routine. The WHO, in particular, has made significant strides in researching the issue of violence against women by their intimate partners and in establishing ethical and methodological standards for investigating violence against women.[23] Demographic and health surveys now include optional questions on female genital mutilation, as well as other forms of violence against women.

International and national agencies, academic institutions, and nongovernmental organizations also have developed and implemented data-collection strategies, and the scope of their work is positively illustrated by the statistics contained in this book. Most recently, a

United Nations General Assembly resolution in December 2003 commissioned an "in depth study on all forms of violence against women."[24] UNDAW is responsible for the implementation of this study, which will not only detail existing data, but also provide recommendations for improving comprehensive and comparable data collection around the world.

The United Nations Special Rapporteur on Violence Against Women estimated in 2003, however, that "it will be another decade before adequate information can be collated."[25] Comparison of data that has been collected is hampered by the use of different frameworks, methods and time-spans, and prevalence research on various types of gender-based violence is often limited to selected areas as opposed to entire countries. In many nations surveyed by UNIFEM, "there is no comprehensive and systematic mechanism for collecting reliable data on violence against women."[26] In the absence of representative statistics, analysts are forced to rely on victims' reports to health and social services agencies and to the legal sector.[27] Because most victims never report their crimes, service-delivery statistics are not an accurate indication of the scope of the problem.

Raising awareness

Efforts to raise awareness and educate the public about violence against women and its roots in broader gender inequalities have been significant in recent decades, at both the national and local levels. Activists have employed different media — from posters to television dramas, and from video cassettes to the Internet — to convey messages aimed at combating violence.[28] Informing women of their rights has been central to their efforts. Key messages within the campaigns have included women's rights to be free from violence, to demand that partners use condoms, and to decide when and with whom they wish to have sex.[29] Awareness-raising has also focused on encouraging women to report incidents of violence and urging families and neighbours to take action if they know women who are being abused.[30] Some successful strategies from around the world have been documented by UNIFEM and others and widely distributed in media toolkits.

> The failure by the healthcare and legal sectors to offer free, confidential and safe advice and care, the absence of standards for the sensitive and accurate collection of forensic evidence, and prevailing victim-blaming attitudes discourage victims from seeking assistance.

Police training in Islamabad, 2005. Despite efforts to sensitise law enforcement officers, Pakistan, along with other countries, struggles to implement national law on violence against women.

Image: Evelyn Hockstein/IRIN

Welcome to Liberia: Young men and boys with guns in a climate of impunity and civil dislocation often contribute to high incidents of rape and sexual abuse of women and girls.

Image: Brent Stirton

Reviewers of campaigns to raise awareness still cite the lack of media expertise and adequate resources as a serious constraint. Even where governments have undertaken national education on violence against women, the level of funding they have devoted to the effort is low compared to allocations they have made to other public-health campaigns.[31] The Special Rapporteur assessed in 2003 that "... very little has changed in the lives of most women. A few women have benefited [...] but for the vast majority violence against women remains a taboo issue, invisible in society and a shameful fact of life."[32]

Involving men

Because male perceptions of masculinity and power relations with women act as collective reinforcement and perpetuate violence against women, targeting men is a crucial element of awareness-raising strategies.[33] Approaches have included community-education campaigns, men's activism against violence and perpetrator programmes.[34] While recognising that not all males are perpetrators, research suggests that "all men can influence the culture and environment that allows other men to be violent."[35] Educational campaigns have attempted to redefine masculinity as nonviolent by providing an alternative construction of male identity.[36] The White Ribbon Campaign, launched in Canada in 1991 and now established in many countries, is a well-known example of a campaign run by men that encourages other men to condemn violence against women.[37] Studies of men's relationships with other men have suggested that such relations can promote notions of male responsibility for ending violence against women.[38] Men's groups committed to combating violence against women can be found all over the world: In the United States alone, there are over 100 such groups linked to the White Ribbon Campaign.[39]

Empowering women

The issue of empowerment of women is a key element in "measuring the world's gender gap." When women advance in five critical areas — economic participation, quality of employment, political representation, educational attainment, and health and wellbeing — they are better equipped to challenge the unequal power relations that preserve male dominance.[40] Research suggests that women who are more empowered in these areas are at lower risk of violence.[41] Empowerment with regard to skills and resources also promotes financial independence, a sense of

social value and improved self-esteem. Another by-product of increased participation by women is a sense of solidarity with other women gained through greater access to social-support networks.

Undeniably, positive changes have occurred in the last 50 years in the status and role of women in many countries. Women have entered the labour market in great numbers, giving them unprecedented economic decision-making power. Increases in women's access to finance have enhanced their control over household resources.[42] In many settings girls have achieved parity with boys, and sometimes exceeded boys, in terms of access to education. Women also have been major actors in the rise of civil society throughout the world, with the current levels of female participation in economic, political and social processes the highest they have ever been.[43]

Despite these advances, the economic, political, social and educational development of women is highly uneven throughout the world. For example, on average 15.6 percent of political representatives in combined houses of parliament around the world are female — but this

> "... very little has changed in the lives of most women. A few women have benefited [...] but for the vast majority violence against women remains a taboo issue, invisible in society and a shameful fact of life."

figure is as low as 6.8 percent in Arab states and as high as 39.7 percent in the Nordic states.[44] The 2005 report by the World Economic Forum, "Women's Empowerment: Measuring the Global Gender Gap," which ranks 58 countries according to gender equality in the five areas mentioned above, highlights the significant differences between countries at the top of the ranking (Sweden, Norway and Iceland) and those ranked at the bottom (Pakistan, Turkey and Egypt).[45]

While it would be wrong to understate the significant and steady progress made in recent years, it would also be wrong to overstate the benefits. Too often, activities to advance women's rights and safety are constrained by limited resources and a lack of influence. Even the United Nations Trust Fund to Eliminate Violence Against Women, an inter-agency effort with a global mandate, that is administered by UNIFEM, labours under severely restricted funding. To end violence against women in this context can sometimes be a Herculean task. Positive change is hard-won and often fragile. n

This book should serve as disturbing testimony of the global disparity between the sexes in relation to equality and human rights abuses. Although the inclusion of images and case studies brings some individual lives into sharp focus, a burden of truth-telling remains. This burden is the weight of the millions of untold stories, of unnoticed suffering, of secret pain and unchallenged assaults on women's minds and bodies. It is also the burden of the endless assaults on women's and girls' dreams and potential.

"Perpetrated by men, silenced by custom, institutionalised in laws and state systems and passed from one generation to the next," the continued and unrelenting violence visited upon women and girls is the "most universal and most unpunished crime of all."[46] With increased evidence of violence against women comes the obligation to act. History will no doubt judge this and subsequent generations harshly if comprehensive action to reject all forms of violence against women is not taken.

Everyone has a role to play because the challenge implicates every community and nation of the world and involves all women and, more pointedly, all men. Ending violence against women and girls is a struggle of historic and universal dimensions. The battle is already underway. And once won, humanity's place on earth will more aptly — and honestly — be called "civilisation".

In one initiative to offer recreation and alternative experiences of solidarity for young commercial sex workers in Sierra Leone, an international nongovernmental organization launched a sports programme of monthly soccer matches.

Image: Brent Stirton

endnotes

introduction

[1] United Nations Development Fund for Women (UNIFEM), *Not a Minute More: Ending Violence Against Women* (New York, 2003), 15.

[2] L. Heise, M. Ellsberg and M. Gottemoeller, "Ending Violence Against Women," *Population Reports* Series L No. 11 (Baltimore, 1999), 1.

[3] Sen, 1990, cited in N. Hatti, T. Sekhar and M. Larsen, "Lives at Risk, Declining Child Sex Ratios in India," *Lund Papers in Economic History* No. 93 (2004), 1; Oxfam, "Towards Ending Violence Against Women in South Asia," Briefing Paper No. 66 (Oxford, September 2003).

[4] S. Kapoor, "Domestic Violence Against Women and Girls," *Innocenti Digest* Vol. 6 (Florence, June 2000).

[5] International Labour Organization (ILO), 2000, cited in United Nations Special Rapporteur (UN Spec. Rapp.) on the Sale of Children, Child Prostitution, and Child Pornography, *Rights of the Child*, United Nations Commission on Human Rights E/CN.4/2004/9 (Geneva, January 2004).

[6] United States Department of State, *Trafficking in Persons Report*, Publication 11252 (Washington, DC, June 2005). Available from: www.state.gov/g/tip.

[7] N. Toubia, *Caring for Women with Circumcision: A Technical Manual for Health Care Providers* (New York, 1999); J. Carr, "Theme Paper on Child Pornography for the Second World Congress on Commercial Sexual Exploitation of Children" (December 2001). Available from: www.ecpat.net/eng/Ecpat_inter/projects/monitoring/wc2/yokohama_theme_child_pornography.pdf

[8] Kapoor, 2000.

[9] International Alert, Réseau des Femmes pour un Developpement Associatif and Réseau des Femmes pour la Defence des Droits et la Paix, *Women's Bodies as a Battleground: Sexual Violence Against Women and Girls during the war in the Democratic Republic of Congo* (2005), 11.

[10] Dixon-Mueller, cited in Conway-Turner and Cherrin, cited in N. Otoo-Oyortey and S. Pobi, *Early Marriage and Poverty: Exploring Links for Policy and Programme Development*, The Forum on Marriage and the Rights of Women and Girls (London, November 2003).

[11] J. Bruce, 2002, cited in Otoo-Oyortey and Pobi, 2003.

[12] United Nations Development Programme (UNDP), 1997, cited in Amnesty International (AI), *Violence Against Women: Worldwide Statistics*. Available from: www.amnesty.org.nz/web/pages/home.nsf/; VicHealth, *The Health Costs of Violence: Measuring the Burden of Disease Caused by Intimate Partner Violence*, Department of Human Services (Melbourne, June 2004).

[13] World Health Organization (WHO), *Violence Against Women Information Pack: A Priority Health Issue*, 3. Available from: www.who.int/frh-whd/VAW/infopack/English/VAW_infopack.htm

[14] UNIFEM, 2003, 8.

[15] UN Spec. Rapp. on Violence Against Women, *Further Promotion and Encouragement of Human Rights and Fundamental Freedoms, Including the Question of the Programme and Methods of Work of the Commission*, United Nations Economic and Social Council E/CN.4/1997/41 (Geneva, February 1997).

[16] L. Post, N. Mezey, C. Maxwell and W. Novales Wibert, "The Rape Tax: Tangible and Intangible Costs of Sexual Violence," *Journal of Interpersonal Violence* Vol. 17 No. 7 (July 2002), 773-782, 779.

[17] C. Spindel, E. Levy and M. Connor, *With an End in Sight*, UNIFEM (New York, 2000), 14.

[18] Office of the United Nations High Commissioner for Human Rights (OHCHR), *Declaration on the Elimination of Violence Against Women* (December 1993). Available from: www.ohchr.org/english/law/eliminationvaw.htm.

[19] OHCHR, 1993.

[20] OHCHR, 1993.

[21] UN Spec. Rapp., *Integration of the Human Rights of Women and the Gender Perspective: Violence Against Women: Intersections of Violence Against Women and HIV/AIDS*, UN Commission on Human Rights E/CN.4/205/72 (Geneva, January 2005), 8.

[22] M. Valchova and L. Biason, eds., *Women in an Insecure World: Violence Against Women Facts, Figures and Analysis*, Centre for the Democratic Control of Armed Forces (DCAF) (Geneva, 2005).

[23] A. Lopez-Claros and S. Zahidi, *Women's Empowerment: Measuring the Global Gender Gap*, World Economic Forum (Geneva, 2005).

[24] Valchova and Biason, eds., 2005.

[25] UNICEF Press Release, "Despite Gains in Girls' Education Worldwide, Far Too Many Still Missing Out" (April 18, 2005). Available from: www.unicef.org/media/media_26028.html.

[26] Lopez-Claros and Zahidi, 2005.

[27] Valchova and Biason, eds., 2005.

[28] B. Scholz and M. Gomez, *Bringing Equality Home: Promoting and Protecting the Inheritance Rights of Women*, Centre on Housing Rights and Evictions (Geneva, 2004).

[29] Lopez-Claros and Zahidi, 2005, 2.

[30] E. Krug, L. Dahlbeg, J. Mercy, A. Zwi and A. Wilson, "Chapter 9, The Way Forward: Recommendations for Action," in E. Krug, L. Dahlberg, J. Mercy, A. Zwi, R. Lozano, eds., *World Report on Violence and Health*, World Health Organization (Geneva, 2002), 245.

[31] Spindel et al, 2000, 13.

[32] OHCHR, 1993.

[33] OHCHR, 1993.

[34] B. Scholz and M. Gomez, 2004.

[35] Lopez-Claros and Zahidi, 2005, 1.

[36] Lopez-Claros and Zahidi, 2005, 1.

chapter 1 — son preference

[1] Ramananna, 1980, cited in R. Patel, "The Practice of Sex Selective Abortion in India: May You Be the Mother of a Hundred Sons," *Carolina Papers in International Health* No. 7 (Fall 1996), 6; United Nations Special Rapporteur (UN Spec. Rapp.) on Violence Against Women, *The Integration of the Human Rights of Women and the Gender Perspective, Cultural Practices in the Family that Are Violent Towards Women*, United Nations Economic and Social Council E/CN.4/2002/83 (Geneva, January 2002), 23.

[2] UN Spec. Rapp., 2002, 23.

[3] UN Spec. Rapp., 2002; S. Kapoor, "Domestic Violence Against Women and Girls," *Innocenti Digest* Vol. 6 (Florence, June 2000).

[4] Sen, 1990, cited in N. Hatti, T. Sekhar and M. Larsen, "Lives at Risk, Declining Child Sex Ratios in India," *Lund Papers in Economic History* No. 93 (2004), 1; Oxfam, "Towards Ending Violence Against Women in South Asia," Briefing Paper No. 66 (Oxford, September 2003).

5 Office of the High Commissioner for Human Rights (OHCHR), "Harmful Traditional Practices Affecting the Health of Women and Children," Fact Sheet No. 23 (Geneva). Available from: www.unhchr.ch/html/menu6/2/fs23.htm.

6 OHCHR, Fact Sheet No. 23.

7 P. Newell, "Children and Violence," *Innocenti Digest* Vol. 2 (Florence, September 1997).

8 Goodkind, 1996 and 1999, cited in F. Arnold, S. Kishor and T.K. Roy, "Sex-Selective Abortions in India," *Population and Development Review* Vol. 28 No. 4 (December 2002), 759-785, 763.

9 M. Das Gupta, J. Zhenghua, L. Bohua, X. Zhenming, W. Chung and B. Hwa-Ok, *Why Is Son Preference So Persistent in East and South Asia? A Cross-Country Study of China, India, and the Republic of Korea*, Policy Research Working Paper 2942, The World Bank Development Research Group, Public Services and Rural Development (December 2002); Hatti et al, 2004.

10 Arnold et al, 2002.

11 Saundrapandiyan, 1985, cited in S. Surreender, R. Rao and S. Nivanjan, "Attitude Towards Female Foeticide: Does it Influence the Survival Status of Female Children?" *Indian Association of Social Science Institutions Quarterly*, Vol. 16 No. 3 & 4 (1997), 106-114.

12 US State Department, 2000, cited in S. Kapoor, 2000.

13 G. Aravamudan, "Born to Die," *The Rediff Special* (October 24, 2001). Available from: www.rediff.com/news/2001/oct/24spec.htm.

14 A. Krishnakumar, "Scanning for Death," *Frontline* Vol. 15 No. 25 (December 5-18, 1998), 109-112.

15 Freed, 1989, cited in Patel, 1996, 5.

16 Arnold et al, 2002.

17 Patel, 1996.

18 Ravindra, 1986, cited in Patel, 1996.

19 Ramanamma, 1980, cited in Patel, 1996, 6.

20 Das Gupta et al, 2002.

21 Aravamudan, 2001.

22 Arnold et al, 2002.

23 M. Das Gupta and L. Shuzhuo, "Gender Bias in China, South Korea and India, 1920-90: Effects of War, Famine and Fertility Decline," *Development and Change*, Special Issue on Gendered Poverty and Wellbeing (forthcoming).

24 Patel, 1996, 11.

25 Census of India, various years, cited in Hatti et al, 2004.

26 Patel, 1996, 26.

27 United States Department of State, *Trafficking in Persons Report*, Office of the Under Secretary for Global Affairs Publication 11252 (Washington, D.C., June, 2005), 20.

28 R. Devraj, "A Murderous Arithmetic" (July, 2003). Available from: www.indiatogether.org/cgi-bin/tools/pfriend.cgi.

29 Das Gupta et al, 2002.

30 "Case Study: Female Infanticide." Available from: www.gendercide.org/case_infanticide.html.

31 C. Wei, *Sex-Selective Abortions: Evidence From Rural East China*, Paper Prepared for the International Union for the Scientific Study of Population, XXV International Population Conference (Tours, France, July 18-23, 2005).

32 Gendercide Watch, "Case Study: Female Infanticide" (1999-2000). Available from: www.gendercide.org.

33 Wei, 2005.

34 Wei, 2005.

35 H. French, "As Girls 'Vanish,' Chinese City Battles Tide of Abortions," *New York Times* (February 17, 2005).

36 French, 2005.

37 US Department of State, 2005, 20.

38 Gendercide Watch, 1999-2000.

39 Aravamudan, 2001.

40 Kusum, 1993, cited in Patel, 1996, 10.

41 B. Gu and K. Roy, "Sex Ratio at Birth in China, with Reference to Other Areas in East Asia: What We Know," *Asia-Pacific Population Journal*, Vol. 10 No. 3 (1995), 7-42.

42 Das Gupta et al, 2002, 5.

43 Gu and Roy, 1995.

44 Banister, 1995, cited in Gu and Roy, 1995.

45 Marie, 1990, cited in Sureender et al, 1997.

46 Das Gupta et al, 2002; Das Gupta and Shuzhuo, forthcoming.

47 S. Kishor, "'May God Give Sons to All': Gender and Child Mortality in India," *American Sociological Review*, Vol. 58, No. 2 (April, 1993), 247-265.

48 Miller, 1981, cited in Patel, 1996.

49 Oxfam, 2003.

50 Singh, 1992, cited in Patel, 1996, 9.

51 Gu and Li, cited in Gu and Roy, 1995, 13.

chapter 2 — sexual abuse of children

1 F. Haque, "Marital Sexual Violence Is a Terrifying Experience," *Family Health International* Vol. 23 No 4 (2005), 12.

2 R. Dominguez, C. Nelke, and B. Perry, "Child Sexual Abuse," *Encyclopedia of Crime and Punishment* Vol. 1 (Thousand Oaks, 2002).

3 P. Newell, "Children and Violence," *Innocenti Digest* No. 2 (Florence, September 1997).

4 L. Heise, M. Ellsberg, and M. Gottemoeller, "Ending Violence Against Women," *Population Reports* Vol. 27 No 4 (Baltimore, December 1999); Dominguez et al, 2002; D. Finkelhor, "The International Epidemiology of Child Sexual Abuse," *Child Abuse and Neglect* Vol. 18 No. 5 (1994), 409-417.

5 D. Runyan, C. Wattam, R. Ikeda, F. Hassan and L. Ramiro, "Chapter 3: Child Abuse and Neglect by Parents and Other Caregivers," in E. Krug, L. Dahlberg, J. Mercy, A. Zwi and R. Lozano, eds., *World Report on Violence and Health*, World Health Organization (Geneva, 2002).

6 M. Ellsberg and L. Heise, *Researching Violence Against Women: A Practical Guide for Researchers and Advocates*, Program for Appropriate Technology in Health and World Health Organization (Geneva, forthcoming).

7 Ellsberg and Heise, forthcoming.

8 Finkelhor, 1994; also see Medical Research Council, *Fourth Meeting of the International Research Network on Violence Against Women* (Johannesburg, January 2001).

9 K. Best, "Non Consensual Sex Undermines Sexual Health," *Family Health International* Vol. 23 No. 4 (2005).

10 United Nations Children's Fund (UNICEF), *Profiting From Abuse: An Investigation into the Sexual Exploitation of Our Children* (New York, November 2001).

11 Finkelhor, 1994.

12 Dominguez et al, 2002.

13 United Nations Division for the Advancement of Women, *Background Information*, Prepared for Expert Group Meeting on Violence Against Women (Geneva, April 2005). Available from: www.un.org/womenwatch/daw/Review/english/responses.htm.

14 S. Kapoor, "Domestic Violence Against Women and Girls," *Innocenti Digest* No. 6 (Florence, June 2000); UNICEF, 2001.

15 Kapoor, 2000.

16 I. Intebi, 1998, cited in International Society for Prevention of Child Abuse and Neglect (ISP-CAN), "A Summary of the Literature on Child Sexual Abuse and Exploitation" (December 2001). Available from: www.ispcan.org/resources.

17 Heise et al, 1999.

18 Finkelhor, 1994.

19 Newell, 1997; A. Jordan, "Commercial Sex Workers in Asia: A Blind Spot in Human Rights Law," *Women and International Human Rights Law* Vol. 2 (Ardsley, 2000); D. Bowley and G. Pitcher,

"Motivation Behind Infant Rape in South Africa," *The Lancet* Vol. 359 (January 2002).

[20] R. Jewkes, L. Marin, and P. Loveday, "The Virgin Cleansing Myth: Cases of Child Rape are Not Exotic," *The Lancet* Vol. 359 (February 2002).

[21] Bowley and Pitcher, 2002, 274-275.

[22] Human Rights Watch, *Suffering in Silence: The Links Between Human Rights Abuses and HIV transmission to Girls in Zambia* (New York, November 2002).

[23] Human Rights Watch, 2002, 9.

[24] H. Mayell, "Thousands of Women Killed for Family Honor," *National Geographic News* (February, 2002). Available from: www.news.nationalgeographic.com.

[25] RAINN Statistics. Available from: www.rainn.org/statistics.html.

[26] WHO Fact Sheet, "Violence Against Women: Health Consequences, Family and Reproductive Health" (Geneva, 1997).

[27] A. Browne and D. Finkelhor, 1986, cited in A.C. Donnelly and K. Oates eds., *Classic Papers in Child Abuse* (Thousand Oaks, 2000).

[28] Convention of the Rights of the Child, 1989, cited in Newell, 1997, 3.

[29] J. Davidson, "The Sex Exploiter," Theme Paper for the Second World Congress Against Commercial Exploitation of Children (December 2001). Available from: www.ecpat.net/eng/Ecpat_inter/project/monitoring/wc2/yokohama_theme_sex_exploiter.pdf.

[30] A. Erulkar, "The Experience of Sexual Coercion Among Young People in Kenya," *International Family Planning Perspectives* Vol. 30 No. 4 (December 2004), 187.

[31] "South Africa Unable to Deal With Child Abuse," Reuters (April 2002).

[32] Amnesty International, "Making Violence Against Women Count: Facts and Figures" (March 2004). Available from: web.amnesty.org/library/print/ENGACT770362004.

[33] RAINN Statistics. Available from: www.rainn.org/statistics.html.

[34] Amnesty International, "Unheard Voices" (April 2005). Available from: web.amnesty.org/library/print/ENGAFR440042005.

[35] Heise et al, 1999.

[36] "Rape A 'Way of Life' on Pitcairn," BBC News (October 2004). Available from: news.bbc.co.uk/go/pr/fr/-/1/hi/world/asia-pacific/3705988.stm.

[37] "Pitcairn Sex Trial Men Sentenced," BBC News (October 2004). Available from: news.bbc.co.uk/2/hi/asia-pacific/3963863.stm.

chapter 3 — child prostitution and pornography

[1] United Nations Children's Fund (UNICEF), *Profiting from Abuse: An Investigation into the Sexual Exploitation of Our Children* (New York, 2001).

[2] UNICEF, 2001.

[3] A. Jordan, "Commercial Sex Workers in Asia: A Blind Spot in Human Rights Law," *Women and International Human Rights Law*, Askin and Koenig, eds., Vol. 2 (New York, 2000).

[4] UNICEF, 2001.

[5] M. Healy, "Child Pornography: An International Perspective", End Child Prostitution, Child Pornography and Trafficking of Children for Sexual Purposes (ECPAT) (Stockholm, August 1996).

[6] UNICEF, "Facts on Children: Child Protection" (Geneva, 2005). Available from: www.unicef.org/media/media_9482.html.

[7] International Labour Organization (ILO) (2000), cited in United Nations Special Rapporteur (UN Spec. Rapp.) on the Sale of Children, Child Prostitution, and Child Pornography, *Rights of the Child*, United Nations Commission on Human Rights E/CN.4/2004/9 (Geneva, January 2004).

[8] B. Willis and B. Levy, "Child Prostitution: Global Health Burden, Research Needs, and Interventions," *The Lancet* Vol. 359 (April 2002), 1417-1422.

[9] UNICEF, 2001.

[10] J. Carr, "Theme Paper on Child Pornography for the Second World Congress on Commercial Sexual Exploitation of Children" (December, 2001). Available from: www.ecpat.net/eng/Ecpat_inter/projects/monitoring/wc2/yokohama_theme_child_pornography.pdf.

[11] UNICEF, 2001, 30.

[12] M. Taylor and E. Quayle, *Child Pornography: An Internet Crime* (Hove, February 2003).

[13] E. Azaola, *Boy and Girl Victims of Sexual Exploitation in Mexico*, UNICEF (Geneva, June 2000), 8.

[14] R. Estes and N. Weiner, *The Commercial Sexual Exploitation of Children in the United States*, Canada, and Mexico, University of Pennsylvania Center for the Study of Youth Policy (Philadelphia, September 2001).

[15] Estes and Weiner, 2001.

[16] UNICEF, 2001.

[17] J. Davidson, "The Sex Exploiter," Theme Paper for the Second World Congress Against Commercial Exploitation of Children (December 2001), 24. Available from: www.ecpat.net/eng/Ecpat_inter/projects/monitoring/WC2/Yokohama_theme_sex_exploiter.pdf

[18] Davidson, 2001.

[19] Estes and Weiner, 2001.

[20] UN Spec. Rapp. on the Sale of Children, Child Prostitution, and Child Pornography, *Rights of the Child*, United Nations Commission on Human Rights E/CN.4/2003/79 (Geneva, January 2003).

[21] Davidson, 2001.

[22] Willis and Levy, 2002.

[23] International Tribunal for Children's Rights (ITCR), *Global Report - International Dimensions of the Sexual Exploitation of Children*, International Bureau for Children's Rights (Montreal, 1999), 22.

[24] Willis and Levy, 2002.

[25] Jordan, 2000.

[26] ITCR, 1999, 22.

[27] Jordan, 2000.

[28] United Nations Special Rapporteur (UN Spec. Rapp.) on Violence Against Women, *Integration of the Human Rights of Women and the Gender Perspective: Violence Against Women: Intersections of Violence Against Women and HIV/AIDS*, UN Commission on Human Rights E/CN.4/205/72 (Geneva, January 2005).

[29] Chikwenya et al, 1997, cited in Davidson, 2001, 21.

[30] M. Koenig, I. Zablotska, T. Lutalo, F. Nalugoda, J. Wagman and R. Gray, "Coerced First Intercourse and Reproductive Heath Among Adolescent Women in Rakai, Uganda," *International Family Planning Perspectives* Vol. 30 No. 4 (Baltimore 2004); H. Lary, S. Maman, M. Katebila and J. Mbwambo, "Exploring the Association Between HIV and Violence: Young People's Experiences with Infidelity, Violence, and Forced Sex in Dar Es Salaam, Tanzania," *International Family Planning Perspectives* Vol. 30 No. 4 (Baltimore, 2004); N. Luke, "Confronting the 'Sugar Daddy' Stereotype: Age and Economic Asymmetries and Risky Sexual Behavior in Urban Kenya," *International Family Planning Perspectives* Vol. 30 No. 4 (Baltimore, 2004).

[31] UN Spec. Rapp., 2004.

[32] UNICEF, 2001.

[33] Integrated Regional Information Networks (IRIN), "IRAQ: Focus on Boys Trapped in Commercial Sex Trade" (2005). Available from: www.irinnews.org/report.asp?ReportID=48485&SelectRegion=Middle_East&SelectCountry=IRAQ.

[34] Davidson, 2001; Wood, 2001, cited in Davidson, 2001, 19.

[35] Healy, 1996.

[36] Carr, 2001.

[37] Healy, 1996.

[38] Carr, 2001.

[39] Carr, 2001.

[40] ECPAT International, "Child Pornography: Record of a Crime" (December 2001). Available from: www.ecpat.net/eng/Ecpat_inter/projects/monitoring/wc2/briefing_note4asp; Healy, 1996.

[41] Carr, 2001.

42 Healy, 1996.
43 Healy, 1996.
44 ECPAT International, 2001.
45 Carr, 2001.
46 Carr, 2001, 3.
47 Carr, 2001.
48 UNICEF, 2001.
49 Carr, 2001, 16.
50 ITCR, 1999, 31.
51 Davidson, 2001, 10.
52 United States Department of State, *Trafficking in Persons Report*, Office for the Under Secretary for Global Affairs Publication 11252 (Washington, DC, June 2005); ITCR, 1999; Carr, 2001.
53 UN Spec. Rapp., 2003.
54 UN Spec. Rapp., 2003; UN Spec. Rapp., 2004.
55 UN Spec. Rapp., 2004, 9.
56 ITCR, 1999, 42.
57 Willis and Levy, 2002.

chapter 4 — female genital mutilation

1 N. Toubia, *Caring for Women with Circumcision: A Technical Manual for Health Care Providers*, Rainbo (New York, 1999); D. Carr, *Female Genital Cutting: Findings from the Demographic and Health Surveys Program*, Macro International (Maryland, September 1997).
2 Toubia, 1999.
3 World Health Organization (WHO), *Female Genital Mutilation: An Overview* (Geneva, 1998).
4 WHO, 1998, 6.
5 WHO, 1998.
6 WHO, 1998.
7 "Female Genital Mutilation: Legal Prohibitions Worldwide," Center for Reproductive Rights (February 2005). Available from: www.crlp.org/tools; Toubia, 1999.
8 Carr, 1997.
9 J. Aldous and G. Boyle, "Forewarned, men may remain foreskinned," *The Australian* (June 15, 1999).
10 M. Schoofs, S. Lueck and M. Phillips, "Findings From South Africa May Offer Powerful Way to Cut HIV Transmission," *The Wall Street Journal* (July 5, 2005).
11 WHO, 1998.
12 Center for Reproductive Rights, 2005.
13 Integrated Regional Information Networks (IRIN), "Razor's Edge: The Controversy of Female Genital Mutilation" (Kenya, 2005), 16.
14 Carr, 1997.
15 S. Igras, personal communication (August 30, 2005).
16 WHO, *Programmes to Date: What Works and What Doesn't: A Review*, Department of Women's Health, Health Systems and Community Health (Geneva, 1999).
17 Carr, 1997.
18 IRIN, 2005, 21.
19 Carr, 1997.
20 Andu, 1993, cited in Carr, 1997, 34.
21 WHO, 1998.
22 IRIN, 2005, 24.
23 WHO, 1999.
24 Carr, 1997; Toubia, 1999
25 IRIN, 2005, 30.
26 WHO, 1998.
27 WHO, 1999.
28 J. Munala, "Combating FGM in Kenya's Refugee Camps," *Human Rights Dialogue* (Fall 2003), 17-19, 17.
29 IRIN, 2005, 26.
30 Center for Reproductive Rights, 2005.
31 Center for Reproductive Rights, 2005; "Female Genital Mutilation in Africa: Information by Country," Amnesty International (1998). Available from: www.amnesty.org/ailib/intcam/femgen/fgm9.htm.
32 CARE, *Integrating Rights-based Approaches into Community-based Health Projects: Experiences from the Prevention of Female Genital Cutting Project in East Africa* (USA, August 2002).
33 Toubia, 1999, 10.
34 Toubia, 1999; Munala, 2003; CARE, 2002.
35 CARE, 2002.
36 Munala, 2003.
37 Carr, 1997.
38 J. Masterson and J. Swanson, *Female Genital Cutting: Breaking the Silence, Enabling Change*, International Center for Research on Women and the Center for Development and Population Activities (Washington, DC, 2000); CARE 2002.
39 A. Mohamud, K. Rignheim, S. Bloodworth and K. Gryboski, "Girls at Risk: Community Approaches to End Female Genital Mutilation and Treating Women Injured by the Practice," *Reproductive Health and Rights: Reaching the Hardly Reached* Article 8, Program for Appropriate Technology in Health (2002), 69-85.
40 IRIN, 2005; Mohamud et al, 2002.
41 Munala, 2003.
42 Masterson and Swanson, 2000.
43 UNICEF Technical Note, *Kenya FGM/C Country Profile* (New York, February 2005).
44 WHO, 1999.
45 United States Agency for International Development, *Information on Female Genital Cutting: What Is Out There? What Is Needed?* (Washington DC, July 2004).

chapter 5 — child marriage

1 S. Mathur, M. Greene and A. Malhotra, *Too Young to Wed: The Lives, Rights, and Health of Young Married Girls*, International Center for Research on Women (ICRW) (2003); M. Black, "Early Marriage: Child Spouses," *Innocenti Digest* Vol. 7 (Florence, March 2001).
2 IAC, 1993, cited in C. Somerset, *Child Marriage: Whose Right to Choose?*, Forum on Marriage and the Rights of Women and Girls (United Kingdom, May 2000), 6.
3 Black, 2001.
4 Barnes et al, 1998, cited in Somerset, 2000, 25.
5 Daily Star, 1999, cited in Somerset, 2000, 24.
6 S. Behgam and W. Mukhtar, *Child Marriage in Afghanistan: A Preliminary Briefing*, medica mondiale Afghanistan (May 2004).
7 J. Bruce, 2002, cited in N. Otoo-Oyortey and S. Pobi, *Early Marriage and Poverty: Exploring Links for Policy and Programme Development*, The Forum on Marriage and the Rights of Women and Girls (London, November 2003).
8 Mathur et al, 2003.
9 Demographic Health Surveys, 1996-2001, cited in "Child Marriage Hotspots," ICRW (2003). Available from: www.icrw.org/photoessay/pdfs/childmarriagehotspots.pdf.
10 Otoo-Oyortey and Pobi, 2003.
11 Otoo-Oyortey and Pobi, 2003.

[12] Black, 2001.
[13] Black, 2001.
[14] Black, 2001, 7.
[15] Black, 2001, 8.
[16] Black, 2001.
[17] Black, 2001, 8.
[18] Black, 2001.
[19] Segni, 2002, cited in Otoo-Oyortey and Pobi, 2003.
[20] Black, 2001.
[21] Mahmud, 2000, cited in Somerset, 2000, 12.
[22] Black, 2001.
[23] Sen, cited in Ouattara et al, 1998, cited in Somerset, 2000.
[24] Rubeihat, 1994, cited in Black, 2000.
[25] Otoo-Oyortey and Pobi, 2003.
[26] UNICEF, 2001, 9.
[27] Behgam and Mukhtar, 2004, 8.
[28] Otoo-Oyortey and Pobi, 2003.
[29] Black, 2001, 9.
[30] United Nations Special Rapporteur (UN Spec. Rapp.) on Violence Against Women, *Integration of the Human Rights of Women and the Gender Perspective: Violence Against Women: Intersections of Violence Against Women and HIV/AIDS*, UN Commission on Human Rights E/CN.4/205/72 (Geneva, January 2005).
[31] UN Spec. Rapp., 2002.
[32] Black, 2001.
[33] UNICEF, 1994, cited in Black, 2001.
[34] Otoo-Oyortey and Pobi, 2003, 26.
[35] Black, 2001.
[36] Dixon-Mueller, cited in Conway-Turner and Cherrin, cited in Otoo-Oyortey and Pobi, 2003.
[37] UNICEF, 1998, cited in Black, 2001.
[38] Otoo-Oyortey and Pobi, 2003.
[39] United Nations Population Fund (UNFPA) Press Release, "UNFPA Launches Two-Year Campaign to Fight Obstetric Fistula in Sub-Saharan Africa" (November 1, 2002). Available from: www.unfpa.org/news/news.cfm?ID=45&Language=1.
[40] Otoo-Oyortey and Pobi, 2003, 34.

chapter 6 — violence against girls in schools

[1] United Nations Children's Fund (UNICEF), *Breaking Silence: Gendered and Sexual Identities and HIV/AIDS in Education* (2003).
[2] Human Rights Watch (HRW) interview with WH, age 13, cited in Human Rights Watch, *Scared At School: Sexual Violence Against Girls in South African Schools* (New York, 2001).
[3] HRW interview with AC, age 14 (Mitchell's Plaine, April 15, 2000), cited in HRW, 2001.
[4] HRW interview with AC, cited in HRW, 2001.
[5] HRW interview with MC, age 15 (Johannesburg, March 18, 2000), cited in HRW, 2001. HRW, 2001.
[6] S. Rossetti, *Children in School: A Safe Place?*, United Nations Educational, Scientific and Cultural Organization (UNESCO) (Botswana, 2001).
[7] J. Mirsky, *Beyond Victims and Villains: Addressing Sexual Violence in the Education Sector*, Panos Report No. 47 (London, 2003), 22.
[8] HRW, 2001, 49.
[9] UNESCO, *Leap to Equality* (2003).
[10] UNESCO, 2003.
[11] HRW, 2001, 48.
[12] UNICEF, 2003.
[13] Rosetti, 2001.
[14] M. Dunne, S. Humphreys and F. Leach, *Gender and Violence in Schools*, Background paper for UNSECO-EFA Monitoring Report (2003).
[15] Dunne et al, 2003.
[16] HRW interview with MC, age 15 (Johannesburg, March 18, 2000), cited in HRW, 2001.
[17] Government of North West Frontier Province, UNICEF and Save the Children, *Disciplining the Child: Practices and Impacts* (Pakistan, 2005).
[18] N. Stein, 1995, cited in Mirsky, 2003, 24.
[19] HRW interview with WH, age 13, cited in HRW, 2001.
[20] D. Warwick and F. Reimers, *Hope or Despair? Learning in Pakistan's Primary Schools* (Westport, 1995).
[21] G. Atinga, *Beginning Teachers' Perceptions and Experiences of Sexual Harassment in Ghanaian Teacher Training Institutions*, Unpublished PhD dissertation, McGill University (Montreal, 2004).
[22] Action Aid, *Stop Violence Against Girls in Schools* (Johannesburg, 2004).
[23] American Association of University Women, *Hostile Hallways: Bullying, Teasing and Sexual Harassment in School* (Newton, 2001).
[24] N. Duncan, *Sexual bullying: Gender conflict and pupil culture in secondary schools* (London, 1999).
[25] Rossetti, 2001.
[26] United Nations High Commissioner for Refugees and Save the Children UK, *Note for Implementing and Operational Partners on Sexual Violence and Exploitation: The Experience of Refugee Children in Guinea, Liberia and Sierra Leone* (2002). Available from: www.unhcr.org.
[27] HRW, 2001.
[28] Dreyer, 2004. For further details, contact Abigail Dreyer: adreyer@uwc.ac.za.
[29] O. Mlameli, V. Napo, P. Mabalene, V. Free, M. Goodman, J. Larkin, C. Mitchell, H. Mkhize, K. Robinson and A. Smith, *Opening our Eyes: Addressing Gender-based Violence in South African Schools*, Canada-South Africa Educational Management Program (Montreal, 2001). For further details, contact Claudia Mitchell: Claudia.mitchell@mcgill.ca.
[30] J. Kirk & R. Winthrop, *Changing the gendered dynamics of refugee classrooms in West Africa*, International Rescue Committee (New York, 2005).

chapter 7 — sex trafficking in women and girls

[1] Amnesty International (AI), "So Does It Mean That We Have the Rights?" (May 2004), 2. Available from: web.amnesty.org/library/Index/ENGEUR700102004.
[2] AI, 2004.
[3] A. Rossi, "Trafficking in Human Beings, Especially Women and Children, in Africa," *Innocenti Insight* (Florence, September 2003), 3.
[4] United States Department of State, *Trafficking in Persons Report*, Office for the Under Secretary for Global Affairs Publication 11252 (Washington, DC, June 2005).
[5] Protection Project, "Global Trafficking in Women: Modern Day Slavery and the Movement to End it," International Women's Day Address at Bradley University (United States, March 8, 2004). Available from: www.protectionproject.org.
[6] United States Department of State, 2005.
[7] International Labour Office, *A Global Alliance Against Forced Labour*, International Labour Conference Report I(B) (Geneva, 2005), 51.
[8] M. Gimon, N. Kazi, D. Mikhail, J. Mueller, P. Ryan and K. Sloehr, *Not for Sale: Child Trafficking Prevention in South Eastern Europe*, United Nations Children's Fund (UNICEF) and Columbia University School of International and Public Affairs (Geneva, May 2003).

9 B. Benninger et al, 1999, cited in R. Jewkes, P. Sen, C. Garcia-Moreno, "Chapter 6: Sexual Violence," in E. Krug, L. Dahlberg, J. Mercy, A. Zwi and R. Lozano, eds., *World Health Organization World Report on Violence and Health*, World Health Organization (Geneva, 2002).

10 Protection Project, cited in J. Carr, "Theme Paper on Child Pornography for the Second World Congress on Commercial Sexual Exploitation of Children" (December, 2001). Available from: www.ecpat.net/eng/Ecpat_inter/projects/monitoring/wc2/yokohama_theme_child_pornography.pdf.

11 Protection Project, cited in Carr, 2001.

12 N. Levenkron, "The Right to a Call Girl" (January 2005). Available from: www.haaretz.com/hasen/spages/522645.html

13 International Organization for Migration, 1995, cited in Jewkes et al, 2002.

14 C. Makino, "Japan Installs Caution Signal for Sex Traffic" (July 2005). Available from: www.womensenews.org/article.cfm?aid=2378.

15 United States Department of State, 2005.

16 L. Ros, "Image Reference LRO00013NIG" (2003). Available from: www.panos.co.uk.

17 J. Frederick and M. Brown, "Export Commodities: Trafficking from Nepal to India" (May 2004). Available from: www.tdhnepal.org/html/newsletters/.

18 United States Department of State, 2005.

19 United States Department of State, 2005.

20 C. Zimmerman, K. Yon, I. Shuab, C. Watts, L. Trappolin, M. Treppete, F. Bimbi, B. Adams, S. Ciraporn, L. Beci, M. Albrecht, J. Binder and L. Kegan, *The Health Risks and Consequences of Trafficking in Women and Adolescents: Findings from a European Study*, London School of Hygiene and Tropical Medicine (London, 2003).

21 United Nations Special Rapporteur on Violence Against Women, *Integration of the Human Rights of Women and the Gender Perspective: Intersections of Violence Against Women and HIV/AIDS*, United Nations Commission on Human Rights E/CN.4/205/72 (Geneva, January 2005).

22 United States Department of State, 2005.

23 Zimmerman et al, 2003.

24 United States Department of State, 2005.

25 United States Department of State, 2005.

26 Zimmerman et al, 2003; United States Department of State, 2005.

27 Protection Project, 2004; United States Department of State, 2005.

28 Zimmerman et al, 2003, 29.

29 Protection Project, *Global Trafficking in Women*, 2004.

30 Frederick and Brown, 2004.

31 UNICEF, *Profiting from Abuse: An Investigation into the Sexual Exploitation of Our Children* (New York, 2001).

32 UNICEF, 2001.

33 International Labour Office, 2005.

34 Carr, 2001.

35 Carr, 2001.

36 United States Department of State, 2005, 10.

37 J. Madslien, "Sex Trade's Reliance on Forced Labor," BBC News (May 2005).

38 Carr, 2001; United States Department of State, 2005; Rossi, 2003.

39 International Organization for Migration, 2003, cited in BBC News, 2005.

40 M. Clark, *Mail-order Brides: Exploited Dreams*, Testimony to the US Senate Committee on Foreign Relations (Washington, DC, July 2004). Available from: www.protectionproject.org.

41 Clark, 2004.

42 M. Mattar, *A Regional Comparative Legal Analysis of Sex Trafficking and Sex Tourism*, Protection Project, Johns Hopkins University School of Advanced International Studies (Singapore, April 25-27, 2005).

43 United States Department of State, 2005, 12.

44 United States Department of State, 2005, 6.

45 Mattar, 2005.

46 UNICEF, 2001.

47 United States Department of State, 2005.

48 C. Zimmerman and C. Watts, *World Health Organization Ethical and Safety Recommendations for Interviewing Trafficked Women*, World Health Organization (London, 2003).

49 Zimmerman et al, 2003, 111.

50 United Nations Special Rapporteur on Trafficking in Persons, *Integration of the Human Rights of Women and the Gender Perspective*, United Nations Commission on Human Rights E/CN.4/2005/71 (Geneva, December 2004), 2.

51 UNICEF, 2001, 16.

52 Protection Project, *Global Trafficking in Women*, 2004.

chapter 8 — dowry crimes and bride-price abuse

1 A. Hitchcock, "Rising number of dowry deaths in India," World Socialist Web Site (July 4, 2001). Available from: www.wsws.org/articles/2001/july2001/ind-j04.shtml.

2 J. Rudd, "Dowry-Murder: An Example Of Violence Against Women," *Women's Studies International Forum* Vol. 24 No. 5 (2001), 513-522.

3 P. Srinivasan and G. Lee, *The Dowry System in India: Women's Attitudes and Social Change*, Working Paper Series 02-15, Center for Family and Demographic Research, Bowling Green State University (2002).

4 H. Thakur, "Are our sisters and daughters for sale?" India Together (June 1999). Available from: www.indatogether.org/wehost/nodowri/stats.htm.

5 S. Kapoor, "Domestic Violence Against Women and Girls," *Innocenti Digest* Vol. 6 (Florence, June 2000).

6 K. Sharma, "Rooted Custom," *India Together* (November 2002). Available from: www.indiatogether.org/opinions/kalpana/dowvict.htm.

7 A. Aguirre, "Dowry: Killing Wives and Crushing Spirits," *Iran Dokht* (2002). Available from: www.irandokht.com.

8 L. Suran, S. Amin, L. Huq and K. Chowdury, *Does Dowry Improve Life for Brides? A Test of the Bequest Theory of Dowry in Rural Bangladesh*, Working Paper No. 195, Policy Research Division, Population Council (2004).

9 Suran et al, 2004.

10 Zhang and Chan, 1999, cited in S. Anderson, "Why Dowry Payments Declined with Modernization in Europe But Are Rising in India," *Journal of Political Economy* Vol. 111 No. 2 (April 2003), 269-310.

11 P.N. Mari Bhat and S. Halli, "Demography of Brideprice and Dowry: Causes and Consequences of the Indian Marriage Squeeze," *Population Studies* Vol. 53 No. 2 (July 1999), 129-148.

12 M. N. Srinivas, *The Cohesive Role of Sanskritization and Other Essays*, Oxford University Press (Delhi, 1989).

13 Anderson, 2003.

14 Rajaraman, cited in V. Rao, "The Rising Price of Husbands: A Hedonic Analysis of Dowry Increases in Rural India," *Journal of Political Economy* Vol. 101 No. 4 (August 1993); Rudd, 2001.

15 Caldwell, Reddy and Caldwell, 1983, cited in Anderson, 2003.

16 F. Bloch and V. Rao, "Terror as Bargaining Instrument: A Case-Study of Dowry Violence in Rural India," *American Economic Review* Vol. 92 No. 4 (September 2002), 1029-43.

17 Bloch and Rao, 2002.

18 Verma and Collumbiean, 2003, cited in Suran et al, 2004.

19 Suran et al, 2004, 2.

20 Kapoor, 2000.

21 Murdock, 1967, cited in Anderson, 2003.

22 S. Tambiah, "Bridewealth and Dowry Revisited: The Position of Women in Sub-Saharan

Africa and North India," *Current Anthropology* Vol. 30 No. 4 (August-October 1989), 413-435.

23 Boserup, 1970, cited in Anderson, 2000; M. Das Gupta and L. Shuzhuo, "Gender Bias in China, South Korea and India, 1920-90: Effects of War, Famine and Fertility Decline," *Development and Change*, Special Issue on Gendered Poverty and Wellbeing (forthcoming).

24 U. Kistner, *Gender-based Violence and HIV/AIDS in South Africa: A Literature Review*, Centre for AIDS Development, Research and Evaluation (CADRE), Department of Health (South Africa, January 2003), 46.

25 R. Rinaldo, "Culture - Uganda: A Price Above Rubies," Inter Press Service News Agency (February 18, 2004).

26 Rinaldo, 2004.

27 C. Wendo, "African Women Denounce Bride Price," *The Lancet* Vol. 363 (February 2004), 716.

28 Wendo, 2004; J. Ward, "Because Men Are Really Sitting on Our Heads and Pressing Us Down," A Preliminary Assessment in South Sudan on behalf of the United States Agency for International Development, unpublished document (March 2005).

29 Feel Free Network, "Bride Price: African Pride or Prejudice?" (2003). Available from: www.feelfreenetwork.org/text_only/bride_price_text_only.htm; Rinaldo, 2004.

30 Feel Free Network, 2004.

31 Sharma, 2002; Rinaldo, 2004.

32 Wendo, 2004.

33 Rinaldo, 2004.

34 Thakur, 1999.

35 A. Mynott, "Fighting India's Dowry Crime," BBC News (November 14, 2003).

36 Mynott, 2003.

37 Rinaldo, 2004.

38 Wendo, 2004; Sharma, 2002.

39 Thakur, 1999.

40 M. Kishwar, "Destined to Fail: Inherent Flaw in the Anti-Dowry Legislation," *Manushi* No 148 (May – June 2005).

chapter 9 — intimate-partner violence

1 Amnesty International (AI), "Making Violence Against Women Count: Facts and Figures" (March 2004). Available from: web.amnesty.org/library/print/ENGAFR440042005; M. Mollmann, "A Test of Inequality: Discrimination Against Women Living with HIV in the Dominican Republic," *Human Rights Watch* Vol. 16 No. 4 (B) (New York, 2004).

2 L. Heise, M. Ellsberg and M. Gottemoeller, "Ending Violence Against Women," *Population Reports* Series L No. 11 (Baltimore, 1999).

3 L. Walker, "Psychology and Domestic Violence Around the World," *American Psychologist* Vol. 54 No. 1 (1999), 23.

4 Heise et al, 1999; L. Heise and C. Garcia Moreno, "Chapter 4: Violence by Intimate Partners," in E. Krug, L. Dahlberg, J. Mercy, A. Zwi and R. Lozano eds., *World Report on Violence and Health*, World Health Organization (Geneva, 2002); S. Kishor and K. Johnson, *Profiling Domestic Violence: A Multi-country Study*, ORC Macro (Calverton, June 2004); W. Parish, T. Wang, E. Laumann, S. Pan, and Y. Luo, "Intimate Partner Violence in China: National Prevalence, Risk Factors, and Associated Health Problems," *International Family Planning Perspectives* Vol. 30 No. 4 (2004); AI, 2004.

5 Heise and Garcia Moreno, 2002.

6 H. Johnson and K. Au Coin, eds., *Family Violence in Canada: A Statistical Profile 2003*, Canadian Centre for Justice Statistics (Ottawa, June 2003).

7 Heise and Garcia Moreno, 2002; Heise et al, 1999.

8 Heise and Garcia Moreno, 2002, 95.

9 N. Duvvury, *Domestic Violence in India: Rooting for Change*, International Center for Research on Women (ICRW), Fourth Meeting of the International Research Network on Violence Against Women (Johannesburg, January 2001).

10 M. Ellsberg and L. Heise, *Researching Violence Against Women: A Practical Guide for Researchers and Advocates*, Program for Appropriate Technology in Health and World Health Organization (Geneva, forthcoming).

11 Kishor and Johnson, 2004; L. Heise, J. Pitanguy and A. Germain, *Violence Against Women: The Hidden Health Burden*, World Bank Discussion Paper 255 (Washington, DC, 1994).

12 M. Ellsberg, R. Pena, A. Herrera, J. Lilgestrand and A. Winkvist, "Candies in Hell: Women's Experiences of Violence in Nicaragua," *Social Science and Medicine* Vol. 51(2000), 1595-1610, 1605.

13 Heise and Garcia Moreno, 2002.

14 M Kimmel, "Gender Symmetry in Domestic Violence," *Violence Against Women* Vol. 8 No. 11 (November 2002), 1332-1363.

15 G. Charowa, Personal Correspondence (May 9, 2005).

16 Heise et al, 1999, 9.

17 World Health Organization (WHO), "Sexual Violence Fact Sheet" (2002). Available from: www.who.int/violence_injury_prevention.

18 WHO, 2002; C. Watts and S. Mayhew, "Reproductive Health Services and Intimate Partner Violence: Shaping a Pragmatic Response in Sub-Saharan Africa," *International Family Planning Perspectives* Vol. 30 No. 4 (2004), 207-213.

19 Heise et al, 1999; J. Csete, *Policy Paralysis: A Call for Action on HIV/AIDS-Related Human Rights Abuses Against Women and Girls in Africa*, Human Rights Watch (New York, 2003), 30.

20 I. Weiser, Personal Correspondance (August 13, 2005).

21 Ellsberg et al, 2000, 1602.

22 UNDP Human Development Report (1997), cited in AI, "Violence Against Women: Worldwide Statistics." Available from: www.amnesty.org.nz/web/pages/home.nsf/.

23 AI, *Violence Against Women: Worldwide Statistics*.

24 VicHealth, *The Health Costs of Violence: Measuring the Burden of Disease Caused by Intimate Partner Violence*, Department of Human Services (Victoria, June 2004), 10.

25 S. Kapoor, "Domestic Violence Against Women and Girls," *Innocenti Digest* Vol. 6 (Florence, June 2000).

26 Heise and Garcia Moreno, 2002; WHO 2000, cited in VicHealth, 2004.

27 Human Rights Watch, "Uzbekistan Turns Its Back on Battered Women" (July 2001). Available from: hrw.org/english/docs/2001/07/10/uzbeki72.htm.

28 Ellsberg et al, 2000.

29 Family Health International, "Non-Consensual Sex," *Network* Vol. 23 No. 4 (2005).

30 World Health Organization Department of Gender, Women and Health, *Violence Against Women and HIV/AIDS: Critical Intersections*, WHO Information Bulletin Series No. 1 (Geneva, 2004).

31 L. Karanja, "Just Die Quietly," *Human Rights Watch* Vol. 15 No. 15 (A) (2003), 24.

32 M. Mollmann, 2004, 15.

33 U. Kistner, *Gender-based Violence and HIV/AIDS in South Africa: A Literature Review*, Centre for AIDS Development, Research and Evaluation (CADRE), Department of Health (South Africa, January 2003); Csete, 2003.

34 United Nations Division for the Advancement of Women, *Background Information*, Prepared for the Expert Group Meeting, (Geneva, April 2005). Available from: www.un.org/womenwatch/daw/review/english/responses.htm.

35 J. Seager 2003, cited in AI, 2004.

36 Heise and Garcia Moreno, 2002.

37 Mollmann, 2004.

38 Kapoor, 2000.

39 K. Asling-Monemi, R. Pena, M. Ellsberg and L. Persson, "Violence Against Women Increases the Risk of Infant and Child Mortality: A Case Reference Study in Nicaragua," *Bulletin of the World Health Organization* Vol. 81 No. 1 (2003), 10-16; WHO, 2002.

40 Heise and Garcia Moreno, 2002; B. Araya, *Domestic Violence Needs Assessment: The Central Zone,* Eritrea, University of Asmara (Asmara, July 2001).

41 Heise and Garcia Moreno, 2002.

42 N. Duvvury, C. Grown, J. Redner, *Costs of Intimate Partner Violence at the Household and Community Levels: An Operational Framework for Developing Countries,* International Center for Research on Women (Washington, DC, 2004).

43 Duvvury et al, 2004.

44 Araya, 2001.

45 L. Heise, "Violence Against Women: An Integrated Ecological Framework," *Violence Against Women* Vol. 4 (1998).

46 Heise and Garcia Moreno, 2002.

47 L. Michau and D. Nakar, *Mobilising Communities to Prevent Domestic Violence: A Resource Guide for Organisations in East and Southern Africa,* Raising Voices (Uganda, 2003), 7.

48 Kishor and Johnson, 2004, 25.

49 N. Abraham, R. Jewkes and R. Laubsher, 1999, cited in Kistner, 2003, 62.

50 Heise and Garcia Moreno, 2002, 113.

chapter 10 — crimes of "honour"

1 United Nations Special Rapporteur (UN Spec. Rapp.) on Extrajudicial, Summary or Arbitrary Executions, *Civil and Political Rights, Including Questions of Disappearances and Summary Executions,* United Nations Economic and Social Council E/CN.4/2000/3 (January, 2000).

2 UN Spec. Rapp., 2000.

3 UN Spec. Rapp. on Violence Against Women, *Integration of the Human Rights of Women and the Gender Perspective, Cultural Practices in the Family that are Violent Towards Women,* United Nations Economic and Social Council E/CN.4/2002/83 (January, 2002).

4 UN Spec. Rapp., 2000.

5 Amnesty International (AI), *Women Confronting Family Violence* (2004). Available from: web.amnesty.org/library/print/ENGEUR440132004.

6 UN Spec. Rapp., 2002.

7 AI, 2004.

8 International Secretariat of Amnesty International, "Afghanistan: Stoning to Death – Human Rights Scandal," AI News (April 26, 2005).

9 UN Spec. Rapp., 2002, 12.

10 UN Spec. Rapp., 2000; UN Spec Rapp., 2002.

11 H. Mayell, "Thousands of Women Killed for Family 'Honor'," *National Geographic News* (February 12, 2002).

12 D. Farouki, *Violence Against Women: A Statistical Overview, Challenges and Gaps in Data Collection and Methodology and Approaches for Overcoming Them,* Paper Prepared for Expert Group Meeting, United Nations Division for the Advancement of Women (Geneva, April 2005); K. Peratis, "Honoring the Killers: Justice Denied for 'Honor' Crimes in Jordan," *Human Rights Watch* Vol. 16 No. 1 (E) (New York, 2004).

13 UN Spec. Rapp., 2002.

14 Integrated Regional Information Networks (IRIN), *Jordan: Special Report on Honour Killings* (2005). Available from: www.irinnews.org/print.asp?ReportID=46677; Farouki, 2005.

15 AI, 2004.

16 UN Spec. Rapp., 2002.

17 Mayell, 2002.

18 G. Bedell, "Death Before Dishonor," *The Observer* (November 21, 2004).

19 Mayell, 2002.

20 UN Spec. Rapp., 2002, 13.

21 UN Spec. Rapp., 2002, 13.

22 T. Kahn, 1999, cited in Mayell, 2002, 2.

23 UN Spec. Rapp., 2000.

24 UN Spec. Rapp., 2002, 13.

25 AI, 2004.

26 J. Borger, "In Cold Blood," *Manchester Guardian Weekly* (November 16, 1997); Mayell, 2002.

27 UN Spec. Rapp., 2000.

28 UN Spec. Rapp., 2002.

29 A. Jones, " 'Honour' Killings of Women." Available from: www.genercide.org

30 L. Brand, *Women, the State, and Political Liberalization: Middle Eastern and North African Experiences* (New York, 1998), 133.

31 Amnesty International (AI), *Honour Killings of Girls and Women* (1999). Available from: web.amnesty.org/library/print/ENGASA330181999.

32 AI, 1999.

33 Peratis, 2004.

34 Peratis, 2004.

35 UN Spec. Rapp., 2002; AI, 2004.

36 Peratis, 2004; AI, 2004.

37 UN Spec. Rapp,. 2002.

38 UN Spec. Rapp., 2000; L. Welchman, *Roundtable on Strategies to Address "Crimes of Honour": Summary Report,* Women Living Under Muslim Law Occasional Paper No. 12 (London, 2001). Available from: www.mluml.org.

39 IRIN, 2005.

40 UN Spec. Rapp., 2002.

41 AI, 2004.

42 Bedell, 2004.

43 IRIN, 2005, 2.

44 UN Spec. Rapp., 2000; Welchman, 2001.

45 L. Pervizat, "In the Name of Honor," *Human Rights Dialogue* (Fall 2003), 30-31; AI, 2004.

46 A. Foster, "Tunisia," *Women's Issues Worldwide: The Middle East and North Africa.,* B. Sherif-Trask, ed. (Westport, CT, 2003), 381-410.

47 Z. Daoud, "Les Femmes Tunisiennes: Gains Juridiques et Statut Economique et Social," Monde Arabe Maghreb Machrek, (145), 27-48.

48 Bedell, 2004.

chapter 11 — sexual assault and harassment

1 K. Wood, *Defining Forced Sex, Rape, Stream-Line and Gang-Rape: Notes from South African Township,* Fourth Meeting of the International Research Network on Violence Against Women, Medical Research Council (Johannesburg, January 2001), 25.

2 A. Abbey, P. McAuslan, T. Zawacki, A. Clinton and P. Buck, "Attitudinal, Experiential, and Situational Predictors of Sexual Assault Perpetration," *Journal of Interpersonal Violence* Vol. 16 No. 8 (2001), 784-807.

3 Abbey, et al., 2001.

4 L. Heise, K. Moore, and N. Toubia, "Sexual Coercion and Reproductive Health: A Focus on Research," Population Council (1995).

5 Heise et al, 1995.

6 I. Anderson and V. Swainson, "Perceived Motivation for Rape: Gender Differences in Beliefs About Female and Male Rape," Current Research in Social Psychology Vol. 6 No. 8 (2001).

7 L. Heise, J. Pitanguy and A. Germain, Violence Against Women: The Hidden Health Burden, World Bank Discussion Papers 255 (Washington, DC, 1995), iii.

8 R. Jewkes, P. Sen, C. Garcia-Moreno, "Chapter 6: Sexual Violence," in E. Krug, L. Dahlberg, J. Mercy, A. Zwi and R. Lozano, eds., *World Health Organization World Report on Violence and Health*, World Health Organization (Geneva, 2002).

9 R. Jewkes and N. Abrahams, "The Epidemiology of Rape and Sexual Coercion in South Africa: An Overview," *Social Sciences and Medicine* Vol. 55 (2002), 1231-1244.

10 Jewkes et al, 2002, 149.

11 Jewkes et al, 2002, 149.

12 Minnesota Advocates for Human Rights (MAHR), "Stop Violence Against Women" (2003). Available from: www.stopvaw.org/.

13 United Nations Special Rapporteur (UN Spec. Rapp.) on Violence Against Women, *Further Promotion and Encouragement of Human Rights and Fundamental Freedoms, Including the Question of the Programme and Methods of Work of the Commission*, UN Economic and Social Council E/CN.4/1997/41 (February 1997), 11.

14 K. Koestner & B. Sokolow, cited in Minnesota Advocates for Human Rights, "Stop Violence Against Women" (2003). Available from: www.stopvaw.org/.

15 P. Rozec, cited in Heise et al, 1995.

16 L. Heise, M. Ellsberg and M. Gottemoeller, "Ending Violence Against Women," *Population Reports* Series L No. 11 (Baltimore, 1999), 11.

17 S. Jejeebhoy and S. Bott, *Non-Consensual Sexual Experience of Young People: A Review of the Evidence From Developing Countries*, Regional Working Papers No. 16, Population Council (New Delhi, 2003), 23.

18 B. Fisher, F. Cullen and M. Turner, *The Sexual Victimization of College Women*, United States Department of Justice (Washington, DC, 2002).

19 N. Toubia, cited in Heise et al, 1995.

20 M. Koss, cited in Heise et al, 1995.

21 Jewkes et al, WHO, 2002.

22 M. Koss, C. Gidyez and N. Wisniewski (1987) and D. Kilpatrick, C. Edmunds and A. Seymour (1992), cited in World Health Organization (WHO), *Violence Against Women: A Priority Health Issue, Family and Reproductive Health* (Geneva, 1997).

23 Jewkes et al, 2002.

24 M. Randall and L. Haskell (1995), cited in WHO, 1997.

25 R. Elman, "Confronting the Sexual Abuse of Women with Disabilities" (January 2005). Available from: www.vaw.umn.edu/documents/vawnet/arsvanddisability/arsvanddisalitly.html.

26 Jewkes et al, 2000, cited in L. Bennett, L. Manderson and J. Astbury, *Mapping a Global Pandemic: A Review of Current Literature on Rape, Sexual Assault, and Sexual Harassment of Women*, Consultation on Sexual Violence Against Women, University of Melbourne (Melbourne, 2002).

27 C. Yimin, L. Shouqing, Q. Arzhu and Z. Yuke, *Sexual Coercion Amongst Chinese Unmarried Adolescent Abortion Seekers*, Fourth Meeting of the International Research Network on Violence Against Women, Medical Research Council (Johannesburg, 2001).

28 M. Koenig, I. Zablotska, T. Lutalo, F. Nalugoda, J. Wagman and R. Gray, "Coerced First Intercourse and Reproductive Health Among Adolescent Women in Rakai, Uganda," *International Family Planning Perspectives* Vol. 30 No. 4 (2004), 156-63.

29 Jejeebhoy and Bott, 2003.

30 M. Ellsberg and L. Heise, *Researching Violence Against Women: A Practical Guide for Researchers and Advocates*, Program for Appropriate Technology in Health and World Health Organization (Geneva, forthcoming).

31 Jewkes et al, 2002, 157.

32 A. Erulkar, "The Experience of Sexual Coercion Among Young People in Kenya," *International Family Planning Perspective* Vol. 30 No. 4 (2004), 182-189.

33 WHO, "Sexual Violence Fact Sheet" (2002). Available from: www.who.int/violence_injury_prevention.

34 Family Health International, "Non-consensual Sex Undermines Sexual Health," *Network* Vol. 23 No. 4 (2005).

35 A. Abbey, "Lessons Learned and Unanswered Questions About Sexual Assault Perpetration,"

Journal of Interpersonal Violence Vol. 20 No. 1 (2005), 39-42, 39.

36 D. Scully and J. Marolla, "Riding the Bull at Gilley's: Convicted Rapists Describe the Rewards of Rape," *Social Problems* Vol. 32 No. 3 (1985), 251-263.

37 Jewkes and Abrahams, 2002, 1242.

38 Scully and Marolla, 1985, 252.

39 M. Koss and K. Leonard 1984, cited in Scully and Marolla, 1985.

40 N. Malamuth 1989, cited in Abbey, 2005; Scully and Marolla 1985.

41 J. Goodchilds and G. Zellman, 1984, cited in Abbey et al., 2001.

42 Abbey et al, 2001.

43 Bennett et al, 2002.

44 Heise et al, 1999, 11.

45 Scully and Marolla, 1985, 261.

46 Anderson and Swainson, 2001.

47 Scully and Marolla, 1985.

48 Jejeebhoy and Bott, 2003.

49 N. Kristoff, "Raped, Kidnapped, and Silenced," *New York Times* (June 14, 2005).

50 M. Koss, 1993, cited in Jewkes and Abrahams, 2002.

51 Statistics Canada, 1993, cited in L. Kelly, *Promising Practices Addressing Sexual Violence*, Paper Prepared for Expert Group Meeting on Violence Against Women, United Nations Division for the Advancement of Women (Geneva, April 2005).

52 Jewkes and Abrahams, 2002.

53 T. Luo, "Marrying My Rapist?!: The Cultural Trauma Among Chinese Rape Survivors," *Gender and Society* Vol. 14 No. 4 (2000), 581-597.

54 Amnesty International (AI), "Nigeria: Unheard Voices" (May 2005). Available from: web.amnesty.org/library/print/ENGAFR440042005.

55 J. Fleischman, *Suffering in Silence: The Links Between Human Rights Abuses and HIV Transmission to Girls in Zambia*, Human Rights Watch (New York, 2002), 34.

56 UN Spec. Rapp., 1997.

57 Oxfam, "Towards Ending Violence Against Women in South Asia," Briefing Paper No. 66 (Oxford, September 2003).

58 UN Spec. Rapp., 1997.

59 UN Spec. Rapp., 1997.

60 Heise et al, 1995.

61 R. Mollica and L. Son (1989), cited in R. Fischback and B. Herbert, "Domestic Violence and Mental Health: Correlates and Conundrums Within and Across Cultures," *Social Science Medicine* Vol. 45 No. 8 (1997), 1161-1176, 1166.

62 Luo, 2000.

63 Bennett et al, 2002.

64 UN Spec. Rapp., 1997, 14.

65 Scully and Morolla, 1985, 262.

66 Minnesota Advocates for Human Rights (MAHR), Women's Rights Center and Georgetown University Law Center, *Employment Discrimination and Sexual Harassment in Poland* (Washington, DC, 2002), 29.

67 UN Spec. Rapp., 1997, 14.

68 U. Kompipote, *Sexual Harassment in the Workplace: A Report from Field Research in Thailand*, International Labor Rights Fund and Rights for Working Women Campaign (Washington, DC, 2002).

69 MAHR et al, 2003.

70 C Piotrkowski, "Sexual Harassment" (May 2002). Available from: www.ilo.org/public/english/protection/safework/gender/encyclo/psy14ae.htm.

71 "Sexual Harassment in the Workplace in Nepal," *Nepal News* (August 31-Sep 06, 2001). Available from: www.nepalnews.com.np; Minnesota Advocates for Human Rights (MAHR), *Sex Discrimination and Sexual Harassment in the Workplace in Bulgaria*, Women's Rights Center, Georgetown University Law Center (Washington, DC, 1999); "Sexual Harassment in Central and Eastern Europe: Brief Article," *New York Times* (January 2000). Available from:

www.findarticles.com/p/articles/mi_m2872/is_2_26/ai_62140815.
72 International Labour Organization (ILO), "Government, Employer, and Worker Representatives Gather in Penang to Combat Risk of Sexual Harassment at Work" (October, 2001). Available from: www.ilo.org/public/english/region/asro/bangkok/newsroom/pr0112.htm.
73 Z. Ming, "China's First Sexual Harassment Lawsuit" (March 2002). Available from: www.chinatoday.com.cn/English/20023/lawsuit.htm; ILO, 2001.
74 MAHR et al, 1999.
75 UN Spec. Rapp., 1997, 16.
76 Anderson and Swainson, 2001, 26.
77 UN Spec. Rapp., 1997.
78 L. Apizar, "Impunity and Women's Rights in Ciudad Juarez," Human Rights Dialogue (2003), 27-29; P. Donohoe, "Sexual Assault and Murder of Women and Girls aged 11-25 in Juarez" (2005). Available from: www.womenofjuarez.com/background.html.
79 UN Spec. Rapp., 1997, 4.
80 Bennett et al, 2002.
81 Garcia Moreno and Watts, 2000, cited in Bennett et al., 2002.
82 C. Rennison, 2002, cited Kelly, 2005.
83 Jewkes et al, 2002.
84 UN Spec Rapp, 1997.
85 Jewkes et al, 2002.
86 AI, "Casualties of war: Women's Bodies, Women's Lives" (October 2004). Available from: web.amnesty.org/library/Index/ENGACT770722004?open&of=ENG-373.
87 Jewkes and Abrahams, 2002, 1242.

chapter 12 — abuse of older women

1 B. Katayama, "Sexual Abuse of the Elderly," Forensic Nurse (September/October 2005). Available from: www.forensicnursemag.com.
2 World Health Organization (WHO)/ International Network for the Prevention of Elderly Abuse (INPEA), Missing Voices: Views of Older Persons on Elder Abuse (Geneva, 2002), 9.
3 J. Teitelman and P. O'Neill, "Elder and Adult Sexual Abuse: A Model Curriculum for Adult Services/Adult Protective Services Workers," Journal of Elder Abuse and Neglect Vol. 11 (3) (1999), 93.
4 Global Action on Aging, International Plan of Action on Ageing 2002, Unedited Version (Madrid, April 2002).
5 WHO/INPEA, 2002.
6 B. Penhale, "Bruises on the Soul: Older Women, Domestic Violence, and Elder Abuse," Journal of Elder Abuse & Neglect Vol. 11 No. 1 (1999), 1-22, 5.
7 Pillemer and Finkelhor, 1988, cited in B. Fisher, T. Zink, B. Rinto, S. Regan, S. Pabst, and E. Gothelf, "Overlooked Issues During the Golden Years: Domestic Violence and Intimate Partner Violence Against Older Women," Violence Against Women Vol. 9 No.12 (2003), 1409-16.
8 J. Y. Kim and K. Sung, "Marital Violence Among Korean Elderly Couples: A Cultural Residue," Journal of Elder Abuse and Neglect Vol. 13 No. 4 (2001), 73-89.
9 Zink, Regan, Goldenhar and Pabst, cited in Fisher (2003), cited in Fisher, 2003.
10 Fisher et al., 2003, 17.
11 F. Clark, "Elder Abuse: A Hidden Reality," Ageways: Practical Issues in Ageing and Development Issue 59, HelpAge International (April 2002), 4-5, 4.
12 Older woman, cited in Keikelame and Ferreira, 2000, cited in HelpAge International, Gender and Ageing Briefs, Five: Violence and Older People – The Gendered Dimension (2002), 11.
13 K. Quinn, "APS Program Spotlight. Older Women: Hidden Sexual Abuse Victims," Illinois Coalition Against Sexual Assault (ICASA) Coalition Commentary (1994).
14 HelpAge International, State of the World's Older People (London, 2002).
15 M. Safarik, J. Jarvis and K. Nussbaum, "Sexual Homicide of Elderly Females: Linking Offender Characteristics to Victim and Crime Scene Attributes," Journal of Interpersonal Violence Vol. 17 No. 5 (May 2002), 500-525, 503.
16 Safarik et al, 2002, 500-501.
17 Safarik et al, 2002, 501.
18 Clark, 2002; HelpAge International, Gender and Ageing Briefs, 2002.
19 HelpAge International, State of the World's Older People, 2002, 69.
20 R. Ayres, 1998, cited in HelpAge International, State of the World's Older People, 2002, 65.
21 HelpAge International, Gender and Ageing Briefs, 2002.
22 P. Teaster, K. Roberto, J. Duke, K. Myeonghwan, "Sexual Abuse of Older Adults: Preliminary Findings of Cases in Virginia," Journal of Elder Abuse and Neglect Vol. 12 No. 3-4 (2000).
23 K. Vierthaler, "Elder Sexual Abuse: The Dynamics of Problem and Community-Based Solutions," National Center on Elder Abuse Newsletter Vol. 6 No. 7 (April 2004), 2.
24 J. Appleby, "Sexual assaults haunt families of elderly victims" USA Today (May 26, 2004).
25 Vierthaler, 2004, 3.
26 United Nations Economic and Social Council, Report of the Secretary-General, Abuse of Older Persons: Recognizing and Responding to Abuse of Older Persons in a Global Context (January 2002).
27 WHO/INPEA, 2002, 14.
28 HelpAge International, State of the World's Older People, 2002.
29 World's Women, 2000, cited in United Nations, Trends and Statistics, 2000, cited in HelpAge International, State of the World's Older People, 2002.
30 J. Natarajan, "Sati Versus Murder," The Hindu (December 3, 1999).
31 Natarajen, 1999.
32 M. Letsch, "De Weduwen van Kashi (The Widows of Kashi)," Onze Wereld (November 1996), 9-13.
33 "Magisterial Inquiry Ordered into 'Sati' Incident," Rediff.com (August 7, 2002). Available from: www.rediff.com/news/2002/aug/07mp.htm.
34 Natarjan, 1999.
35 Natarajan, 1999, 11.
36 Kenya Ministry of Health and National AIDS Control Council, AIDS in Kenya: Background, Projections, Impact, Interventions and Policy 6th Edition (Nairobi, 2001).
37 S. Buckley, "Wife Inheritance Spurs AIDS Rise in Kenya," The Washington Post Foreign Service (November 8, 1997); M. Nyakudya, "Health-Zimbabwe: 'Wife Inheritance' " Tradition Spreads AIDS, Inter Press News Service (August 3, 1998).
38 E. Wax, "Kenyan Women Reject Sex 'Cleanser': Traditional Requirement for Widows Is Blamed for Aiding the Spread of HIV/AIDS," The Washington Post Foreign Service (August 18, 2003), A12.
39 S. LaFraniere, "AIDS Now Compels Africa to Challenge Widows' Cleansing," The New York Times (May 11, 2005).
40 Wax, 2003.
41 LaFraniere, 2005.
42 Wax, 2003.
43 LaFraniere, 2005.
44 LaFraniere, 2005.
45 R. Mukumbira, "Shock Treatment for Widows as Pandemic Ravages Zimbabwe," News from Africa (March 2002).
46 WHO/INPEA, 2002.
47 Clark, 2002.
48 WHO/INPEA, 2002, 13.
49 HelpAge International, "Policy and Advocacy: Ten Actions to End Age Discrimination: Action Six: Put an End to Violence Against Older People." Available from: www.helpage.org/advocacy/CampState6/CampState6middle.html.
50 J. Lowick Russel Avalos, 1999, cited in HelpAge International, State of the World's Older People, 2002, 66.
51 Vierthaler, 2004.

52 "Nexus: Speaking the Unspeakable, An Interview About Elder Sexual Assault with Holly Ramsey-Klawsnik," *Nexus* Vol. 4 Issue 1 (April 1998).

53 J. Schaffer, "Older and Isolated Women and Domestic Violence Project," *Journal of Elder Abuse and Neglect* Vol. 11 No.1 (1999), 59-77, 66.

54 Global Action on Ageing, 2002.

55 Fisher et al., 2003.

56 Teitelman and O'Neill, 1999, 94.

57 *Nexus*, 1998.

58 R. Wolf, L. Daichman and G. Bennet, "Chapter 5: Abuse of the Elderly," in E. Krug, L. Dahlberg, J. Mercy, A. Zwi and R. Lozano, eds., *World Report on Violence and Health*, World Health Organization (Geneva, 2002).

59 HelpAge International, *State of the World's Older People*, 2002, 57.

60 HelpAge International, *Gender and Ageing briefs, Three: Participation of Older Women and Men in Development* (2002), 6.

61 Wax, 2003.

62 S. Abraham, "The Deorala Judgment Glorifying Sati," *The Lawyers Collective* Vol. 12 No.16 (June 1997), 4-12.

63 Natarajan, 1999.

64 LaFraniere, 2005.

chapter 13 — sexual violence in times of war

1 Human Rights Watch (HRW), 1995, cited in M. Hynes and B. Lopes-Cardozo, "Sexual Violence Against Refugee Women," *Journal of Women's Health and Gender-based Medicine* Vol. 9 No. 8 (2000), 819-23.

2 Avega, 1999, cited in J. Ward, *If Not Now, When?, Reproductive Health for Refugees Consortium* (RHRC) (New York, April 2002).

3 Hynes and Lopes Cardozo, 2000.

4 A. Benton, *Research Report: Prevalence of Gender-based Violence Among Liberian Women in Three Refugee Camps*, International Rescue Committee (IRC) (Sierra Leone, February 2004) unpublished report; also cited in IRC, *Situation Analysis of Gender-based Violence* (Liberia, April 2004).

5 Reproductive Health Response in Conflict Consortium, Liga de Mujeres Desplazadas, Red de Empoderamiento de Mujeres de Cartagena y Bolivar Sindicato de Madres Comunitrias, *A Determination of the Prevalence of Gender-based Violence Among Women Displaced by Internal Armed Conflict*, Preliminary Report (Cartagena, Colombia, January 2005).

6 United Nations Special Rapporteur (UN Spec. Rapp.) on Violence Against Women, 2005, cited in J. Ward, "Gender-based Violence among Conflict-affected Populations: Humanitarian Program Responses," *Listening to the Silences: Women and War* (Konnklikje Brill, Netherlands, 2005), 67.

7 S. Brownmiller (1975), cited in M. Hynes, J. Ward, K. Robertson and C. Crouse, "A Determination of the Prevalence of Gender-based Violence among Conflict-affected Populations in East Timor," *Disasters* Vol. 28 No. 3 (2004), 294-321.

8 S. Swiss and J. Geller, "Rape as a Crime of War: A Medical Perspective," *Journal of the American Medical Association* Vol. 279 No. 8 (1993), 625-629; World Health Organization (WHO) (1997), cited in Hynes and Lopes Cardozo, 2000; T. McGinn, "Reproductive Health of War-Affected Populations: What Do We Know?" *International Family Planning Perspectives* Vol. 26 No. 4 (December 2000), 174-80; Ward, 2002.

9 J. Gardam and M. Jarvis (2001), cited in Amnesty International (AI), *Lives Blown Apart: Crimes Against Women in Times of Conflict* (London, 2004).

10 E. Rehn and E. Johnson Sirleaf, "Women, War, Peace," *Progress of the World's Women* 2002 Vol. 1 (2002), 4.

11 M. Vlachova and L. Biason, eds., *Women in an Insecure World: Violence Against Women, Facts, Figures, and Analysis*, Geneva Centre for the Democratic Control of Armed Forces (Geneva, 2005), 114.

12 United Nations Security Council, *Report of the Secretary General on Women, Peace and Security* S/2002/1154 (October 2002), 1.

13 T. McGinn, 2000; AIDS Weekly Plus, 1996, cited in Hynes and Lopes Cardozo, 2000.

14 Médicins Sans Frontières (MSF) Press Release, "MSF Shocked by Arrest of Head of Mission in Sudan" (Khartoum/Amsterdam, May 30, 2005).

15 Hynes et al, 2004.

16 Avega, 1999, cited in Ward, 2002.

17 International Alert Press Release, Panel on The Causes and Consequences of Sexual Violence Against Women and Girls in South Kivu, Democratic Republic of Congo (New York, March 2004).

18 International Alert, Réseau des Femmes pour un Developpement Associatif and Réseau des Femmes pour la Defence des Droits et la Paix, *Women's Bodies as a Battleground: Sexual Violence Against Women and Girls During the War in the Democratic Republic of Congo* (2005).

19 International Alert et al, 2005, 34.

20 International Alert et al, 2005, 34.

21 HRW 2000, cited in Ward, 2002, 36.

22 Physicians for Human Rights (PHR), *War-related Sexual Violence in Sierra Leone: A Population-based Assessment* (Boston, 2002).

23 International Alert, 2005, 11.

24 Integrated Regional Information Networks (IRIN), *Our Bodies, Their Battleground: Gender-based Violence in Conflict Zones*, IRIN Web Special on Violence Against Women and Girls During Armed Conflict (September 2004).

25 Oxfam UK, 2001, cited in Ward, 2002.

26 R. Ojiambo Ochieng, *The Efforts of Non-governmental Organizations in Assessing the Violations of Women's Human Rights in Situations of Armed Conflict: The Isis-WICCE Experience*, Paper Prepared for Expert Group Meeting on Violence Against Women, United Nations Division for the Advancement of Women (Geneva, April 2005), 11.

27 AI, *Sudan, Darfur Rape as a Weapon of War: Sexual Violence and Its Consequences* (London, 2004), 15.

28 Rehn and Johnson Sirleaf, 2002, 2.

29 Shan Women's Action Network and Shan Human Rights Foundation, *License to Rape* (2002).

30 UN Spec. Rapp. on Violence Against Women, *Integration of the Human Rights of Women and the Gender Perspective*, United Nations Economic and Social Council E/CN.6/2001/2 (January 2001), 27.

31 UN Spec. Rapp. January 2001, 28.

32 Watchlist on Children and Armed Conflict, *Colombia's War on Children* (New York, February 2004).

33 Ward, 2002.

34 Rehn and Johnson Sirleaf, 2002, 17.

35 AI, *Sudan*, 2004, 12.

36 International Alert, 2005, 46.

37 IRIN, 2004, 22.

38 M. Hobson, *Forgotten Casualties of War: Girls in Armed Conflict*, Save the Children (London, 2005).

39 Watchlist, 2004.

40 AI, *Liberia: No Impunity for Rape, A Crime Against Humanity and a War Crime* (London, December 2004).

41 AI, *Casualties of War: Women's Bodies, Women's Lives: Stop Crimes Against Women in Armed Conflict* (London, October 2004), 3.

42 Watchlist on Children and Armed Conflict, *Caught in the Middle: Mounting Violations Against children in Nepal's Armed Conflict* (New York, January 2005), 39.

43 Hobson, 2005, 10.

44 United Nations High Commissioner for Refugees (UNHCR), *Refugees By Numbers (2005 Edition)* (2005). Available from: www.unhcr.ch.

45 United Nations Security Council, *Report of the Secretary-General on Women, Peace and Security* S/2002/1154 (October 2002), 2.

[46] AI, *Forgotten Casualties of War*, 2005.

[47] Vlachova and Biason, eds., 2005.

[48] Vlachova and Biason, eds., 2005.

[49] Watchlist, 2004; Ward, 2002.

[50] Ward, 2002.

[51] Watchlist, 2004.

[52] Human Rights Documentation Unit and Burmese Women's Union, 2000, cited in Ward, 2002.

[53] S. Olila, S. Igras and B. Monahan, 1998, cited in T. McGinn, 2000.

[54] AI, *Liberia*, 2004, 4.

[55] AI, *Forgotten Casualties of War*, 2004.

[56] S. Nduna and L. Goodyear, *Pain Too Deep for Tears: Assessing the Prevalence of Sexual and Gender Violence Among Burundian Refugees in Tanzania*, IRC (New York, 1997).

[57] AI, *Liberia*, 2004.

[58] United Nations Children's Fund (UNICEF), IRC, Christian Children's Fund, Legal Aid Project, *Protected Yet Insecure*, unpublished document (November 2004), 20.

[59] Reproductive Health Response in Conflict Consortium et al, 2005.

[60] M. Hynes et al., 2003 and M. Hynes 2004, cited in Reproductive Health Services for Refugees and Internally Displaced Persons, *Report of an Inter-agency Global Evaluation 2004* (November 2004), 39; RHRC et al, 2005.

[61] UN Spec. Rapp., 2001, 29.

[62] UN Spec. Rapp., 2001, 22.

[63] Ward, 2002, 48.

[64] A. Naik, "Protecting Children from the Protectors: Lessons from West Africa," *Forced Migration Review* Vol. 15 (October 2002), 17.

[65] A. Naik, "UN investigation into sexual exploitation by aid workers," *Forced Migration Review* Vol. 16 (January 2003).

[66] Human Rights Watch, *Iraq: Insecurity Driving Women Indoors* (New York, July 2003).

[67] AI, *Lives Blown Apart*, 2004.

[68] Hobson, 2005, 21.

[69] AI, *Lives Blown Apart*, 2004.

[70] IRIN, 2004.

[71] AI, *Rwanda: "Marked for Death," Rape Survivors Living with HIV/AIDS in Rwanda* (April 2004), 9.

[72] RHRC, *Gender-based Violence: Key Messages*. Available from: www.rhrc.org/rhr_basics/gbv.

[73] AI, *Lives Blown Apart*, 2004.

[74] AI, *Lives Blown Apart*, 2004.

[75] United Nations, *Children and Armed Conflict: Report of the Secretary General pursuant to Security Council Resolution 1261* (July 2000), cited in UNICEF, *The Impact of Conflict on Women and Girls in West and Central Africa and the UNICEF Response* (February 2005), 21.

[76] African Rights, *Broken Bodies, Torn Spirits: Living with Genocide, Rape and HIV/AIDS*, Press Release (Kigali, April 2004), 4.

[77] AI, *Lives Blown Apart*, 2004.

[78] Hynes et al, 2003 and Hynes, 2004, cited in Reproductive Health Services for Refugees and Internally Displaced Persons, 2004, 39; Reproductive Health Response in Conflict Consortium et al, 2005.

[79] MSF, 2005, 6.

[80] African Rights, 2004, 4.

[81] African Rights, 2004, 5.

[82] UNHCR, *Sexual and Gender Based Violence Against Refugees, Returnees and Internally Displaced Persons: Guidelines on Prevention and Response* (Geneva, May 2003).

[83] Ward, 2002.

[84] Rehn and Johnson Sirleaf, 2002, xii.

[85] UN Inter-Agency Standing Committee, *Action to Address Gender Based Violence in Emergencies: IASC Statement of Commitment* (January 2005).

[86] K. Burns, personal correspondence (July 11, 2005); AI, *Lives Blown Apart*, 2004.

[87] K. Burns, personal correspondence (July 11, 2005).

[88] P. Donovan, "Rape and HIV/AIDS in Rwanda," *The Lancet* Vol. 360 Supplement: Medicine and Conflict (December 2002), 18.

chapter 14 — perpetrators

[1] E. Still, *Biology & Society* 5 (1988), ix.

[2] J. Carr, "Theme Paper on Child Pornography for the Second World Congress on Commercial Sexual Exploitation of Children," (December, 2001). Available from: www.ecpat.net/eng/Ecpat_inter/projects/monitoring/wc2/yokohama_theme_child_pornography.pdf; A. Jordan, Askin and Koenig, eds., "Commercial Sex Workers in Asia: A Blind Spot in Human Rights Law," *Women and International Human Rights Law* Vol. 2 (New York, 2000); L. Heise, K. Moore, and N. Toubia, "Sexual Coercion and Reproductive Health: A Focus on Research," *Population Council* (1995).

[3] H. Wakefield and R. Underwager, "Female Child Sexual Abusers: A Critical Review of the Literature," *American Journal of Forensic Psychology* Vol. 9 Issue 4 (1991).

[4] M. Flood, "Deconstructing the Culture of Sexual Assault," Presentation to Practice and Prevention: Contemporary Issues in Adult Sexual Assault, University of Technology (New South Wales, Sydney, Australia, February 12-14, 2003).

[5] D. Counts, J. Brown and J. Campbell, eds., "Sanctions and Sanctuary: Cultural Perspectives on the Beating of Wives" (Boulder, Colorado, 1992), 268, cited in *International Planned Parenthood Federation Newsletter* (Winter 2001), 4.

[6] Flood, 2003.

[7] Miedzan, cited in Heise et al, 1995.

[8] International Centre for Research on Women (ICRW), *Men, Masculinity and Domestic Violence in India* (2002).

[9] P. Tjaden and N. Thomas, *Prevalence, Incidence and Consequences of Violence Against Women: Findings from the National Violence Against Women Survey*, National Institute of Justice, United States Department of Justice (November 1998).

[10] M. Flood, "Engaging Men: Strategies and dilemmas in violence prevention education among men," *Women Against Violence: A Feminist Journal* Vol. 13 (2002-2003), 25-32.

[11] Tjaden and Thomas, 1998.

[12] David Gilmore, 1990, cited in Heise et al, 1995.

[13] M. Miedzam, cited in Heise et al, 1995.

[14] M. Flood, 2002-2003.

[15] R. Connell, Men and Violence, University of Sydney, 1985, 6.

[16] M. Miedzian, *Boys Will Be Boys: Breaking the Link Between Masculinity and Violence* (New York, 1991).

[17] S. LaFranier, "Entrenched Epidemic: Wife Beating in Africa," *New York Times* (August 11, 2005).

[18] LaFranier, 2005.

[19] Agger, 1994, cited in Heise et al 1995, 104.

[20] M. Flood, 2003-2004.

[21] S. Romans, M. Poore and J. Martin, "The Perpetrators of Domestic Violence," *The Medical Journal of Australia* (2000).

[22] La Franier, 2005.

[23] L. Walker, "Psychology and Domestic Violence Around the World," *American Psychologist* (January 1999), 24.

[24] J. Belknap and H. Melton, "Are Heterosexual Men Also Victims of Intimate Partner Abuse?," National Online Resource Center on Violence Against Women, Applied Research Forum,

National Resource Centre for Domestic Violence (2005).

25 M. Kimmel, " 'Gender Symmetry' in Domestic Violence: A Substantive and Methodological Research Review," *Violence Against Women, Special Issue: Women's Use of Violence in Intimate Relationships*, Part 1.8 No. 11 (November, 2002).

26 M. Testa, "The Role of Substance Use in Male-to-Female Physical and Sexual Violence," *Journal of Interpersonal Violence* Vol. 19 No. 12 (Dec 2004).

27 Heise, 1998, 272.

28 Heise, 1998, 273.

29 Reuters, "Five Pakistanis Arrested Over 'Honour' Rape" (July 6, 2005).

30 Al-Fanar, *Women Against Fundamentalism Journal* No. 6 (1995), 37-41.

31 Heise et al, 1995.

32 M. Spatz, "A Lesser Crime: A Comparative Study of Legal Defenses for Men Who Kill Their Wives," *Columbia Journal of Law and Social Problems* (1991).

33 Ward (1983), cited in D. Scully and J. Marolla, "Riding the Bull at Gilley's": Convicted Rapists Describe The Rewards of Rape," *Social Problems* Vol. 32 No. 3 (February 1985).

34 Amnesty International (AI), *Making Violence Against Women Count: Facts and Figures*, AI Index: ACT 77/036/2004 (March 2004).

35 S. Xenos and D. Smith, "Perceptions of Rape and Sexual Assault Among Australian Adolescents and Young Adults," *Journal of Interpersonal Violence* Vol. 16 No. 11 (2001).

36 D. Scully and J. Marolla, "Riding the Bull at Gilley's: Convicted Rapists Describe the Rewards of Rape," *Social Problems* Vol. 32 No. 3 (1985).

37 Scully and Marolla, 1985, 256.

38 Scully and Marolla, 1985, 256.

39 Scully and Marolla, 1985.

40 Scully and Marolla, 1985.

41 Heise et al 1995.

42 S. Vir Tyagi from Toronto, Canada; quoted on film in the documentary, *The Children We Sacrifice* (Shakti Productions).

43 Vir Tyagi, *The Children We Sacrifice*.

44 D. Russell, *The Secret Trauma: Incest in the Lives of Girls and Women* (Basic Books, 1986), 216.

45 NGO Group for the Convention of the Rights of the Child and ECPAT International Briefing Note, *People Who Prey on Children*, Second World Congress Against the Commercial Sexual Exploitation of Children. Available from: www.ecpat.net.

46 C. Ford, "Infant Rape and the Deconstruction of Predatory and Impulsive Masculinity," Sex and Secrecy Conference (2003). Available from: www.princesstrust.com/news_files/infant_rape.htm.

47 M. Glassner and L. Kolvi, "Cycle of Child Sexual Abuse: Links between Being a Victim and Becoming a Perpetrator," *British Journal of Psychiatry* 178 (2001), 178: 482-494.

48 Heise, 1998, 267-268.

49 M. Flood, "Men's Collective Struggles for Gender Justice: The Case of Anti-Violence Activism," *The Handbook of Studies on Men and Masculinities*, M. Kimmel, J. Hearn, and R.W. Connell, eds. (Thousand Oaks, CA, 2005).

50 L. Salas, cited in L. Heise et al, *Violence Against Women: The Hidden Burden*, World Bank (Washington, 1994).

chapter 15 — turning the tide

1 S. Vieira de Mello, "Violence Against Women — What Next?," Paper Prepared for the Symposium Sponsored by the United Nations (UN) Office of the High Commissioner for Human Rights (OHCHR) and the Nongovernmental Organization Committee on the Status of Women (April 2003).

2 United Nations Committee on the Elimination of All Forms of Discrimination against Women, "Statement to Commemorate the 25th anniversary of the Convention on the Elimination of All Forms of Discrimination against Women" (October 2004).

3 UN Committee on the Elimination of All Forms of Discrimination against Women, 2004.

4 Universal Declaration of Human Rights, Preamble and Article 1 (December 10, 1948). Available from: www.un.org/Overview/rights.html.

5 Universal Declaration of Human Rights , Articles 3, 4, 5, 7, and 16 (December 10, 1948).

6 United Nations Special Rapporteur (UN Spec. Rapp.) on Violence Against Women, *Integration of the Human Rights of Women and the Gender Perspective: Violence Against Women*, United Nations Commission on Human Rights E/CN.4/2003/75 (January 6, 2003).

7 UN Spec. Rapp., 2003, 5.

8 C. Spindel, E. Levy and M. Connor, *With an End in Sight: Strategies from the UNIFEM Trust Fund to Eliminate Violence Against Women*, United Nations Development Fund for Women (UNIFEM) (2000); M. Valchova and L. Biason, eds., *Women in an Insecure World: Violence against Women Facts, Figures and Analysis*, Centre for the Democratic Control of Armed Forces (DCAF) (Geneva, 2005).

9 R. Jewkes, P. Sen and C. Garcia-Moreno, "Chapter 6: Sexual Violence," in E. Krug, L. Dahlberg, J. Mercy, A. Zwi and R. Lozano, eds., *World Report on Violence and Health*, World Health Organization (WHO), (Geneva, 2002), 169.

10 Spindel et al, 2003, 90-94.

11 UN Spec. Rapp., 2003.

12 Spindel et al, 2003, 41.

13 Spindel et al, 2003, 42, 90-94.

14 Amnesty International (AI), "Justice not excuses." Available from: web.amnesty.org/actforwomen/justice-index-eng.

15 B. Scholz and M. Gomez, *Bringing Equality Home: Promoting and Protecting the Inheritance Rights of Women*, Centre on Housing Rights and Evictions (Geneva, 2004).

16 Human Rights Watch (HRW), *What Will it Take? Stopping Violence against Women – Challenge for Governments* (2000).

17 Spindel et al, 2003, 45.

18 A. Rahman and N. Toubia, 2000, cited in Vlachova and Biason, eds., 2005, 30.

19 UN Spec. Rapp., 2003, 11, 13.

20 World Health Organization, 2002, 73, 136-137.

21 L. Heise, M. Ellsberg and M. Gottemoeller, "Ending Violence Against Women," *Population Reports* Series L No. 11 (Baltimore, 1999), 26-28.

22 UNIFEM 2003, 38.

23 *Putting Women First: Ethical and Safety Recommendations for Research on Domestic Violence Against Women*. Available from: www.who.int/gender/violence/en/womenfirtseng.pdf

24 United Nations General Assembly, *In-depth Study on all Forms of Violence Against Women*, Resolution A/RES/58/185 (March 2004).

25 UN Spec. Rapp., 2003, 20.

26 UNIFEM, 2003, 63.

27 UNIFEM, 2003, 11.

28 World Health Organization Department of Gender, Women and Health, *Violence Against Women and HIV/AIDS: Critical Intersections*, Information Bulletin Series, No 1 (Geneva, 2004) 4.

29 UNIFEM, *Picturing a Life Free of Violence: Media and Communications Strategies to End Violence Against Women* (New York 2001).

30 UNIFEM, 2001.

31 UNIFEM, 2003, 34.

32 UN Committee on the Elimination of All Forms of Discrimination against Women (October 2004).

33 M. Flood, "Engaging Men: Strategies and Dilemmas in Violence Prevention Education Among Men," *Women Against Violence* Vol. 13 (2002-2003).

34 M. Flood, 2002-2003, 25.

[35] M. Flood, *Changing Men: Best Practice in Violence Prevention Work with Men*, Paper Prepared for Home Truths Conference: Stop Sexual Assault and Domestic Violence: A National Challenge (Melbourne, September 2005), 15-17.

[36] P. Welsh, *Men Aren't from Mars: Unlearning Machismo in Nicaragua*, Catholic Institute for International Relations (London, June 2001).

[37] www.whiteribboncampaign.org.

[38] UNIFEM, 2003, 70.

[39] WHO, 2002. 169.

[40] S. Zahidi and A. Lopez-Claros, *Women's Empowerment: Measuring the Global Gender Gap*, World Economic Forum (Geneva, 2005), 2.

[41] R. Jewkes, "Intimate partner violence: causes and prevention", *The Lancet* Vol 359 (2002) 1.

[42] Vlachova and Biason, eds., 2005.

[43] Vlachova and Biason, eds., 2005, 277.

[44] Inter-Parliamentary Union, *Women in National Parliaments* (2004). Available from: www.ipu.org/wmn-e/world.htm.

[45] Zahidi and Lopez-Claros, 2005, 8-9.

[46] R. Carrillo, *Planting the Seeds of Change* in *With and End in Sight*, UNIFEM (2000), 11; United Nations Development Fund for Women (UNIFEM), *Not a Minute More: Ending Violence Against Women* (New York, 2003), 15.

A self-help group of women in Sierra Leone — all survivors of sexual violence and torture. They posed for this photo - wanting the world to know of their needs and the abuse they suffered. Thousands of women like these struggle to find a future after living through years of brutal conflict.

Image: Brent Stirton

"The day will come when men will recognize woman as his peer, not only at the fireside, but in councils of the nation. Then, and not until then, will there be the perfect comradeship, the ideal union between the sexes that shall result in the highest development of the race." Susan B. Anthony

"When you are a mother … left behind with children who are boys, there is one amongst your children … he wants to sleep with you and wants that you not talk about it … You are afraid because you do not have the strength. He does that thing as he pleases." Older woman victim the victim of sexual abuse perpetrated by her son, South Africa

"Women are the victims of this patriarchal culture, but they are also its carriers. Let us keep in mind that every oppressive man was raised in the confines of his mother's home." Shirin Ebadi

"The delivery of the child I have just lost lasted three days. It was during the delivery that the fistula occurred. … I wept and wept. … " Sixteen-year-old girl, forced into marriage at the age of 14, Niger

"We have to stop this violence. We have to make the political nature of the violence clear, that the violence we experience in our own homes is not a personal family matter, it's a public and political problem. It's a way that women are kept in line, kept in our places." Patricia Ireland

"He pulled me from the bed to the floor and started trampling on me. … He used his hands to beat me, his fists and his feet. … He took a piece of wood and hit me on the head and in the lower stomach. It broke in two pieces." Twenty-two-year-old survivor of intimate-partner violence, Democratic Republic of Congo

"Crosscultural research demonstartes that gender inequality is the most significant cause of men's violence against women. The policy implications for reducing gendered violence seem clear from this research. We need to reduce the gender power inequality between men and women if we are going to effectively address the problem of men's violence". Bob Pease

"He used to tell me, 'You're an animal, an idiot, you're worthless.' That made me feel even more stupid. I couldn't raise my head. I think I still have scars from this … I accepted it, because after a point, he had destroyed me by blows and psychologically." Survivor of intimate-partner violence, Nicaragua

"We must acknowledge that violence is not the same as anger. While anger is an emotion, violence is a behaviour. We must also acknowledge that violence is always a choice, noting that most men who are violent towards their partners do not usually display similarly violent or abusive behaviour towards others." Danny Blay

"There must be no impunity for gender based violence. Let me be clear. What we are talking about is not a side issue. It is not a special interest group of concern to only a few. What we are talking about are not only women's rights but also the human rights of over one half of this globe's population … Violence against women concerns not only women but above all the rest of us." Sergio Vieira de Mello

"There are so many girls where I come from who have been raped and are living a life like I did. If anyone wants to help, we desperately need a shelter for these children to escape to — a shelter that can offer vocational skills training and give them a chance for a better life." Fourteen-year-old girl, who had worked as a child prostitute, Kenya

"There is nothing nobler or more admirable than when two people who see eye to eye keep house as man and wife, confounding their enemies and delighting their friends." Homer

"You want to have a liking for a man to have sex, not to have someone force you. But I had no choice, knowing the whole village was against me." An older woman, forced to undergo a widow cleansing ritual, Malawi

"Whenever women protest and ask for their rights, they are silenced with the argument that the laws are justified under Islam. It is an unfounded argument. It is not Islam at fault, but rather the patriarchal culture that uses its own interpretations to justify whatever it wants." Shirin Ebadi

"We are going to shout about bride price across Africa and we are going to say 'No' to the sale of women!" Atuki Turner, the director of a nongovernmental organization in Uganda that helps victims of intimate-partner violence

"As a human rights issue, the effort to end violence against women becomes a government's obligation, not just a good idea." Charlotte Bunch

"My master treated me so badly and often raped me. He used to tell me that his traditional doctor said that if he slept with a slave he would be cured from illness." Female slave, Niger

"A great many people think they are thinking when they are just rearranging their prejudices." William James

"The boys never meant any harm against the girls. They just wanted to rape." Deputy principal describing a gang of male students at her school who killed 19 schoolgirls and raped 71 others. Kenya

"Do not wait for leaders; do it alone, person to person. Be faithful in small things because it is in them that your strength lies." Mother Teresa